D1593358

COMMANDOS FROM THE SEA

**NAVAL
INSTITUTE
SPECIAL
WARFARE
SERIES**

COMMANDOS FROM THE SEA

Soviet Naval Spetsnaz in World War II

YURIY FEDOROVICH STREKHNIN

Translated, with Introduction and Notes,
by James F. Gebhardt

Naval Institute Press • Annapolis, Maryland

Originally published in Russian under the title *Otryad "Boroda"* (Detachment of "The Beard") by DOSAAF Publishers, Moscow, in 1962.

Library of Congress Cataloging-in-Publication Data
Strekhnin, IUrii.
    [Otriad Borody. English]
    Commandos from the sea : Soviet naval spetsnaz in World War II /
Yuriy Fedorovich Strekhnin ; translated, with introduction and notes by
James F. Gebhardt.
        p. cm. — (Naval Institute special warfare series)
    Includes bibliographical references and index.
    ISBN 1-55750-832-1 (alk. paper)
    1. Soviet Union. Voenno-Morskoi Flot. Baltiiskii flot. Otriad Borody.
2. World War, 1939–1945—Naval operations, Soviet. 3. World War,
1939–1945—Reconnaissance operations, Soviet. 4. Special forces
(Military science)—Soviet Union. I. Title. II. Series.
D779.R9S7313 1996
940.54'5947—dc20   96-23216

CONTENTS

CONTENTS

TRANSLATOR'S INTRODUCTION

Commandos from the Sea: Soviet Naval Spetsnaz in World War II is this translator's second work that describes the combat actions of Soviet naval special operations forces in World War II. The first volume, *Blood on the Shores: Soviet Naval Commandos in World War II* (Annapolis, Md.: Naval Institute Press, 1993), recounted the exploits of Viktor Leonov's Northern and Pacific Fleet detachments in combat against the Germans on the Murmansk front and the Japanese army in northern Korean ports. The introduction to *Blood on the Shores* clearly established this elite World War II force as the forebear of the Soviet, and now Russian, naval *spetsnaz* of the modern era.

Such forces also existed in other fleets of the Soviet navy. The Black Sea Fleet reconnaissance detachment was formed in the late summer or early fall of 1941, made up of enlisted and officer personnel of naval and naval infantry units of the Sevastopol area.[1] The detachment trained in general and special skills at the fleet school and deployed on its first combat operation in November of that year. In May 1942, the group was split into three parts: one group of men remained in Sevastopol to aid in the defense of the city; another was assigned to the Azov Flotilla base at Novorossiysk; the third went to Tuapse, south of Novorossiysk on the east shore of the Black Sea.

This account of the combat actions of the Black Sea Fleet and later Danube Flotilla reconnaissance detachment is based on *Detachment of "The Beard"* by Yu. F. Strekhnin.[2] "The Beard" was Senior Lieutenant Viktor Kalganov, a naval infantry officer who joined the Black Sea Fleet reconnaissance detachment in late 1942 while it was deployed along the east coast of the Black Sea near Tuapse. Strekhnin's account was published in 1962, five years after Viktor Leonov's memoir on the Northern Fleet scouts appeared and one year after memoirs of the Baltic Fleet and Black Sea Fleet reconnaissance detachments were published.[3]

The book opens with a combat vignette of a Soviet naval ground reconnaissance unit somewhere on the north Caucasus coastline near Tuapse. This unidentified unit was assigned to the Black Sea Fleet, whose ground forces were at this time engaged in the desperate attempt to retain Soviet control of the north Caucasus region in the face of a determined southward German offensive. The action soon shifts to the Crimean peninsula and to the Black Sea Fleet reconnaissance detachment, which began coast-watching and partisan operations against the German occupation forces there in the summer of 1943.

In the summer of 1944, as the Soviet-German front inexorably moved westward, many of the personnel of the Black Sea Fleet reconnaissance detachment were reassigned to the reconnaissance detachment of the Danube River Flotilla. Viktor Kalganov was named to command this detachment. The Danube Flotilla, which had been chased out of Bessarabia by the invading Germans in June 1941, had been dissolved as a standing force in November 1941, and its sailors and vessels were reassigned to the Kerch Naval Base and Azov Flotilla.[4] The Danube Flotilla was reestablished on 13 April 1944, on the base of the now uncommitted Azov Flotilla, in preparation for entering the Danube River to conduct riverine operations in support of the offensive against German forces and their allies in southeast Europe. Rear Admiral S. G. Gorshkov, then commanding the Azov Flotilla, was named to command the Danube Flotilla. He brought his primary staff with him, including his chief of staff, Captain First Rank A. V. Sverdlov.

When it entered the Danube River estuary in August 1944, the Danube Flotilla consisted of the Armored Cutter Brigade (twenty-two armored cutters and twenty smaller vessels), the 4th Separate Brigade of River Vessels (fourteen armored cutters, twelve mortar boats, twenty-two minesweeping craft, and fifteen rubber boats), several ground artillery units equipped with a total of fourteen 122mm and eight 152mm artillery pieces, a separate antiaircraft artillery battalion (twelve 85mm guns), the 369th Separate Naval Infantry Battalion, and assorted headquarters and support units. Although the vessels of the Danube Flotilla came from the Azov Flotilla, its reconnaissance detachment came directly from the Black Sea Fleet reconnaissance detachment.

From August 1944 to April 1945, the Danube Flotilla fought its way along the Danube River as it passed through Romania, Yugoslavia, Hungary, Austria, and Czechoslovakia, conducting combat and combat support operations while subordinated to the Third Ukrainian *Front*, commanded by Marshal of the Soviet Union F. I. Tolbukhin.

Although Strekhnin's work is the most comprehensive concerning the Danube Flotilla reconnaissance detachment, there is another account from this group that bears discussion: *Zapiski razvedchika* [Notes of a scout] (Moscow: Voyenizdat, 1981), by A. A. Chkheidze. Chkheidze was accepted into Kalganov's detachment as a seventeen-year-old naval infantry scout in the fall of 1944, just before the detachment entered Yugoslavia. He first appears in Strekhnin's account in the author's foreword and is found throughout the book as a participant in many of the detachment's combat escapades. At the war's end, Chkheidze was grievously wounded by an explosion while clearing the Danube channel of mines en route back to the Black Sea.

Strekhnin's book contained not a single footnote in its original Russian form. Therefore, I have added notes to offer explanations of Russian terms or to share information gleaned from other accounts.

Here, then, is Yuriy Strekhnin's account of Soviet naval special operations forces in World War II.

FOREWORD

This book is based on actual events. It recounts the combat feats of a detachment of naval scouts during the Great Patriotic War.[1] This detachment operated at the front and in the enemy rear, carrying out missions assigned by the Black Sea Fleet staff and, later, the staff of the Red Banner[2] Orders of Nakhimov and Kutuzov[3] Danube Flotilla.

The pages of this book capture the heroism of these naval scouts and are alive with their combat deeds. In the example of one small detachment, it uncovers the beauty of the spirit of the Soviet youth who gave unsparingly of themselves in the defense of their Motherland and for victory over the enemy. The detachment of "the Beard" was one of the many detachments of young people raised up by the Communist Party and Komsomol.[4]

When the enemy was attempting to enslave us and lay waste to our land with fire and sword, the best sons and daughters of our people went to front-line reconnaissance detachments and to other extremely difficult and dangerous assignments. The principal goals of the sailor scouts, whose stories this book conveys, were to uncover the enemy's intentions ahead of time, to find the weak links in his forces, and, in doing so, to aid the forces of the *front*[5] and the ships and units of the fleet in discerning the enemy's plan and defeating him.

The glorious combat path walked by the detachment of "commander's scouts" is of particular interest because they accomplished their missions in a great variety of conditions: at the forward edge and in the enemy rear in the mountains of Crimea and the Caucasus, in active association with the partisan movement, in battles of our ships and troops during the liberation of Romania, Bulgaria, Yugoslavia, Hungary, Czechoslovakia, and Austria, and in combat cooperation with the peoples of these countries during the common struggle to liberate them from the fascist yoke.

The combat activity of the reconnaissance detachment yielded significant results. The successes of the scouts made possible the destruction of many enemy ships by naval air forces, the landing of assault forces in the enemy's rear and flanks, and the defeat of the enemy at Novorossiysk, Sevastopol, Belgrade, Budapest, and Vienna. The efforts of the scouts prevented the detonation of enemy mines by our vessels; the majority of these mines were placed by the enemy along the entire trace of the Danube. The naval scouts deserve their fame. The combat awards and decorations that adorn their chests are testimony to this glory.

This book abounds with examples of the bravery, determination, discipline, and soldierly skill of the detachment's scouts. I want to express to them my heartfelt thanks for their remarkable combat deeds.

—*Captain First Rank A. V. Sverdlov,*
Former Chief of Staff of the Red Banner, Orders of
Nakhimov and Kutuzov Danube Flotilla

PREFACE

I would like to explain how this book came into being. The telephone rang one day. Someone was speaking in an unfamiliar voice, and he was somewhat hard of hearing.

"I fought on the Danube. I would like to meet with you."

"Well, then, come to my place," I said, and asked, "What is your name?"

"Chkheidze. Aleksey Chkheidze."

While waiting for the day of our meeting, I tried to recall who he was. I knew many of the Danube Flotilla sailors. But no matter how I strained my memory, I could not recall this man's name. Why did he want to meet with me? Perhaps he had read my outline of the Danube Flotilla's battles[1] and wanted to discuss some of his impressions? Perhaps he was a retiree on pension, who wanted my help in writing his memoirs? But I already had urgent work on my desk that would keep me busy for several months. "Well, okay," I thought. "He will come, and we will talk, but not for long, I hope."

The agreed-upon time arrived, and at the exact minute a knock sounded at the door. Two men came in, one leading the other, who was slightly behind. My heart sank. In front of me stood a person of thirty-five years, with a closely shaved head and immobile, unseeing eyes. On his right cheek and close to his mouth were gnarled scars, which gave his enegertic, lean face a sense of urgency

xiii

and will. Lifeless hands, covered in black leather gloves, extended from the arms of his modest brown jacket. I could guess immediately that these were prostheses. It also struck me that his guide, a black-haired, dark-complected man with southern features, had almost no fingers on his right hand.

"My friend Carlos," Chkheidze introduced him.

Had I only known ahead of time of Chkheidze's condition! Of course, I would have gone to him. But what led him to me?

"I was a sailor in the flotilla headquarters reconnaissance detachment," he began to explain.

"Is that so?" I was surprised. I had heard about the amazing activities of this detachment's sailors, but this man was the first of them that I had laid eyes on.

"I am looking for my comrades," Chkheidze continued. "I very much want to meet with them. Perhaps you know some of them? You have written a book about the Danube sailors."

"Alas," I replied, "almost nothing is known about the men of your detachment. The archival documents also contain little information."

"The war was on, and not everything was recorded in documents." My guest smiled. "At the same time, very few were supposed to know about our activities. At that time, we ourselves did not like to talk. Correspondents were offended by us."

"You can tell the story!" I didn't hold back. In front of me was sitting one man from the detachment about which legends traveled down the Danube. "Tell me about it now!"

He talked hesitantly at first, only answering my questions. But later he became more animated. I heard and saw him not as he was sitting before me but as a clear-eyed seventeen-year-old lad, as he was almost twenty years ago, with a Komsomol pin on his sailor's blouse and a submachine gun in his hands, his *beskozyrka* [saucer cap with ribbon tail] tilted to one side. I saw him with his comrades, walking through a foreign city at night, where there was danger in every step. I saw him breaking into an enemy headquarters.

I listened to him, and the desire began to burn in me to retell everything that I was hearing. To tell the generation of young people

who perhaps are the same age as he and his friends in the detachment were when, following the command of their hearts along the
Komsomol path, sometimes straight from school, they departed
into the fires of war.

So I gathered up the unfinished manuscript from my desk,
which I hadn't intended to put aside even for a day—this manuscript can wait!

Already I was unable not to write about these brave young men
and women.

Aleksey sat with me a long time that first day. At the end of our
conversation, I suggested to him, "Let's look for your comrades
in arms together."

A year passed. I inspected hundreds of pages of reports and
intelligence summaries in the military archives, finding many
from the headquarters reconnaissance detachment. On the table
in front of me were notes of our conversations, letters from veter-
ans, and old wartime photographs. I picked up one picture. Against
the background of the thick paper are sitting tall young men in
fatigues and canted *pilotkas* [garrison hats]. They are holding
their weapons with pride—sniper rifles. The letters *ChF*—Black
Sea Fleet—are visible on their shoulder boards. Each has an
anchor on his sleeve—the emblem of naval infantry—and on their
belts a grenade and a knife. This is an amateur front-line photograph, or perhaps one taken by a wartime newspaper correspon-
dent who had showed up to gather materials about distinguished
soldiers and posed them on a bright summer day somewhere at the
front. They are happy—have they had a combat success?

In the middle, with a bandaged head and binoculars on his
chest, is their commander. He is distinguished not only by shoulder boards with three small stars but also by a beard, which does
not in any way make him look older.

There was a story behind this beard. On the first day of the
war, *komsomolets* Viktor Kalganov, an electrician at one of
Moscow's factories, declared: "I will not shave until we have
defeated Hitler!"

He became a soldier of a detachment of young men, created for operations in the enemy rear. He passed through his first combat schooling in the snowy forests around Moscow and later in the swamps around Leningrad, already in the naval infantry, and became a commander of a detachment of scouts.

This photograph was taken in the summer of 1943, in the coastal mountains near Novorossiysk. Later, the sailors of the detachment of "the Beard," as his comrades nicknamed Kalganov, operated in Crimea and on the Danube.

In the pages of this book you will become acquainted with the detachment's heroes; you will see that the young sons of many peoples—Russians, Ukrainians, Byelorussians, Georgians, and Tatars—fought shoulder to shoulder. At various times, there were Spaniards, Romanians, and several Yugoslavs along with them in the detachment.

The scouts had many voluntary helpers in the cities along the Danube and in the villages of each of the countries to which these men were among the first to arrive as liberators.

You will see that all the detachment's scouts were brave, enduring, capable soldiers. During their school years, many of them were outstanding athletes, attracted to rifle marksmanship, swimming, wrestling, and track. All this was to their advantage in the war. The scouts had to operate as snipers, fight in hand-to-hand combat, conduct parachute jumps, climb up steep mountain slopes, drive motor vehicles, steer small boats, swim in the icy waters of the Danube, and capture "tongues."[2]

Don't think that the people who made up this detachment were out of the ordinary. During the war years, many of our Soviet people committed acts of heroism no less remarkable at the front and in the enemy rear. Having learned how self-confidently the scouts of this detachment operated, however, you will call them heroes, although their missions were not always successful.

But form your opinion of these people not only in the results of any one reconnaissance patrol. Also consider the bravery they displayed as they conducted any dangerous task assigned to them.

Perhaps in reading this book you will doubt its truthfulness. But unbelievable things happen in war. I didn't make anything up. In this regard, I want to relate only those events that were made known to me from the scouts themselves, from their former commanders, and from some sparsely worded archives.

It is possible that the narrative will seem too terse, that you will want to know more about each soldier in the detachment. But the limits of this book did not permit me to recount everything about everyone. A separate narrative could have been written about any of the detachment's scouts—a narrative about a person who picked up a weapon in still young hands and with a firm step went down the most risky of all wartime roads, the road of a scout.

This book does not contain a narrative about everyone. Nor does it contain a full, exhaustive history of the detachment. There were too many glorious deeds to be recounted in one book. I have written only about the incidents that to me were the most characteristic. I have told only several of the most interesting, in my opinion, stories associated with the scouts. Therefore, do not judge me sternly if you do not learn all that you want to learn about the detachment and its people from this book or you do not find the names of everyone who fought in the detachment.

I didn't know what to call this book—a narrative, a collection of stories, or simply sketches. Is it important under which literary rubric this book will be released? I want only one thing—that you learn about these people.

Let the up to now almost unknown feats of these young people in sailors' *tel'nyashkas*[3] become a never-fading example.

Through the pages of this book you will move along with the detachment of scouts in the enemy rear in the mountains of the Caucasus and Crimea; sail the Danube, whose waters were mixed with fire and blood; fight your way across bridges blown up by the enemy and over mines concealed in the depths; fight your way first into Belgrade with the scouts. Gathering up all your courage, you will penetrate with them into the floating stench of the underground labyrinth of Budapest, greet the radiant Victory

Day [9 May 1945] together with them far beyond Vienna, marvel at their combat adventures, and be carried away with their bravery, resourcefulness, and endurance.

And may you have the desire to be as faithful a son of the Motherland as was each of them.

COMMANDOS
FROM THE SEA

CHAPTER ONE

TO THE AID STATION

Three horsemen in Red Army uniforms with submachine guns[1] slung over their shoulders rode at a trot along the rocky, potholed cart track that wound between yellowed scrub trees, exposed to the southern sun. None of them appeared to be above the age of twenty. The blue and white stripes of their sailors' *tel'nyashkas* showed from under the flapping collars of their fatigues. By the way all three sat in their saddles, one could guess that they were not particularly skilled cavalrymen. A small armored car with a machine gun sticking out of its open-top turret followed behind the horsemen, lurching across the ruts. Two heads in faded *pilotkas* could be seen above the edge of the armor. The driver's young but bearded face showed through the propped-open windshield.

The beard's owner, Lieutenant Kalganov, commander of a platoon of scouts, was moving out on a regular search mission with his soldiers. The platoon and its parent naval infantry battalion had arrived from Leningrad to the Tuapse area two months earlier, in April 1942.[2] It was not easy for the scouts to operate on unfamiliar terrain. In the confusion of forest groves, gullies, and ravines, they had to identify what was ours and what was no-man's land, where the enemy was, and where the enemy dugouts and trench lines were concealed behind the foliage.

Their task had become even more difficult now that the Germans had begun their offensive to capture Tuapse and break out from the coast. The situation was changing continuously, and new information on the enemy was required all the time. The scouts rarely rested.

Their current mission was particularly difficult: they not only had to discern what positions the advancing enemy was fortifying but also determine what forces he was bringing forward.

The road grew increasingly narrow and more winding, becoming more like a trail. The armored car proceeded with difficulty. Finally, the lieutenant stopped the vehicle. He ordered the driver, to whom he had been giving directions, and one of his sailors, Yumachev, "Camouflage the vehicle here, stand watch at the machine gun, and wait for us."

The lieutenant deployed in this manner in case the enemy detected the scouts and attempted to pursue them. The vehicle would then be able to provide cover.

Kalganov mounted his horse. Borisov had been riding it and now moved on foot. Two other sailors, Krivda and Yusupov, continued up the trail on horseback.

It was quiet in the forest. Nothing suggested the presence of the enemy. But moving slowly along the narrow path, the scouts vigilantly inspected and attentively listened. The enemy could be near. The trail wandered deeper into the forest thicket. Kalganov referred to his map and compass more and more frequently. Somewhere, not far up ahead, was the village of Chilipsi. Was it occupied by the enemy?

Only a short distance remained to Chilipsi, by Kalganov's calculations, when he noticed some men in civilian clothes in the bushes up ahead. They apparently had already seen the scouts but were standing quietly. Two of them, rifles in hand, came out onto the trail.

"Partisans!" the sailors exclaimed with pleasure and halted their horses.

The partisans informed them that the Germans were rushing new reinforcements toward the rail lines and highways leading to Tuapse. But they did not know to what sectors of the front these units were headed.

"Well, we'll wait and find out," and Kalganov asked the partisan how best to penetrate through the enemy front line positions into his rear.

The partisans explained, cautioning him that although the German positions were not continuous through the forest, there were patrols, ambushes, and observation posts everywhere.

"Just the same, we have to get through," said Kalganov. "We need information."

"Perhaps our prisoners can help you?" asked the partisans.

"What kind of prisoners?"

"Take a look!"

They led the sailors into the bush, where ten dark-complected eastern types in German uniforms sat under guard of two partisans. One was wearing a German *pilotka*, the others lambskin caps.

"Where did you get them?" asked Kalganov.

"They're from the Islamic Legion.[3] We captured them today."

Yusupov, standing next to Kalganov, threw the captives a question in the Tatar language. One of them, also as dark complected and with the same high cheekbones as Yusupov, answered immediately, smiling broadly. But Yusupov was not happy. His eyes flashed angrily, and he reached for his submachine gun.

"You traitor! Dog! You shame our people!"

"Don't get excited, Sayfulla," Kalganov held him back. "I will interrogate your countrymen."

The prisoners could tell nothing instructive about the enemy. But during the conversation, Kalganov came up with a good idea.

"These scum are worthless to us," he said to the partisans, "but we can use their uniforms."

Kalganov sent Krivda with the horses back toward the armored car, ordering him to bring it and the horses to the forest ravine that was their rally point by evening.

Kalganov, Borisov, and Yusupov put the uniforms taken from the "legionnaires" on over their own fatigues, replaced their own *pilotkas* with the sheepskin caps, and took their identification papers. They asked the partisans to give them their wagon and harnessed team. Kalganov and Borisov bandaged their arms and heads so the bandages were visible, hid the submachine guns in the bottom of the wagon, and laid down in it. Kalganov said to Yusupov:

"You have the personality most resembling a 'legionnaire.' Sit on the driver's seat as though you are hauling us from the front line to the hospital. Act very important."

Yes, the position to which the commander had appointed him was very important. As the driver, he would be the first to engage the Germans in conversation if they encountered any, and he had to conduct himself decisively and discreetly. But the lieutenant could rely on Yusupov. He knew this *komsomolets* would not let him down. Yusupov was composed and decisive.

Saying goodbye to the partisans, the scouts set off through the thicket in the direction of the road that led into the German-occupied village. Kalganov figured that no one would suspect the "wounded," and his team, giving the appearance of looking for a German hospital, would be able to find out much. If they were lucky, they would also capture a "tongue."

At the same time, Krivda, leading two horses by the reins, rode back toward the armored car. He attentively looked over everything with a scout's observant eye. When he had almost arrived at the site where the armored car was hidden, he saw the clear, fresh imprint of a German boot on the clay soil of the path. Even the impression of the nails in the heel were clearly visible. When the scouts had moved down this trail a short time ago, these tracks did not exist!

Turning into the bushes, Krivda left his horses and began to follow the tracks. He saw not only the imprints of German boot heels but also trampled grass and broken branches. The tracks led toward where the armored car was parked. The sailor's heart skipped a beat.

Here the tracks divided—the enemy was surrounding the armored car. Germans! Krivda saw their backs appearing and disappearing in the bushes. Their submachine guns were at the ready. This meant they were closing in. But perhaps he could still manage to help his comrades, to warn them.

Bypassing the enemy through the bushes, but keeping them in view, Krivda quickly and noiselessly, trying not to shake the thick branches, hurried toward the armored car. There it was! Yunachev, not suspecting anything, was looking up out of the turret and smoking. The Germans would soon begin shooting or throwing grenades. They could not delay for a second! Krivda shouldered his submachine gun and fired a burst into the bushes toward the advancing enemy. Rifle fire cracked in return.

Looking around, Krivda spotted Yunachev's head diving into the turret, followed immediately by the chattering of the armored car's machine gun.

The exchange of fire was brief. The Germans, realizing that they would be unable to capture the armored car by surprise, were forced back, driven by the bursts from the armored car's machine gun and Krivda's submachine gun. Krivda crawled up to the armored car and said to Yunachev and the driver:

"Drive into the gully! We'll pick up our horses on the way."

At the same time, the wagon with the three "wounded" was unhurriedly lumbering along the rural track, already in the enemy's rear. They passed through the villages of Chilipsi and Shaumyan, confirming that they were full of the enemy. Outside of the villages, they saw several German artillery batteries and made note of their location. They also noted the site where ammunition crates were stacked near the road under some trees, in what direction the telephone cable was strung, and the direction of movement of trucks and horse-drawn wagons and the nature of their cargo. Several times they encountered Germans heading toward the front line on trucks or wagons or walking. The scouts were ready. But the Germans riding and walking by did not pay any attention to the wagon with the "wounded."

Up ahead was a railroad and beyond it, past the grade crossing, the white huts of Goytkh. This village also interested the scouts because it was located along the path of the enemy's offensive.

While still far off, the scouts noted that a patrol of two German soldiers was standing near the railroad track. When the wagon approached the grade crossing, one of the Germans stopped it with a hand paddle, commanding:

"Halt!"

"Hospital! Hospital!" responded Yusupov, pointing at the "wounded." But the German, suspiciously looking into the wagon, demanded:

"*Ausweis* [Documents]!"

Yusupov handed him three soldiers' identification booklets the partisans had taken from the prisoners. The German turned the booklets over in his hand, then handed them back, cursing: "*Dumkopf!*" he pointed. "*Nach lazaret-faren zo!*" [The hospital is that way.]

The scouts surmised that the patrol cursed them because they were traveling in the wrong direction. It was a nuisance, but they had to comply. Nonetheless, they had to reach Goytkh!

Yusupov turned the wagon around, and as soon as the grade crossing disappeared from view behind the trees, on the lieutenant's instruction he steered the wagon straight through the bushes toward Goytkh. Their objective was to intersect the railroad at another crossing where, perhaps, there would be no sentries.

They drove for some time along a narrow, rocky cart track, then through a ravine along the mountain stream Pshish, which passed close to Goytkh. The road finally came out of the thickly overgrown ravine, and up ahead once again the white huts of Goytkh on the opposite side of the village could be seen. It was a large village.

Dusty bushes pressed in on both sides of the road. Stunted trees with leaves dried out by the sun grew thickly, in places weighed down by liana and wild grapevines. The scouts were cautious—a German patrol could stop them here. There were probably many Germans in Goytkh itself, as in the other two villages that they had passed through a short time before.

When just a short distance remained to the first buildings, Kalganov instructed Yusupov to turn the wagon into the bushes.

Before they drove into the settlement, they needed to check it out. All three dismounted and, grabbing their weapons, began cautiously to move toward the village through the bushes along the road.

They walked a little way, and Kalganov gave a sign to stop. The scouts froze. Someone was coming down the road toward them, not hurrying. The heels of this lone walker struck the road with a regular beat.

Carefully, not disturbing a leaf, Kalganov peered out from behind a bush. A German!

He was already close. A private, the collar of his uniform unbuttoned, his *pilotka* on the back of his head—it was hot! He had his rifle slung across his shoulder—what was there to be afraid of here in the rear?

"We must take him!" Kalganov made a snap decision. The German was coming from Goytkh. Perhaps he was even a headquarters runner with a pouch.

Stunned by a blow of a buttstock, the German fell. They grabbed him and dragged him off into the bushes. They found a soldier's identification booklet and several letters in his pocket.

The prisoner did not regain consciousness. They bandaged his head and placed him in the wagon. Now they had a genuine wounded man in the wagon, with blood showing on his bandage. When the German fell, his face struck a rock in the road. They bandaged his mouth especially diligently so that when he regained consciousness he could not cry out.

Kalganov did not abandon his plan to go into Goytkh and look around to see what was happening there—the more so now that the presence of a wounded German in the wagon would likely diminish the suspicion of any onlooker.

But another patrol stopped them at the other entrance to the village, two soldiers who also asked for their documents. Yusupov handed them over with a calm face, including the documents of the captured German. The patrol looked long and hard at the documents, talking between themselves, glancing suspiciously at the people sitting in the wagon in German uniforms.

Attentively monitoring the soldiers, Kalganov discreetly began to grope for his submachine gun under his side.

One of the soldiers moved off to the side, brought up his rifle, and commanded:

"*Stehen* [Stay where you are]!"

The other soldier, the one with the identification booklets in his hands, ran somewhere, probably to report.

There was no time to waste. Pulling his submachine gun out from under himself, Kalganov fired a short burst at the German. Borisov fired a burst at the same time.

"Sayfulla, take off!" shouted Kalganov.

Yusupov turned the wagon around sharply and lashed the horses. Bouncing and careening on the stones, the wagon raced off away from the village. They heard firing and shouts behind them—the chase was on.

"To the left!" commanded Kalganov.

The wagon flew into the bushes.

"Stop!" Kalganov jumped down and grabbed the German prisoner.

"We will carry him!"

It was difficult to move through the prickly underbrush with their heavy burden. But a lifesaving gully was up ahead. They would soon reach it. The bullets were already whistling over their heads.

The three scouts were stubbornly pushing straight through the bushes with their catch. This "tongue" could give valuable information. How could they abandon him?

The pursuers were closing in. Another minute or two and they would have to fight. The bullets were slapping through nearby bushes. The increasingly distinguishable, excited voices of the pursuers could be heard approaching.

"Get rid of him!" Kalganov commanded, with pain in his voice.

The "tongue" was left lying in the bushes. Stripping off the foreign uniforms and hats, the three scouts fired their submachine guns in concert. There was a momentary silence.

"Did we lose the Germans?" Yusupov asked in a whisper.

"No!" Kalganov replied firmly. "We haven't broken away from them. Let's go!"

The now lightened scouts ran into the heart of the forest. It was unfortunate that they had to abandon their "tongue." But, burdened by their load, they might not have escaped their pursuers and could have been killed without delivering the intelligence they had collected. The scouts did not have the option to risk losing already gained information.

They continued their flight until finally they calculated that they had moved past the enemy front line. All around was no-man's land. But the enemy continued to pursue them. The crackling of branches grew louder, and the voices were heard more clearly behind them, in the thick underbrush.

Up ahead above the undergrowth the scouts spotted the lightning-scorched black tree that stood out against the background of forest green. This was a reference point. The tree was on the opposite side of a ravine. Their comrades should be waiting for them there, on a forest trail.

Kalganov, Borisov, and Yusupov, moving through the thorny bushes, descended into the steep ravine, jumped from rock to rock across the stream, and clambered up the opposite bank by holding onto branches and protruding roots. Again, submachine-gun bursts rattled through the trees—perhaps the Germans had seen the scouts when they crossed the ravine. Branches knocked off a dead tree by bullets fell on their heads.

"Krivda! Yunachev!" called Kalganov, charging across the vegetation at the edge of the ravine toward the road.

"Over here!" they shouted from up ahead.

"Start the motor! Get the horses!"

Several seconds later, all three were in their saddles. Ducking to avoid branches and vines overhanging the trail, the three scouts galloped toward our positions.

The armored car followed the horsemen by five minutes. It had delayed so as to fire several machine-gun bursts at the pursuing Germans.

The lieutenant walked with a heavy heart to report to the chief of staff on the results of their reconnaissance. He figured that the search had been conducted unsatisfactorily and was prepared to receive a reprimand. They had been unable to penetrate into Goytkh, and they had struck their "tongue" too hard so that they could not interrogate him in the field. They were unable to drag him back, and in the end, the enemy had detected and almost captured them.

Kalganov certainly didn't expect the chief of staff, after he had received the report, to congratulate him:

"Good work! Thank you for your effort."

Noting the lieutenant's disbelief and look of guilt, the chief of staff smiled, saying:

"You are surprised? But you spent an entire day in the German rear and were in two villages. Your information was valuable." He added, "Don't worry that you didn't accomplish everything you planned. There will come a time when you can execute a mission without a hitch."

CHAPTER TWO

İRON SOUVENİR

İt was the third summer of the war. The front line had remained stable in the mountains of the Caucasus coastline for many months. The enemy had been halted around Tuapse in the fall of 1942. In and around Novorossiysk, the Germans were reinforcing their lines and bringing up more forces, in anticipation of our offensive. Soviet troops were already engaged around Novorossiysk, and, despite the enemy reinforcements, the bridgehead of Myskhako Peninsula, the noted "land of fire," was being stubbornly held by Soviet forces.

Our command needed precise information about the enemy's forces and positions to prepare for the offensive against Novorossiysk. It was not easy to obtain such information. The enemy was digging in, carefully camouflaging his positions and using the terrain. The front line in the Novorossiysk area passed through densely forested mountains. Enemy observers maintained continuous watch over the neutral zone.

The scouts of our units on the Novorossiysk sector of the front had attempted more than once to penetrate beyond the enemy's forward edge. But they had been unsuccessful. The enemy, fearing our offensive, was very vigilant. The sailor scouts of Kalganov's platoon, who by this time had become a senior lieutenant, were sent to the Novorossiysk sector from Tuapse.

Having received the mission to penetrate behind the front line of the enemy's defenses, Kalganov, along with his scouts, began to study the enemy's forward edge to determine where it would be easier to cross it.

The scouts spent days, from dawn to dusk, crawling into the neutral zone, sneaking as close as possible to enemy positions and, skillfully camouflaging themselves, observing for the locations of machine gun nests and how the enemy rotated his observation posts. They noted how much and where work was being done to reinforce the positions. In the evening, when the scouts had returned from the forward edge, they gathered in Kalganov's bunker.

"We see the Germans every day but do not shoot them. This isn't right. We must combine our observation with sniping."

The scouts guardedly supported their commander's suggestion. All of them were fairly good shots and were itching to do something whenever they got a glimpse of a green uniform behind the bushes on the enemy side. They received the sniper rifles requested by Kalganov from the command. Each scout was issued a sniper rifle,[1] on a temporary basis, in exchange for his submachine gun.

The success of a sniper depends not only on how good his eyes are but also on the quality of the scope. Before he can take aim and fire, a sniper, and also a scout, must know how to take up a good position in which he cannot himself be spotted. A sniper must know how to maintain his endurance and composure in any circumstance so that his hands holding the weapon remain steady. The scouts possessed all these qualities. Their commander was their example.

One time, before dawn, Kalganov crawled into the neutral zone. He crept to a tree selected earlier, not far in front of which an enemy communications trench had been spotted that extended out from the rear, from a hill. Thick foliage covered the scout from enemy eyes.

The sun came up but was obscured by the trees. Its rays, penetrating between the branches, gilded the leaves. The communications trench, which was entirely exposed, was empty. But Kalganov waited to see how often the Germans used it. Where were their observers in the immediate area? Could the scouts attempt to cross the German positions at this site?

Some time had passed when Kalganov spotted several German officers coming along the trench from the rear. Looking at them through the scope of his sniper rifle, he noted that the officers were escorting an important superior, who was probably inspecting the position. The temptation was great. Kalganov placed the crosshairs on the chest of this important German, around whom the remaining officers were crowding servilely, and squeezed the trigger. One of the officers rushed to his fallen chief. When the second bullet cut him down, the remainder of the group fled.

Kalganov had not begun to exult in his success when there was a loud crackling over his head.

"They spotted me!" Kalganov dropped like a rock at the base of the tree. A knurled bough knocked down by a machine-gun burst struck him in the back. He threw it off and, pressing to the earth, forcing his way through the tangled forest grass, crawled toward our own position. Machine guns chattered right behind him, with rounds whistling and popping, cutting the leaves off the branches. Mortar bombs were exploding in rapid sequence.

Day after day, the scouts patiently conducted their watch in the neutral zone, simultaneously accomplishing their sniper duties. Their sniper count rose, and they gathered information about the disposition of the enemy's front-line positions. But only at the end of the second week was the scouts' commander finally able to select the site where they would cross into the enemy's rear area. The senior lieutenant decided to go on reconnaissance with a small group so as to remain less noticeable. He took only four sailors on the search with him.

On a moonless July night, five scouts successfully crossed over between the enemy's forward observation posts. They walked the entire night along the tree-covered mountain slopes, penetrated into an enemy-occupied village, and inspected ravines and fields, searching for the locations of artillery batteries, supply dumps, and headquarters. They gathered valuable information.

Morning approached. When they set off on this search, they counted on crossing back through the enemy's forward edge and returning to their own positions before daylight. But they had spent considerably more time on reconnaissance than they had planned.

Dawn caught the scouts in a thick forest, along the edge of which passed a road that led through the immediate rear to the German positions. It was too dangerous to go farther. They made the decision to wait out the day.

They could have withdrawn somewhere into a deep gully and sat until evening. But the scouts did not want to waste the time. German vehicles were moving along the road. It appeared that movement did not stop during the day—the road was covered by the forest. If the road was visible at all from our side of the lines, then much of it was obscured. It was important to determine how the enemy was using this road and what type of vehicles he was moving.

"It may be dangerous to set up right along the road for observation," pondered Kalganov, "and suddenly Germans happen along, and stop for a break. Can we observe from farther away, from the woods? We may not see anything because of the trees."

While deciding, Kalganov looked at the trees that stood thickly on the edge of the forest. The night fog still lay between them, but it was already dissipating, and the sky was showing light.

"We will sit in the trees!" Kalganov decided.

Each scout chose a tree, old, with many branches, thick beech or oak, densely tangled with liana or forest grapevines. Each climbed high in his tree and hid in the thick foliage.

It had already become light. The five scouts observed without exposing themselves. Trucks, horse-drawn wagons, and columns of German soldiers passed by on the road. It was obvious that some kind of regrouping was going on. The scouts' observant eyes took in everything.

The sun was high in the sky when the clank of tracks and the heavy rumble of motors was heard. Tanks? Yes, these were tanks. Three of them pulled up even with the trees in which the scouts sat and, turning off the road, stopped right under them. The motors fell silent, but the opening hatches clanged and rattled. Tankers climbed out of the vehicles and began to spread out on the grass to eat.

Looking down on the tankers, unconcernedly sprawled in the shade of the tree, Kalganov thought to himself: "Could we grab one of them as a 'tongue'?" He did not have the mission to capture a "tongue." The temptation was great, but Kalganov faced too many enemy tankers.

The tanks departed. But the scouts had seen them, determined their type, and noted their direction of movement.

The long summer day dragged on, and five scouts sat between the branches, continuing to observe the road.

Only when the shadows began to fade beneath the trees did Kalganov decide it was time to come down. By the time they reached the forward edge of the German position, where they would be especially vigilant, it would be completely dark. Then it would be possible to cross the front line with minimal risk. The scouts returned to our lines late at night and delivered valuable information about the enemy.

After this search patrol, during the weeks that preceded the launching of our offensive on Novorossiysk, Kalganov and his sailors covertly passed through the enemy's forward positions and conducted other searches in his immediate rear and deeper near Myskhako on numerous occasions. He took young scouts with him, who became more experienced with each patrol, and older scouts such as Yusupov, Borisov, and Yunachev. The scouts carried back important information that helped the command plan strikes against the enemy.

But each time it became more difficult to return. The enemy, disturbed by the scouts' activities, attempted to intercept and destroy them. Frequently, to break off from pursuit or avoid an ambush, the scouts had to deviate from their intended march route and come through regardless of the obstacles. Kalganov had to take a larger number of men with him so he could fight more successfully should the enemy happen to pin his scouts down.

During a return from one search, however, the scouts had no alternative route to escape from the pursuing enemy except to pass between two bunkers. It would be difficult to slip between them unnoticed. But the Germans in the bunkers did not spot the scouts, and Kalganov decided to take advantage of this. Grenades hurled by sailors' powerful arms flew into the embrasure of one of the bunkers. The layer of logs collapsed, burying the German machine gunners beneath it. But at that same moment, machine-gun fire spewed from the neighboring bunker, blocking the path of withdrawal.

"Sayfulla!" Kalganov ordered Yusupov. "You take charge! Take Borisov, Yunachev, and two others, and suppress the machine gun with grenades!"

Yusupov with four sailors behind him crawled toward the bunker. Rushing the embrasure from the flank, they threw several grenades. These exploded in front of the bunker and collapsed the embrasure. But then the machine gun rattled from a second embrasure. The Germans had repositioned their weapon.

The fire prevented the scouts from closing on the bunker to throw more grenades, but the sailors had to accomplish their mission.

"Wait, I'll go alone!" Yusupov stopped his comrades.

"Where to, Sayfulla?"

But Yusupov obstinately shook his head and crawled through the grass, grasping a grenade in his hand. He managed to reach the bunker from a flank where the enemy machine gunners could not see him. Then the others observed as Yusupov lay on top of the bunker, almost over the embrasure, and reached toward the edge of the embrasure with his grenade hand. It was a difficult stretch. Yusupov inched forward, lowering himself a bit, until he was hanging over the embrasure. His hand waved, and Yusupov jerked upward and backward, avoiding his own grenade explosion. There was a muffled thump in front of the embrasure. Yusupov jumped down from the bunker and, as a sign that everything was all right, waved to his comrades with his submachine gun. At that moment, there was a burst of fire from the embrasure directly at Yusupov. How had the machine gun remained intact? With his last effort, the scout threw his now unresponding body at the embrasure and fully masked it.

Komsomolets Sayfulla Yusupov, famed warrior, who had begun his combat path back in 1939 as a fighter in a ski battalion on the Finnish front,[2] did not return to his native Ufa, to the foundry.

Taking advantage of the fact that the embrasure was covered by Yusupov's body and the machine gun could not fire at them, the scouts rushed the bunker's entrance. Their hearts were boiling with pain and anger. Several submachine-gun bursts finished off the Germans in the bunker who had survived Yusupov's grenade. While the scouts were making their way between the two bunkers, however, German submachine gunners found them. They had to be engaged.

The submachine gunners, of which there were several score, went to ground. Returning fire and covering each other, the scouts continued to withdraw. They were already close to the neutral zone. They had only to cross an abatis[3] constructed by the Germans, and then it was a stone's throw to their own positions. Someone had to delay the enemy, even if only for several minutes, while the others negotiated the obstacle.

Yunachev was called forward. He ran into a trench near the bunker where Yusupov had died and opened fire on the pursuers with his submachine gun, covering the withdrawal of his comrades. But there were many of the enemy. They were closing in, running between the bushes and trees. Already a German grenade with a long wooden handle was arching through the air toward Yunachev. It struck the revetment, knocking loose some dirt, and skidded into the trench.

Deftly picking up the grenade, Yunachev hurled it back. He threw his own grenade right behind it, toward the flat-sided gray-green helmets of the submachine gunners he glimpsed between the bushes. Yunachev had two grenades left. He waited until the Germans closed in on him and then threw them. The Germans went to ground again.

The scouts, meanwhile, had reached the obstacle. It was difficult to climb across the logs piled one atop the other, the protruding branches laced with barbed wire, and with bullets whistling overhead. "We will move on the ground," Kalganov decided. On his command, the sailors began to crawl under the tree trunks, between stumps resting on the ground. Yunachev, having accomplished his mission, quickly rejoined them.

Kalganov, hiding a map with reconnoitered enemy positions marked on it under his shirt, crawled at the rear. He had already made it through the log obstacle when something hit near his head that was not a tree or a rock, followed immediately by a sharp hissing. "Grenade!" He instantly buried his face in the tough, sunburned grass.

He regained consciousness in the hospital. His head was bandaged, and it hurt. He learned from the doctor that he had survived by a miracle. The grenade, thrown by a German into the log obstacle, had exploded near his head. Two fragments had struck and wounded him—in the back of the head and the cranium.

Sailors soon arrived to visit with their commander.

"Did you give my map to the headquarters?" Kalganov asked first.

"We passed it along." They calmed him. "We passed on all the information."

They recounted how it had happened. His comrades saw that their commander lay immobile after the explosion of the German grenade. They removed their belts and secured him by the legs—there was no other way under the fire—hauling him back to their own lines. They told how they went back at night to the bunker where Yusupov had died and carried his bullet-ridden body back. They had buried Yusupov with a three-volley salute not far from the forward edge, on a leaf-covered hill between two thick oaks.

After the sailors had visited Kalganov, a tall, black-haired man with generals' shoulder boards on his blouse appeared in the tent. Looking around the tent, he asked:

"Where is our famous scout?"

They pointed to Kalganov.

"Look at you, young man, with a beard!" The general was surprised and, coming over to Kalganov's cot, warmly greeted him.

This was Lieutenant General K. L. Leselidze, commander of the 18th Army.[4] The scouts had conducted their search in the sector of his formations that were preparing for the storm of Novorossiysk. The general was very satisfied with the results of their work and particularly of the last search patrol, during which Kalganov had been wounded.

Leselidze asked Kalganov how he was feeling, thanked him for the intelligence data he had delivered, and said:

"I have coordinated with your fleet command, and I'm awarding you, Comrade Senior Lieutenant, with a ground forces' decoration—the Order of Aleksandr Nevskiy[5]—for successful reconnaissance. No one else in the entire Black Sea Fleet has received this award. You will be the first."

This award became for Kalganov a remembrance of the many difficult days and nights of reconnaissance on the front around Novorossiysk, a remembrance of the daring searches in the enemy's rear and of the battles they had to fight returning from there, a remembrance of the feat of Sayfulla Yusupov, of everything they experienced in the summer of 1943.

But he has still one more remembrance, an iron souvenir: a small grenade fragment stuck in his cranium that remains there to this day, despite the doctors' efforts.

CHAPTER THREE

WATCH OVER THE SEA

It was dark and close in the tightly sealed bomber fuselage. The overcast winter night was black through the glass of a small porthole. Pressed together shoulder to shoulder, Senior Lieutenant Kalganov and the sailor scouts sat in sheepskin coats, with parachutes on their backs. Strapped to their bodies were weapons and equipment—everything they might need in the enemy's rear. When they were preparing for the flight, Kalganov had asked each of them: "Do you need anything? It's not too late to turn it down." No one turned down anything that was offered.

Two were a bit off to the side, in the forward part of the compartment: radio operator Valya Morozova, who was to jump with the rest of them, and a young lieutenant, a parachute instructor,[1] who had trained the scouts for the jump. The two appeared to be acquainted, perhaps more than simply acquainted. Kalganov had noticed while still at the airfield that both were very agitated, although they were trying to hide it. They were anxious as twins would be before parting. This was no simple separation. What unknown events lay ahead for her?

"She's just a girl," Kalganov thought about Valya, "still eighteen years old. Will I have to 'fuss' with her?"

He would not have had these thoughts about Valya, whom he had met just before the flight, if he had known more about her. At the age of fifteen, Valya and her mother had gone into the woods to a partisan detachment when the Germans took over the small Crimean town where they lived. Valya had gone out on recon- naissance and had fought in battles, losing her mother in one of them. She had broken out of the encirclement and survived, gar- nering a wealth of experience. Sick, Valya was taken out to the mainland, and, upon recovery she volunteered to take a radio oper- ator's course so she would be sent into the enemy's rear once again.

The faces of the group were not visible in the darkness. Everyone was quiet; only the rhythmic pulse of the motors was heard. But each was thinking about one thing—what was waiting for them on the ground?

Pulling at his sleeve, Kalganov looked at the illuminated watch face. The second hour of flight. "We have probably already crossed the sea, and the enemy-occupied land is below us," he thought to himself.

"Get ready!"

Kalganov pressed his face to the cold plexiglass of the small porthole. What is below? But only the impenetrable darkness reigned, and he could not distinguish the ground or the sky. Somewhere below was Yalta, and the Germans were there. But no lights were visible.

The aircraft slowly banked and began to circle. Kalganov con- tinued to look out. He was looking for the signal fires that would indicate the drop zone. There were supposed to be five fires, form- ing an "envelope." Where were they?

The aircraft made circle after circle. The motors droned uneasily.

Five fires. The sailors who had parachuted into this area ear- lier, when Kalganov was still at the front around Novorossiysk, were to prepare them. Kalganov's group had to jump from an alti- tude of almost four thousand meters because the aircraft deliver- ing them had come under antiaircraft fire and had been forced to seek altitude in the night sky. The first group of scouts—Seamen Georgiy Veretenik, Gennadiy Konshin, Sergey Menadzhiev, and radio operator Antonina Gromova—had landed in the woods between Black Mountain and Chatyrdag. They had linked up with the partisans who were watching the port of Yalta and the coastal road network. The scouts transmitted regular radio reports and prepared to receive the group that followed.[2]

One day, returning from Yalta, the scouts noticed that a line of Germans was walking through the forest, inspecting each bush. The scouts had to vacate the area quickly. But no matter what direction they tried to move, lines of enemy soldiers came toward them. The ring tightened. To break through it, they had to run across a large glade. They managed to do this, but when Konshin, the last of the group, made his break, German submachine guns fired. The enemy moving toward the glade had spotted the scout. His comrades saw him run into the bush, then heard the Germans shouting from that area. The sailors rushed to assist Konshin. They beat the bushes thoroughly but could not find their comrade.

Several days later, the partisans reported to the sailors that they had found the mutilated body of the sailor on a forest road. His ears had been cut off, his eyes gouged out, and his arms pulled out. The partisans showed the scouts the spot where they had buried him in a gully. The sailors placed a wreath of forest flowers and oak leaves on their battle comrade's grave and fired a ceremonial salute with their submachine guns, promising: "We'll avenge you!"

One of the Germans fell into the hands of partisans a short time later. On interrogation, he revealed that they had captured the seriously wounded sailor and had tried to elicit from him his purpose for being in the hills and where his comrades were. Communist Konshin had refused to answer their questions. Thanks to Konshin's resoluteness, the Germans were unable to track down and destroy the sailor scouts.

A second group landed soon after the first in the same area, around Black Mountain.[3] The group Kalganov led was the third.

Far, far away below, five tiny flashes of dim fires appeared and disappeared, hidden by the wing of the turning aircraft. Four of the fires formed a rectangle, and the fifth was in the middle—the long-awaited envelope.

The roar of the motors, the whistle of the air around the airplane's fuselage, and the sharp wind rushed up from below through the open hatch. The lieutenant instructor stood up, whispered something to Valya, and then shouted loudly:

"First!"

The sailor seated next to Kalganov stood up.

One behind the other, his comrades shuffled past Kalganov and, guided by the instructor, dropped through the open hatch, through which the howling cold night air struck their faces.

Now it was Valya's turn. She was already at the hatch. The lieutenant put his hand on her shoulder with a particularly caring gesture. Kalganov noticed that the lieutenant hesitated. But not Valya! She glanced at the young officer, then jumped through the open hatch.

"Now it's my turn!"

Kalganov crouched, leaning forward on the edge of the hatch, and threw himself head first into the night sky. But he got stuck. He was hung up on his equipment. The air forced its way into his eyes and nose, into his mouth, and into his ears with frightening strength, taking the breath out of him. Kalganov twisted his entire body, trying to get free, to clear the hatch, but in vain. He could not help himself with his hands—he was hanging upside down, caught by his harness. He felt the airplane leaning into a turn so as to cross the drop zone again. One circle, a second, a third. The bomber started into a fourth orbit.

In despair, Kalganov flailed upward with his legs. Perhaps he could kick himself free against something on the aircraft. He felt the toe of his boot strike something. At the same instant, he heard a deep machine-gun chatter. A stream of tracers passed in front of him for a second.

"What have I done?" Kalganov was horrified.

He was in trouble, and his tall height was responsible. Trying to kick himself free, Kalganov had accidentally struck a machine gun mounted near the hatch with his long leg, causing it to fire a short burst. The tracer stream punctured the darkness of the night sky, lighting it up for several seconds. But this was long enough

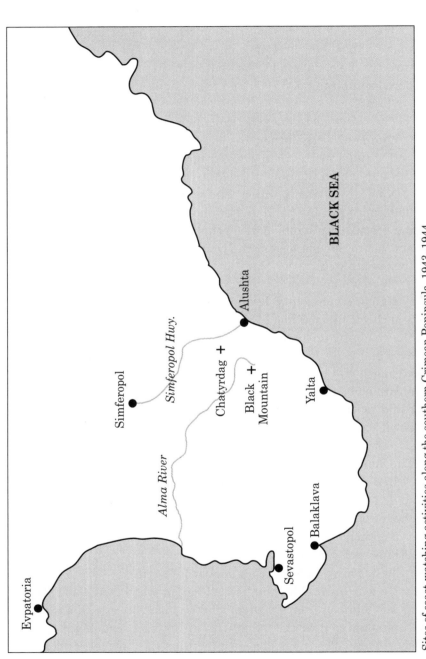

Sites of coast-watching activities along the southern Crimean Peninsula, 1943–1944.

for observers at German antiaircraft batteries positioned outside Yalta to determine the general area where the unidentified aircraft, whose motors they no doubt had long ago heard, was orbiting. Continuing his attempts to kick free of the aircraft, Kalganov saw yellowish-brown explosions flash in the black sky around the aircraft. Twinkling tracers flew up from below, out of the darkness that covered the land, to meet the clumsily turning aircraft.

Kalganov was gripped by fear at the first flak explosions. Not only was he concerned lest the aircraft be shot down with him still stuck in the hatch and he would die with it. He was also frightened that the pilot would turn the aircraft back toward base. The sailors who had already jumped out—who probably had already landed—would be without a commander, without a connection with the mainland, because he, Kalganov, was carrying the cipher tables of the new radio codes, the group's sole means of communication after landing.

"I will let my comrades down!" This fear increased his strength tenfold, but the damned hatch held onto him.

The lieutenant instructor and one of the crew members held Kalganov by the legs and pushed on his parachute-covered back. He felt stabbing pains in his sides. Finally, someone, perhaps in desperation, moved Kalganov with a forcefully applied boot below the back.

How thankful Kalganov was to whoever thought to do this! A powerful but painful blow finally freed him from the hatch.

A thought flashed through his mind in the first seconds of free fall. What if my parachute doesn't open? What if it had been damaged in the trouble in the hatch?

It opened!

Kalganov floated down under the canopy. The antiaircraft gunners fell silent, and the sound of the motors of the aircraft, finally freed of its last cargo, faded. It was pitch dark. The night darkness covered everything—the sky, the sea, and the ground.

Kalganov peered down with a searching look: perhaps the five fires were still burning? No, there was only darkness, impenetrable darkness.

Hanging from the risers, peering into the darkness, he wondered where he would come down. The aircraft had orbited the entire time over the same spot where the fires had been spotted. But perhaps the wind, which he did not sense under the canopy, was pushing him to the side?

Below, in the gloom, some spots gradually began to emerge. The white probably was snow, covering the steep slopes, and the black was the forests or ravines. Kalganov tried to get a bearing on the terrain below him. During the preparation for the flight, he had carefully studied it on the map. He and his group were to have been dropped not far from Yalta, in the area of Black Mountain, into the forest near the village of Biyuk-sala. They were to meet their comrades there. Had they linked up? Perhaps the signal fires marking the landing zone were set not by them but by the Germans? The enemy was clever and insidious and had a nose. Kalganov recalled that the time and place of his group's flight was changed several times to disorient the enemy. He also remembered that the fleet staff chief of intelligence[4] had warned him during his preflight briefing. According to our information, the enemy knew of the landing of two groups of parachutists near Yalta and was concerned that, in addition to partisans, some military detachment had appeared in the mountains. It was possible that the enemy had already captured the rest of his party.

Below, in the half-hidden darkness of the snow-covered ground, which was becoming more discernible as the parachute descended, dark spots could be made out intermingled with the white background. They were trees, and the parachute was carrying him straight toward them.

Kalganov began to pull on the risers to maneuver his parachute and avoid the trees. But he was not very successful. The ground was coming up fast, the parachute dropped inexorably toward the snow cover. Perhaps they had spotted him from below?

The rustling of parachute fabric was followed by the cracking of branches. The silk canopy covered the crown of a tall tree, and Kalganov came down in a crotch of the tree, as in a saddle.

"Did they spot me or not?" He quickly freed himself from his parachute, grabbed onto the main trunk, and climbed down. He looked around. The ground was snow-covered. Nearby stood a half-broken-down fence made of sticks. Beyond it was a dark structure. It was quiet all around. Perhaps no one had seen him. But he must hurry! Someone might come. First, he had to pull his parachute down out of the tree and hide it.

It was not easy to remove the parachute. Its fabric and risers were caught in the branches. It took Kalganov fifteen minutes to pull the parachute down and bury it in the snow at the foot of the tree. He had hardly finished when he heard someone jump heavily across the fence. Kalganov fell like a rock in the snow and made his submachine gun ready to fire in the direction from which he had heard the noise. A swaying dark figure was moving slowly toward him. It became more visible against the backdrop of the snow. Putting down his submachine gun, Kalganov removed his cap from his head and wiped away the sweat. Close by, shaking its mane, hobbled a downcast horse.

Kalganov hurried away from the tree toward a forest, which showed up dark on a steep mountain slope. Burrowing into a thicket, he oriented himself with a compass. Then he set off in the direction the group was to take when they landed. True, he was not sure that he had landed where he needed to or that the small village into which he had almost dropped was Biyuk-sala, the designated rally point. But he walked, looking around at the terrain and listening, anticipating the signals—rifle shots—that one of the parachutists was to fire at a specific time if everyone had not assembled. This was risky—the Germans could hear the shots—but there was no other recourse.

Kalganov waited for the signal shot and walked toward its sound. The shots guided his route. But he had to deviate a bit across a wooded hillside in the night darkness before he encountered the sailors of his group and those who had landed earlier and were now receiving the new arrivals.

By the end of the night, the entire detachment had assembled in a base near Black Mountain, hidden from enemy eyes in a deep, deserted gully between two wooded hills. Holes had been burrowed out for occupation, their entrances camouflaged with white parachute cloth and branches.

Now the scouts were all together: Seamen Grigoriy Kotsar, Mikhail Shabanin, Vladimir Kalinichenko, and Sergey Kondrat'ev, Senior Sailors Aleksey Gura and Ivan Martynenko, Petty Officers First Class Aleksandr Morozov, Vasiliy Globa, Venedikt Andreev, and Gennadiy Chichilo, and radio operators Sonya Dubova, Valya Morozova, Zhenya D'yachenko, and Tonya Gromova, and Veretenik and Menadzhiev, the very first from the detachment to land on Crimean soil.[5] Among the scouts was a single foreigner—Antonio Luis, a radio operator. As a young man during the Spanish Civil War, he ended up in the Soviet Union and now considered it his second home. He was now fighting for his Motherland.[6]

Kalganov still did not know the people with whom he was to operate in the enemy rear. There was not a single person among them who had gone on reconnaissance with him around Tuapse and Novorossiysk. But he knew that these to whom his wartime fate was henceforth connected were not novices in the affairs of war.

When the occupiers arrived in his native Kherson, Georgiy Veretenik, a fourteen-year-old lad, headed across the front to rejoin his people. This *komsomolets* and son of a communist, a combat commander and participant in the civil war and the Great Patriotic War, did not want to remain under the authority of the enemy for even a day. He managed to pass through the front. Some sailors–border guards who were fighting in the Kherson area—took him in, and he became their scout. It was there that Veretenik accomplished his first feat. The Germans placed him, as a "local resident," in a headquarters bus to show them the route. Risking his life, he guided the bus so that it drove into our own positions. All the Germans on the bus were captured. Later, when the enemy burst into the Crimea, the fifteen-year-old scout fell in with the partisans during the retreat. They sent him out to the mainland by air, and he became a fighter in the fleet reconnaissance detachment.[7]

Aleksey Gura was the son of a Donbas miner. He was drafted into the Black Sea Fleet a year before the war, fought from the war's first days, earned the right to become a communist in battle, and then became one. Grigoriy Kotsar had landed along with Gura on the coastline below Novorossiysk to conduct reconnaissance and diversions in the enemy rear. Siberian Venedikt Andreev, who began his naval service the same year as Gura, was initially an artilleryman, then a scout. Aleksandr Morozov, one of the oldest men in the detachment, received his battle christening earlier than the rest. In 1939, he was voluntarily sent to the front as a sailor in a Baltic Fleet rifle brigade and participated in the war with the White Finns. On 22 June 1941, in Ismail, Morozov, then a sailor of the Danube Flotilla, again heard shells bursting, and with this day the war began to turn over new pages in his biography: breakout from Ismail, the battle for Kherson, wounding on Tendrovskiy Spit, hospital, the defense of Sevastopol, another wound, and, after recuperation, service in the Black Sea Fleet reconnaissance detachment, where Morozov went at his own request. Morozov had passed through the combat school of the scout, landed in amphibious assault, captured "tongues," and was wounded three times outside Kerch and Novorossiysk, on the coast, and in the mountain passes.[8]

Like Morozov, Vasiliy Globa chose the difficult and dangerous duty of reconnaissance. Before the war, he had been a lathe operator in the Dnepropetrovsk factory Comintern. Globa also had gone into the enemy rear on more than one occasion around Novorossiysk. Other scouts had equal amounts of combat experience.

Beginning on this memorable night, when the detachment's last reinforcements had landed, the German combat vessels and transports coming into Yalta were subjected to air strikes by our fleet air forces. Soviet aircraft always arrived on station on time. Their bombs managed to catch the enemy ships before they made port. Whose hand so precisely guided these air strikes on enemy shipping? The eyes of the sailor scouts continuously monitored the Yalta port from the countless mountain heights that towered over the city. They conducted watch in small camouflaged groups: observers and one of the radio operators. They stood watch for

several days, rotating for rest, each time in a new place so as not
to attract the enemy's attention.

During a routine watch on one of the winter days, a group went
out commanded by Morozov: Veretenik, Globa, Kalinichenko, and
Sonya Dubova with a radio set. They selected an elevation from
which the entire Yalta port lay before them like the palm of their
hands. Hiding in the thick undergrowth that covered the top of the
hill, they began to observe. Sonya prepared her radio for operation.

Hour after hour passed, but nothing new was seen in the port.
The short winter day passed, then night fell.

Nothing happened the following day either. Perhaps the three
days that remained until their rotation would also pass without
incident. This sometimes happened. But the scouts were patient.
Days and nights passed, and still they waited, passing the binoculars around, never losing sight of the port that lay below.

The fifth and last day of their watch began. An overcast winter
sky slowly lit up the forested mountain height. Veretenik was
looking through the binoculars at the boundless, completely
empty expanse of the sea, still half-concealed by the haze of the
night fog that was slowly lifting. Morozov and Globa with their
submachine guns were intently peering into the naked dark
shrubbery that covered the slopes of the hill and into a gully that
stretched along its base. Had any Germans escaped their notice?
Were they sneaking up on them? Kalinichenko, rolled up under
a bush, was resting after standing night watch. As always, Sonya
sat on the alert alongside her radio set, concealed but prepared
for immediate use. Dressed in quilted fatigues and a black sailor's
shapka [wool hat with ear flaps], with earphones showing, how
different she now appeared than the light-haired girl in a gaily
colored *sarafan* [a sleeveless peasant dress] who, on one of the
dark days in late June 1941, left an x-ray technician training
course and went to the shop floor of a Simferopol factory to make
grenades. One would hardly recognize her as the same girl who
a year earlier had studied at a radio operator course. The features

of her girlish face had become more concentrated and defined; the constant stress had made them more distinct.

Veretenik was observing especially diligently this morning hour. German vessels seldom showed up any later in the day. The Germans were somewhat afraid of our naval air force raids, and their ships sailed primarily at night. But he might still spot a ship hurrying to reach its destination port.

Now the fog was dissipating over the sea, and, as before, it was empty. It would be totally light in sixty to ninety minutes. There was little likelihood that any enemy vessel would appear during the day. Would this last day also pass without success?

Thinking so, Morozov reached over to his rucksack, took out a can, removed his *finka* [Finnish knife] from its sheath, and prepared to eat.

"I see something!" He suddenly heard Veretenik's voice.

"Where?"

"There!" Veretenik pointed.

Morozov looked. Black spots were coming one after another out of the bluish-gray haze, slowly creeping across the flat sea parallel to the coastline.

Hearing voices, Kalinichenko got up. Now everyone, except Globa, who continued intently to observe the approaches to their hill, was looking out to sea.

Not pulling his eyes away from the binoculars, Veretenik counted:

"One, two, three . . . five . . . ten . . . twenty ships!"

"Get ready!" Morozov alerted Sonya. "We will determine their course and then transmit."

"They are turning!" Veretenik said, "toward Yalta!"

"What kind of ships?" asked Morozov.

"I'm looking now." Veretenik moved the binoculars along the formation, strung out in column astern, its ships now clearly visible. "Self-propelled barges. Transports. Submarine chaser escorts."

"Sonya, send it!" Morozov ordered. Glancing at her encoding table, the radio operator hunched over her gray radio set and tapped with her [telegraph] key.

"Transmission complete!" she reported after several minutes.

"Collect your things, we're leaving!" Morozov commanded, tossing the ration can into his rucksack and sheathing his *finka*. It would have been dangerous to remain on the hilltop. German signals intelligence had perhaps already resected their position. They could anticipate a cordon and search.

Moving through the bushes, the scouts climbed another height, from which the port of Yalta was clearly visible. The German convoy had already completed its turn to enter the bay. Remaining camouflaged, the scouts took turns observing through the binoculars. Now the enemy ships were distinctly visible. Stacks of crates, perhaps full of ammunition, were visible on the self-propelled barges, along with closely parked vehicles, guns, and prime movers. German soldiers were crowded on the decks of the transports. Of course, they were glad to be completing this dangerous sea crossing and with anticipation were preparing to disembark onto firm ground.

The scouts waited.

The ships were already in the harbor. Some were moving up to the docks, while others were standing in the channel, awaiting their turn for mooring. The scouts looked worriedly into the already light sky, punctuated by occasional clouds remaining from the night. Everyone was listening with great concern. Were our aircraft inbound? Would the enemy manage to offload his troops and equipment and send them toward Kerch or Perekop?

From far away, beyond the mountaintops, from where the colorless sun was just coming up, they barely heard a flat drone.

"They're ours!"

Aircraft, stretched out in a line, flew in from behind the Yalta range. Here, on the crest, the heavy drone of their motors was already loud, splitting the morning calm.

"Petlyakovs!"[9] Morozov indicated, having raised the binoculars to his eyes. Everyone hurried over to hug Sonya.

"*Molodets* [Atta girl]! You called them!"

"Ura!" someone shouted, forgetting himself. But Morozov put the damper on their celebration.

"Quiet! The Germans are listening!"

Pe-2 bombers, their motors racing loudly, passed over the scouts' heads. One behind the other, they turned over the harbor. The scouts could clearly see from their vantage point as their bombs flew down like black spots and columns of smoke and spray erupted, covering the barges and transports. One barge turned over and quickly disappeared beneath the water. They saw ragged flames on the deck of a transport and small figures dropping into the water off its side. There was another strike, then yet another.

Puffs of black and white smoke dotted the sky around the Petlyakovs as they scurried about above the enemy ships—the German antiaircraft gunners guarding the port had opened fire. But too late! Many self-propelled barges had already disappeared from view on the surface. Some were still afloat but sinking. Brown smoke from the burning transports floated above the harbor, driven out to sea by the wind.

Having dropped their last bombs, the Petlyakovs, accompanied by the explosions of antiaircraft rounds, again flew over the hill-top where the scouts were positioned and disappeared behind the broken line of mountaintops of the Yalta range.

Morozov once again inspected the harbor through the binoculars. On the surface of the water wreckage floated here and there, cutters raced back and forth frantically, and a launch was moving. From his enormous height, it looked tiny, like a six-legged insect. Only a few of the targeted self-propelled barges were tentatively turning in the channel and heading toward the docks. Counting them, Morozov turned to Sonya:

"Transmit to headquarters that fifteen of twenty ships were sunk."

They had passed five wearisome days for a reason. This time the watch was successful! Morozov, Veretenik, Globa, Kalinichenko, and Sonya returned to the base happy.

All watches on the heights above Yalta did not conclude as successfully as this one. The Germans presumed that someone was vectoring our aviation to their ships. They feverishly searched for the secretive "military detachment" that, according to their information, had been dropped by parachute near Yalta.

In a newsletter the Germans published for the local population and in leaflets posted on the streets of Yalta and surrounding villages, they declared that fifty thousand marks would be paid for each captured parachutist. But they were unable to capture a single parachutist.

The occupiers did not poke their noses into the forest overgrowth far from the city, in the mountains. They feared the Crimean partisans. But around Yalta, German patrols moved all the time in the region of the hills from which the sailor scouts observed the port. They positioned permanent guard posts on some heights to watch over the terrain. The scouts had to be on their guard every minute. The smallest oversight could lead to a disaster.

On one particular morning, Morozov, Veretenik, Globa, and Sonya, standing scheduled watch on one of the heights, failed to notice that an emptied ration tin had bounced far below on the slope. They realized their carelessness too late. Excited voices were already calling to each other on the neighboring height. It turned out that a German guard post there had spotted the flashing tin.

Hearing the Germans' voices, the scouts were forewarned. Several minutes later, Germans showed up. Holding their weapons at the ready, they walked toward the foot of the hill. No matter how much the scouts regretted leaving this height, which was good for observation, they had to abandon it. The scouts were not allowed to give their position away or engage the enemy.

Sailors not only monitored enemy shipping from the heights above Yalta. They maintained close liaison with partisans and used the intelligence information the partisans collected. The scouts also had liaison with the underground in Sevastopol, Balaklava, and other Crimean ports.[10] They had informants among the local population in each port, from Alushta to Evpatoria. These patriots, constantly risking capture by the Gestapo, tracked when and how many enemy ships arrived and how many departed to sea. Detachment scouts were constantly going into Yalta and other coastal towns to communicate with these informants. They moved alone and in small groups, which normally included one of the radio operators—Valya, Sonya, Tonya, or Zhenya [all females]. Earlier, well-camouflaged antennae with hidden cables had been installed in the attics of clandestine "safe" apartments. If information gathered from the informants had to be transmitted immediately, the radio operator connected her set to the antenna, established contact with the mainland, transmitted the required message, and then disconnected the antenna.

The group then immediately moved as far away as possible. Each minute of delay harbored deadly danger. The Germans monitored the airwaves closely. Their radio direction finders were able to pinpoint the site where a radio was located just minutes after the scouts began to transmit. Sometimes the scouts had just disassembled their transmitter and left when the block in which the building from which they had transmitted was located was cordoned off by hurriedly arriving police units. The Gestapo combed all the structures, apartments, and attics and inspected every crack, looking for the clandestine transmitter. But the antennae and cables were securely hidden in the rafters and walls, and the scouts were long gone.

Trying to capture the elusive scouts, the Germans not only shadowed them in populated areas but also set up ambushes on roads leading into the mountains.

But the scouts were vigilant. They learned a lesson the enemy taught them. A German agent penetrated their detachment in the guise of a local resident. From the time of his appearance, the frequency of clashes with enemy ambushes on the mountain trails increased. They managed to uncover the agent only a month after his appearance. They shot him, and ambushes dropped off precipitously. Now the Germans did not know by what trails the sailors walked and where it was best to monitor them. Just the same, the scouts could not weaken their vigilance. They normally spotted where enemy ambushes were set up ahead of time and bypassed them, making a fool of the enemy. This was not always the case, however.

On one dark night, Kalganov was returning from Yalta to Black Mountain, to the base, in slushy cold weather. They were moving cautiously, off the path leading out of the city, with flank and advance guards. But the Germans hidden in the night forest saw them coming. German submachine gun bursts rang out. One of the sailors was seriously wounded in the stomach in the first minute, and two others were also wounded. The remaining scouts laid down and returned the fire. Kalganov ordered two sailors to get around the Germans' rear and throw grenades at them. They did this. It sowed confusion among the enemy, enabling the scouts to break contact and escape, carrying their wounded.

The enemy's attempts to interfere with the scouts' work were futile. The faraway mainland headquarters for which the detachment was operating received more and better reports on the enemy.

The soldiers of the German patrol standing on the road leading into Yalta paid no special attention to the tall, light-haired young man in a tattered quilted jacket and wide-legged Tatar trousers who was walking into the city carrying a large apple-filled wicker basket on his shoulders. They gave only a cursory glance at his pass. It was the normal morning hour when people, Russian and Tatar, came into Yalta from the surrounding villages to sell their produce at the bazaar.

Reaching the marketplace, he inquired about the prices and selected a busy spot. The young man put the basket on the ground and began to sell. He sold all of his apples before anyone else, because he sold them cheaper. Then, picking up his empty basket, the young man nonchalantly walked through the bazaar. It seemed as though he had rarely visited the city. He looked all around with curiosity, watching the people walking toward him, especially the young girls. One of them, a fair-haired and shapely girl, was, like him, heading toward the exit from the marketplace. He walked next to her. Evidently, just to strike up a conversation with her, he asked:

"Do you know where a person can buy thread here in the town?"

Giving him a searching look, the young woman answered. It seemed that she was not averse to becoming acquainted. She asked:

"What was it that you sold out of so quickly?"

"I don't like this market business," the young man responded. "I'm not used to it."

"Perhaps you are a stranger to these parts?"

"No, why do you ask?" The young man named the village indicated in his documents.

"A man as young as you," the young woman noted with surprise, "was not called into the army?"

"I was in the army," the young man acknowledged, "and fought here, in Crimea. Well, when the Germans began to press us toward the sea, I saw a bad end coming and I left."

"You mean, you deserted?"

"Think what you want. But your own hide is more precious."

"Are you living with your relatives?"

"What relatives! I fell in with Tatars and married one of theirs."

"Are you happy?"

"No!" sighed the young man. "I'm sorry that I was such a fool. Now I don't know how to get out of it."

They walked along the streets of Yalta, conversing animatedly. With obvious interest, the young man asked his companion, named Lida, about her life. She told him she was working in a theater troupe that was on tour in Yalta when the war started and thus became stuck in Yalta. She complained that the city had recently become particularly tense, and the Germans were checking documents more frequently and conducting night cordon and search operations—they were constantly looking for parachutists. Without noticing, they had reached the last street, which led into the mountains, the steep, forested foothills of which lay directly behind the last row of buildings. They stopped before they reached the German guard post positioned at the end of the street.

"I would like to meet with you again," said the young man.

"Well, I think that's possible." Lida smiled. "When will you be at the marketplace again?"

"The day after tomorrow, in the morning, just like today. But," he stopped short, "there are many people from my village at the bazaar. I don't want them to see us together."

"Are you afraid of your jealous wife?"

"Yes," the young man admitted. Then he asked, "Do you have a pass to leave the city?"

"Yes, but why?"

"It would be better to meet at noon, after I have sold out, over there." The young man pointed at a prominent leafy tree on the slope of the hill, surrounded by thick bushes. "We'll sit and talk."

"Good," Lida agreed.

Pressing her hand firmly in farewell, the young man walked toward the city's exit. He again showed his pass to the German guards, walked a bit farther down the road, then turned off into the bushes. He stopped in a thicket, where he quietly and briefly whistled. He received the same quiet and short whistle in reply. The young man moved off in the direction of the whistler. Several steps farther, he saw an old Tatar man in a black *tyubeteyka* [embroidered skullcap] and clothes made of new material, sitting under a shrub. Two unshaven men in black navy pea jackets, holding submachine guns on their knees, sat near the old man. Seeing the young man, they stood up and joyfully stepped forward to greet him.

"Sasha! Did it go well?"

"Everything is fine."

The young man—it was Morozov—threw the empty basket toward the old Tatar's feet, pulled a wad of green script—occupation marks—out of his pocket, and extended them to the Tatar.

"Take this. I sold your apples."

Picking up his own clothing that he had left with his comrades, Morozov took off the quilted jacket and broad-legged pants and gave them to the Tatar.

"Put this on!"

The Tatar began to take off the pea jacket, but Morozov waved his hand.

"Keep it. I don't need it."

Morozov had gone into Yalta that morning in this fancy jacket and similar trousers, accompanied by two comrades from the detachment. But along the way, they had second thoughts and decided it was too risky to go dressed in such clothes. In them he would stand out among the general population who, under the occupation, were dressed poorly. Before they reached Yalta, Morozov and his comrades stopped the old Tatar, who was carrying a basket of apples to the city marketplace, and Morozov "borrowed" his clothes.

They led the Tatar, who was already garbed in his quilted jacket and wide trousers and had secured the pea jacket given him in his wicker basket, out to the road and released him. Morozov and his two comrades, who had waited half a day for him, returned to the detachment base.

Why did Morozov go to Yalta? Why did the fair-haired girl in the marketplace attract his attention?

In fact, not long before this, they had received instructions by radio from the mainland. They were to find out why no reports had been received from one of our female agents, who for some time had been located in Yalta. The radio message provided a description of the agent and suggested how to find her, how to establish contact with her, and how to use her for collection of needed information. Morozov was given the task of searching out this agent.

Among all the young women he had looked at on the streets of Yalta and in the marketplace, the fair-haired one appeared to him most to resemble his target. The fact that he met her at the bazaar at the height of trade reinforced his feeling that she was the one he was looking for. A female agent, having lost communications with her handlers, would certainly try to regain them and would be looking at everyone, hoping to find the person she needed. Where better to meet people than at the city marketplace?

Because his new acquaintance asked questions and talked about herself, Morozov was almost sure that Lida was the person he was seeking. But the enemy was cunning. Perhaps they had captured the agent and had established a double agent in her place in hopes of catching still other Soviet agents with this "bait."

They had to be cautious. Therefore, Morozov would conduct himself with this young woman as if his only purpose was to court her.

The next day, Morozov arrived at the indicated meeting place—the large tree—at the appointed hour. He did not go alone but with several comrades, who were prepared to come to his assistance if needed. They hid in the bushes for the time being. What if Lida turned out to be a spy and brought Germans with her? Anything was possible. If she was a spy, they had to capture her, to take her away and question her. If this was impossible, they would kill her on the spot. If she was one of them?

"Open up to her, shock her, and I will immediately find out who she is!" Morozov decided.

The bushes rustled, and it turned out to be the young woman, walking toward the tree. "Lida." Morozov looked at her. She was alone. He gave a signal to his comrades waiting in ambush. Then Morozov went out to meet her.

"Aha, are you a sailor?" She was surprised, seeing his sailor's pea jacket and the stripes of his *tel'nyashka* through his open collar.

"Yes, I am a scout from the Black Sea Fleet."

"I guessed it!" Lida exclaimed. "I'm an agent myself. I've been looking for 'our own' for some time, and finally, here you are!"

Morozov saw how happily the young girl's eyes sparkled. But this joy could have a totally opposite explanation. And Morozov hastened to warn her:

"I believe you, but know this: if you're lying, you won't live to tell about it."

"Believe me!" Lida said with fervor. "I can't show you any documents right now that prove I'm telling the truth, but believe me!"

Lida said that her transmitter was broken, and therefore she was unable to communicate with the mainland. But she had continued to collect information about the enemy forces in the hope that she would somehow be able to send it when she finally found someone from "our side."

They agreed that in several days Lida, having collected all the information she could on the enemy forces in Yalta, would record it on paper and place it at a drop site. Walking with her through the forest, Morozov selected a hollow in an old oak tree.

Morozov and his comrades went to the hollow, not on the designated day but later, at night. Although he believed Lida, he decided to take every precaution. What if there were an enemy ambush at the oak tree?

No, Lida did not deceive them. There was no ambush at the oak tree. Sticking his hand down into the hollow, Morozov found an entire notebook. He looked through it right there in the forest, using a flashlight covered with his pea jacket. In the notebook, he saw an accurately drawn sketch of the antiaircraft battery positions in the Yalta area, the antilanding defenses along the coast, and even information on the minefields near Yalta port and the lanes through them. It was easier for Lida to gather all this information than another scout: German officers were not reluctant to chat with this young, fair-haired actress.

All the information that Lida had obtained was quickly passed along to the mainland. The hollow of the old oak tree then served as a "post office box" for new reports from the agent.

At the end of winter [early 1944], the scouts, who had been monitoring not only the south coast ports but also the roads leading toward them, determined that the Germans were hurriedly relocating some units from Simferopol to Yalta. What could this mean? Were the Germans intending to load these forces and move them by ship to another sector of the front? What units were involved? Where were they taken from? All this information was important for our command. The decisive battle for the liberation of Crimea would soon begin.

We had to capture a "tongue." It was not particularly difficult for the scouts to capture any German. They had captured "tongues" in Yalta, in Balaklava, in coastal villages, and on roads. They had captured ten officers, three of them lieutenant colonels. But all these "tongues" were from local garrisons. Now they needed an officer who could give information on the new units being moved on the Simferopol highway toward the coast.

After consulting with his petty officers and sailors, Kalganov made the decision to take a "tongue" on the highway by lying in wait for a staff car. It would certainly contain officers.

At night, Kalganov and ten scouts hid in the bushes, winter bare but sufficiently thick to conceal them well. The scouts chose this position on a steep slope, beneath which, thirty meters below, stretched the gray ribbon of asphalt road. In the opposite direction, on an equally steep hillside, the bushes looked black and grew right up against the road. Kalganov sent two sailors to take up a position two hundred meters to the right and two other sailors the same distance to the left. Skillfully camouflaged, the scouts waited and watched.

The road remained deserted until dawn—the Germans feared the partisans at night. But in the morning it came alive. Breaking the morning quiet of the forest with the deep rumbling of motors, trucks with some kind of cargo passed by every several minutes from the direction of Simferopol. The German soldiers sitting in these trucks were peering cautiously at the terrain.

Kalganov was waiting for any light vehicle and not simply a car. He wanted to wait for an automobile with motorcycle escorts. An escort was a sure sign that it was a staff car and that an important officer was riding in it, from whom they could obtain much information.

Two or three cars had already flashed by on the road coming from Simferopol, but not one of them was traveling with an escort. But then a large, open car came around the corner. It approached and would soon be in the ambush. It too was without accompanying motorcyclists. "Well, let's try this one," Kalganov decided. But just the same, he trained his binoculars on the vehicle to see who was in it. "Aha!" he exclaimed. The German sitting next to the driver was clearly an officer and, judging by his black hat, was not a common officer but from the SS troops.

"Gennadiy!" Kalganov turned toward Petty Officer Second Class Chichilo. "This one!" he reminded him. "Only the motor!"

"Aye, aye!" Chichilo responded in half voice and readied his silenced carbine.

The vehicle was closing in on the ambush site. Only those right next to Chichilo heard the shot from his silenced rifle, no louder than a cork coming out of a bottle. The Germans initially did not understand why their vehicle's motor suddenly fell silent. The car continued on for several meters by inertia and then stopped. The driver slammed his door open, got out, and began to raise the hood. The others—there were two of them—remained seated in the car. But the officer in the black hat anxiously looked around to the flanks. Perhaps he had noticed something alarming in the bushes. He shouted some words in a high, piercing voice and, throwing up the flaps of his cape, jumped from the car. The second jumped out behind him, and the pair hid behind the car.

The tense silence was maintained for several seconds. But then, one after another, two pistol shots cracked out from behind the vehicle, and the dry, short burst of a German submachine gun chattered.

"Don't shoot at the officer!" Kalganov reminded them, and commanded: "Fire!"

Upon hearing the first shots, the sailors posted to the right and left of the main ambush site ran, as was agreed, across the highway. They quickly came up behind the Germans through the bushes on the opposite side and fired their submachine guns at them. Each side fired several more submachine gun bursts. Two shaking arms with open hands were thrust out above the top of the car.

"Cease fire!" Kalganov ordered his sailors.

The arms with outstretched hands were slowly rising from behind the vehicle, followed by the crushed peak of a black service cap with the SS emblem—a skull on the hatband. Beneath the service cap could be seen a pallid, drawn-out face with drooping eyes.

The scouts ran over to the vehicle. The SS officer stood in a long, hanging oilskin cape, his hands upraised in surrender. Near the back wheel, a soldier with SS tabs on his collar lay sprawled in his greatcoat on the asphalt, clutching a submachine gun in his lifeless hands. The driver sat propped up against the front door, pressing his hand to his side.

Picking up the officer, the scouts quickly moved into the forest. They stopped in an overgrown gully, now already far from the highway. Kalganov, who knew some German, interrogated the prisoner. The SS officer, a first lieutenant, indicated that he was a staff officer of an SS regiment being repositioned from the Perekop to reinforce the defenses along the coast. His regiment was to replace a Romanian unit deployed in several coastal villages. The German command feared a Soviet amphibious landing on the south Crimean coast and considered the Romanians unreliable allies. They no longer trusted them with the defense of this important sector. The lieutenant gave us much other valuable information on the composition, disposition, and movement of German forces in Crimea.

The sun grew hotter with each passing day. The soft snow had long ago melted off the open areas on the foothills. The first buds were beginning to swell. The approach of spring was felt more acutely each day.

In anticipation of our offensive, the enemy was feverishly preparing to defend Crimea. New ships stopped daily at Crimean ports with troops, equipment, and ammunition. This was now his only means of reinforcing the peninsula because it had been cut off from the mainland by Soviet forces in the autumn of 1943.

Not all of the German transports were able to reach or depart from one or another south coast port safely. With a precision that infuriated the enemy, more and more air strikes rained down on his ships, especially at night. The Germans did not know that two bomber regiments of Black Sea Fleet air forces remained on alert at distant airfields along the Caucasus coast. As soon as the headquarters received a report from the detachment's radio operators, these aircraft sortied out to bomb the ships designated by the scouts.

The Germans did not know this, but their radio direction finders had often resected unidentified transmitters operating from coastal heights or from the area of Black Mountain, behind Yalta Ridge.

The Germans could not help but see in this a direct link with the very accurate and effective Soviet air raids on their ships in port or at sea along the coast. As time went on, they tried more persistently to draw out in the coastal range not only partisans operating there but also the scouts, whose actions over the past several months had led to the sinking of a score or more of German ships.

The German command, realizing that our offensive into Crimea was inevitable, tried to make their rear, and, foremost of all, the coastline, safe. Specially designated SS and police units were combing the ravines, gullies, heights, and forests on their slopes. More and more often, the scouts noted tracks of German boots with thirty-two nails in the heel in the melting snow of the mountain trails. It became more and more difficult to maintain liaison with informants and to conduct watch on the heights. Everywhere there were more Germans and guard posts. The enemy set up ambushes on paths leading into Yalta and to the heights above it more frequently. German aircraft circled above the forest, hoping to find the partisan and scout bases from the air. The situation with provisions grew worse. True, the Black Sea Fleet command regularly dispatched aircraft to drop supplies to the scouts by parachute. But many of these containers never reached the scouts. They frequently fell into the hands of the enemy, who was blanketing the mountains with his patrols. Sometimes the containers fell in places where it was impossible to recover them without a fight. And on some occasions the scouts had to exchange shots so they could recover a container hanging in a tree. At times, the scouts managed to shoot several rabbits or a deer, and then the detachment had a feast. Sometimes they raided German supply wagons on the Simferopol highway. But this was infrequent—the Germans were providing reinforced security for these wagons.

The situation with food continued to deteriorate. That which they managed to obtain was subject to the strictest rationing. The ration became more and more miserly.

On one of these difficult days, Valya Morozova had her eighteenth birthday. They decided to celebrate this day. Kalganov, with common agreement, apportioned out two handfuls of meal. Valya baked two unsalted flatcakes on the fire and, dividing them, treated her comrades. They insisted that Valya, as the subject of the celebration, take a double portion for herself. No one knew that Valya mentally shared this portion with the man who she knew cared for and missed her from that moment she had felt his hand on her shoulder and looked into his eyes for the last time and then jumped through the open hatch of the aircraft.

It had become very difficult for the scouts, but they continued to do their work. It is no surprise that the majority of them were communists and *komsomolists*. Many of the nonparty members made their declarations for membership to the party or Komsomol. The meetings did not last long. Everyone knew how the applicant conducted himself in combat and in the difficult forest life. They did not observe protocols or hand out party or Komsomol cards—in reconnaissance, it was not smart to be found carrying such documents. But the radio traffic back to the mainland reported who had been accepted into the party or Komsomol. The new members could receive their party or Komsomol cards when they returned from the enemy rear.

The party organization existed, worked, and grew. Political information was disseminated. They found out about the situation at the fronts and about life in the Motherland by radio. On rare occasions, they received newspapers in the food and ammunition containers. Before each significant reconnaissance mission, the party and Komsomol groups assembled.

The party organization showed special concern that a high spirit of combat friendship and iron discipline was maintained in the detachment. Woe to the scout who dared to violate discipline. Immediate and effective measures were taken, but perhaps not always those provided for in the regulations.

A regular sweep, which the enemy had conducted continuously over the course of five days, had just been completed. To escape, the scouts had to march for many kilometers. The meager supplies of food they had taken with them had long since been exhausted, and there was no place to resupply. When the detachment finally reached a safe place and stopped in a thick mountain forest near the stream Al'ma, Kalganov gave the order to unpack the transmitter and communicate with the mainland to report their situation and identify a drop zone for an immediate resupply of food. A radio message received in reply indicated that aircraft would fly out the next night.

When darkness fell, Kalganov dispatched several groups, with three sailors in each, to track the parachute drops, find them, and bring back the supply containers.

The aircraft arrived. The scouts did not light any signal fires at the drop zone so as not to lure the enemy, who had established his posts everywhere. Nevertheless, the parachutes were found. By morning, the groups sent out by Kalganov returned carrying the containers.

Only one group, consisting of Andreev, Volkov, and Zolotukhin, was late. Kalganov had begun to be concerned that something might have happened to them, and, after waiting a while longer, he wanted to send out a search party. But the trio showed up between the trees. Zolotukhin, one of the rookies in the detachment, was walking in front, staggering, frantically looking around.

His face was somber, and he had a big black eye. Behind him, carrying the long cylindrical container with the parachute cloth wound around it, walked Andreev and Volkov. When they reached their waiting comrades, they dropped the container on the ground and with a strong shove pushed the hesitating Zolotukhin ahead.

"Here he is, the scum!"

"What's going on?" asked Kalganov in disbelief.

"He violated our naval forest law!" Andreev pointed at Zolotukhin's bruised eye. "The container broke open when it fell, and biscuits and chocolate spilled out. While we were coming up, he began to gobble them up on the sly! If that weren't enough, he was trying to dig a hole in the ground to lay in his own supply. We caught him in the act!"

A murmur of indignation rose among the sailors. Never before had anyone violated the naval forest law: all provisions, to the smallest crumb, were maintained for distribution to everyone.

There was no justification for anyone to violate this law. To eat anything in secret from one's comrades or hide a piece for oneself was considered treason in the detachment.

"Expel him!" a voice shouted.

"Try him!"

Kalganov brought silence with a wave of his hand. He looked at Zolotukhin, whose face was turning white, which made his black eye stand out even more, and then asked Andreev and Volkov:

"Did you exaggerate any of this?"

They both replied with one voice: "We wouldn't tolerate that."

"Well, all right." Kalganov again glanced at Zolotukhin and ordered him: "Surrender your weapon!"

Zolotukhin extended his submachine gun toward the senior lieutenant and with open hands unfastened the buckle of the belt on which hung his spare drums and grenades.

What should be done with Zolotukhin?

Kalganov could have decided the issue under his own command authority. But he did not want to do this. They discussed Zolotukhin's conduct at a closed meeting of the party and Komsomol members and then reached a decision.

The entire formation was assembled in a forest clearing. Zolotukhin was brought before the formation, unarmed and beltless. He looked at the ground, unable to look his comrades in the face.

"I submit him to your judgment," Kalganov pronounced, pointing at Zolotukhin. "You decide what to do with him."

The formation was silent.

Zolotukhin stood, unable to raise his eyes. His scowling comrades stared at him.

After waiting a minute or two, the senior lieutenant asked:

"What are your suggestions?"

The response was continued silence. Everyone understood what it meant, what was hidden in the commander's question.

Then it fell like a rock: "Shoot him!"

There was a barely noticeable movement in the formation, as if a cold wind had suddenly swayed it.

"Are there any defenders?" Kalganov asked.

"No!" a stern voice from the formation broke the silence.

"There is no defense for this!" affirmed another.

"Shoot him," a third slowly intoned.

"Brothers, how can you do this?" Zolotukhin blurted out.

"Silence!" The senior lieutenant cut him off. "I haven't given you permission to speak."

Zolotukhin was silent. In desperation he looked into the stern faces of his comrades, his hands and knees shaking.

"Who is opposed to a firing squad?" the senior lieutenant asked again.

Not a single voice rose up out of the formation.

Delaying, Kalganov pronounced:

"So, for this looting, the decision of the detachment is the firing squad!"

"Give me pardon! Have mercy on me!" Zolotukhin pleaded, gesturing toward the formation.

"Get back! Stand silent!" his commander ordered.

Zolotukhin stopped. His legs gave in. Kalganov crisply commanded:

"Everyone who concurs with the decision, prepare your submachine gun for firing and take one step forward!"

The clicking of safeties coming off and the rattle of opening bolts seemed especially loud in the tense silence. One after the other, the sailors stepped forward out of the formation. The entire formation quickly moved toward Zolotukhin. Everything went just as it had been decided at the closed meeting. But what happened next depended on how Zolotukhin conducted himself.

"Do you see?" Kalganov indicated the silent formation to him. "This decision is supported by everyone. Do you have any last words?"

"Comrades!" Zolotukhin fell to the ground again, his legs unable to hold him. "Comrades! Forgive me! Let me make it right! I will prove myself!"

The formation was silent.

Zolotukhin, pushing himself off the ground with his arm, turned toward Kalganov and threw him a pleading glance.

"I have not judged you." Kalganov moved away from Zolotukhin and asked:

"Have you said all you have to say?"

Zolotukhin was silent, holding himself off the ground with his arms but unable to stand up. He gulped for air convulsively, and tears flowed down his face.

"Detachment, submachine guns at the ready!" Kalganov gave the command. The black muzzles of the barrels stared at Zolotukhin, who remained seated on the ground. Kalganov moved off to the side.

"For his crime. . . ."

"Brothers, permit me to say something in farewell!" Zolotukhin blurted out with his last strength.

"As you were!" the senior lieutenant commanded. He said to Zolotukhin:

"Get up and talk!"

Swaying, the accused stood up, his voice quivering:

"Forgive me. I don't dare ask for mercy. You are right. I don't blame you. I am the guilty one. But I am not a traitor! I ask you to postpone my firing squad for several days. Give me a chance to exculpate my guilt. Leave me with a pair of grenades and a pistol. I promise you—I will kill myself. But permit me to take several Germans with me. Grant this last request! Let me die not from our own bullets but from German bullets!"

The formation was silent.

"If you do not believe me, then shoot me!" Zolotukhin exclaimed with conviction and covered his eyes with his hands.

"Can we believe him?" Kalganov asked the sailors.

They did not answer. But one after another, they slowly lowered the barrels of their submachine guns that were pointed at Zolotukhin.

"Anyone who can believe him, step back!"

One sailor slowly took a step back, a second, then the entire formation.

Zolotukhin justified their confidence. In subsequent combat, he zealously tried to expiate his guilt, acted bravely, and not once committed even the smallest infraction of discipline.[11]

The detachment's "running score" grew. The number of enemy ships sunk by fleet air forces vectored to their targets by the scouts continued to increase.

But with each day, it became increasingly difficult to evade German cordons and searches. The enemy not only combed the forest, he also mined the forest trails, passages through ravines, and approaches to villages. One time Morozov and Menadzhiev, traveling together, were caught in one of these mine traps. Menadzhiev was wounded in both legs by the detonation of an antipersonnel mine and could not get up. Risking another explosion, Morozov hurried to the aid of his comrade. He carried him from the mined area, put a tourniquet on his wounded legs to stop the blood flow, and then carried him away. The route that he had to travel back to the base was several kilometers long and very difficult. They had to negotiate steep slopes and thickets, bypassing roads and villages to avoid bumping into the enemy.

Despite all this, they did not escape an encounter with Germans who were sweeping the forest. "Leave me here!" Menadzhiev demanded. The two friends fired their submachine guns. Taking advantage of the enemy's confusion, Morozov again put Menadzhiev on his shoulders and carried him off.

On another occasion, the scouts had to abandon their permanent base hurriedly to avoid being caught in the enemy net, not the first time this had happened in recent days. They had to divide into two groups and remain constantly on the move, deceiving the enemy, who was relentlessly pursuing them. Fairly quickly they were forced to "eat grass"—they had left their last food supplies at the base and could not return to retrieve them. They ate roots that they dug up out of the thawing ground. It was a stroke of luck if they managed to find a dead horse. Their legs grew so weak from malnourishment that some scouts had trouble walking. But they had to go on across the mountains, through thorny thickets, forested ravines, and canyons, and cross streams swollen by the spring runoff. They walked day and night to stay out of encirclement, taking only short breaks, not more than thirty minutes, in a gully where the sun had not yet melted the snow or in a forest ditch, in the damp leaves left over from last year.

With each day, the area in which the scouts could maneuver became more limited. The Germans were into a second week of continuous sweeping on the slopes of Black Mountain. It seemed that their command had decided to put an end to the elusive "parachutists," as they had nicknamed the detachment of sailors. New German units joined with those already combing the slopes of Black Mountain, looking for the scouts. And if only recently the scouts had been able to find a place in the mountain forest where they could slip between the enemy formations, now this had become exceedingly difficult.

It was a lovely March day. The spring sky was showing blue above the pine trees joined together at their crowns, above the tops of the oak trees and beeches still in their winter black. Semitransparent, thinning clouds slowly floated across the sky. It was quiet in the forest—the songbirds had not yet made their appearance. There were no strange sounds in the forest, as if no humans were around. A closely packed clump of several people in tattered pea jackets and sheepskin coats, wearing black naval pile caps, each with a submachine gun in hand, silently stood in a small forest ravine. Along the bottom of the ravine ran a barely perceptible trickle of water under a thick layer of last year's leaves, which had only recently showed from under the thawing snow. Exhaustion showed on the scouts' mud-splattered, emaciated faces. Their eyes, full of worried anticipation, were straining at the commander. All awaited his words. They had just climbed down into this ravine. Lines of German soldiers stretched out through the forest behind them, inspecting every bush and depression. The scouts had to move out again, but to where?

Security posts ran up. The enemy lines, five of them one behind the other, were moving in from all sides. The ring was tightening.

There was nowhere to go. Could the scouts break through? Could they fight their way out? There were hundreds of enemy and only tens of scouts. The first German line would soon cross through the ravine. What to do?

"We're ready to meet them," Globa suggested in a whisper, squeezing his submachine gun with thinning hands.

"Don't be in a hurry to die," Kalganov replied just as quietly. The commander suddenly came up with a plan:

"We will attempt to hide."

"Where?" Everyone was bewildered.

"Here!" Kalganov pointed at his own feet. He brushed away the thin layer of old leaves with his boot. "Here! We have no choice." He ordered: "Everyone burrow in! Women first. Hold your submachine guns and grenades at the ready. If they spot us—jump up and break out."

The sailors' hands worked quickly. Last year's leaves lay in a thick layer on the very bottom of the ravine, where the stream trickled. The deeper they dug into the leaves, the wetter they became. The ground under them was cold, swollen by the spring water. But they had to burrow in as deep as possible. They buried Sonya Dubova first, along with her radio transmitter, in an oblong pit. Next was Zhenya and then Valya. Then the sailors helped bury each other. The commander was the last to lie down in the leaves. His was the most difficult task. He had to conceal himself by throwing leaves on himself so that no one could spot him from above. The leaves fell off with each movement of the hand. If only someone could pile them on from above! But there was no one.

Finally, the last handful of leaves was thrown on his chest and face. Carefully, so as not to knock off the leaves, Kalganov moved his hand to feel for the trigger of his submachine gun. The weapon was prepared for battle.

Agonizing minutes passed. They could not move or look around. Were the Germans close? If only they would pass around them! But their security had reported that the enemy lines were combing the forest from all sides; they were coming together, the ring was tightening, and with each minute it was getting more dense. Without fail, the enemy would pass through the ravine.

Straining their ears, the scouts listened: are the Germans coming? They are coming!

Muffled voices filtered through the layer of leaves, becoming more distinct. They were still coming. The sound of the enemy's boots crunching through the deadfall on the forest floor grew louder. "If only I could look around," thought Kalganov. But he couldn't move a muscle—it would give him and everyone else away.

The rustle of leaves grew louder. The forest echoed with the crunch of scores of feet. Quite near, perhaps only several steps away, they heard a muffled, low voice, responding to another. Had they spotted the scouts? Kalganov's hands tightened around his submachine gun. It was important to gain the first seconds. It would be a lightning-fast and merciless fight, without hesitation, face to face.

Now the Germans were descending into the ravine! All of Kalganov's muscles tightened. Is it time? No, not yet.

With a noise that seemed deafening to Kalganov, a heavy German boot compressed the leaves alongside his head. It raised up, crackling through the leaves.

They did not spot the scouts!

It helped that the scouts had buried themselves in the leaves in the gutter-narrow streambed, and many Germans jumped over it without stepping on the scouts.

The crunching grew quieter and moved off in another direction. Then the sounds stopped. But this was only the first line, and there were five! The scouts had to wait for the last.

Quiet, quiet. How quiet could it get in the forest? Or was it quiet only under the leaf piles?

The sheepskin coats became wet in the back; the icy dampness penetrated their bodies. The cold liquid came in over their collars. But they had to remain motionless. Now the second line was approaching. It was closing in! The boots of many German soldiers were crushing the leaves from the same direction. Closer,

closer, ever closer. Kalganov felt as one of the Germans, passing over the top of him, scattered the leaves alongside his leg. Kalganov carefully braced himself on the cold ground with his left hand, prepared to jump up. But the Germans passed by.

A minute, then a second of painful anticipation.

And once again, crackling leaves under hobnailed boots.

The third line.

The fourth.

When the fifth line passed, Kalganov lay waiting for several additional minutes. Perhaps a straggler or a stay-behind from the last line was still coming through?

No, it was quiet.

Kalganov stood up, brushed the heavy, wet leaves from his chest and face, and quietly commanded:

"Get up!"

The sailors got up, as if in a fairy tale, and shook off the wet leaves.

"A German stepped on my elbow."

"They stepped right over me; I was buried right in the stream."

"Now let them figure out where we disappeared to."

Upon completion of such a comprehensive sweep, the Germans would have to report to their command that they had not found any Soviet parachutists in the area of Black Mountain.

Once again, sharp sailors' eyes tracked enemy ships entering Yalta and other ports on the Crimean southern coast. Once again, reports transmitted by the quick and steady hands of the young female radio operators went to the headquarters of the Black Sea Fleet. And once again, fleet air force bombers, taking a course to the targets designated by the scouts, lifted off at night from faraway airfields on the Caucasus coast.

The air strikes became particularly destructive when our attacking forces were approaching the south coast and the German command was dispatching ships to remove their troops and equipment. Already fearing to use Yalta harbor, which was under constant Soviet air bombardment, the Germans were attempting to relocate their forces to Alushta [northeast of Yalta]. But two sailor scouts and radio operator Valya Morozova were standing watch on the heights near Alushta. The enemy received the same treatment in Alushta as in Yalta.

The scouts stood their watch until the last Germans had fled Yalta escaping from our advancing forces. On 13 April 1944, having completed their several-month-long watch in the enemy rear, the sailor scouts left the forest. They spotted Soviet vessels sailing toward the Crimean shore on a sea glittering under the spring sun from the docks of the port of Yalta.

CHAPTER FOUR

TRUST

The battles for Balaklava and Sevastopol were still being fought. Black Sea Fleet submarines, torpedo cutters, and air forces were actively operating along the Crimean coast, cutting the enemy's sea evacuation routes. Our command needed new information on the movement of enemy ships, on the situation in Sevastopol harbor, and on the enemy's coastal defensive positions. Therefore, the scouts continued their work.

Underground formations with whom the scouts had earlier maintained liaison were operating in Balaklava and Sevastopol. In these days it was particularly important to deliver the taskings of the command to members of the underground and receive reports from them in a timely manner. The liaison, of course, had to be accomplished across the front line. For this purpose, Kalganov and several sailors were sent into the area where our forward units attacking Balaklava and Sevastopol were operating. Valya Morozova was also to go through the front lines. She was ordered to go into Sevastopol in the guise of a young woman who had ended up there along with the retreating Germans, get in contact with the underground, and then collect and transmit intelligence data. But on the way toward the front line, Valya was struck by a shell that broke both of her legs. It was a miracle that she survived.

A large shell fragment that struck her in the side was deflected by a pistol she had hidden under her dress.

The situation in the city was difficult. The Gestapo was working feverishly to make the rear of the German Seventeenth Army, which by this time had been pressed up against the sea in Sevastopol, safe.

Liaison with the underground was further complicated because their ranks had been heavily depleted. The scouts already knew that one of their Black Sea Fleet sailors, Gorlov by name, had been picked up in Sevastopol, where he was living illegally after escaping captivity. Through Gorlov, the scouts were connected with the Sevastopol underground headed by V. D. Revyakin.[1] Many members of this group had been arrested simultaneously with Gorlov, including Revyakin himself. It quickly became known that the local police in Balaklava had arrested a man named Burov, a member of the underground working in the port repair facility.

Burov, a clever and self-reliant individual, was particularly closely tied to the scouts. The arrest of such an informant was very keenly felt. And so Kalganov decided to go to Balaklava. He had to obtain information about the enemy, and, in addition, he hoped to rescue Burov if he had not already been moved and was still alive.

When darkness came, Kalganov, Globa, Gura, and Chichilo, dressed in civilian clothes and hiding pistols and grenades under their garments, went through our forward edge north of Balaklava and penetrated undetected past German positions. Along one of the ravines that extended down toward Balaklava Bay, they made their way into an encampment full of German soldiers.

The scouts made their way unnoticed along a back street to a secret rendezvous location known to them. There they met with a member of the underground who, like Burov, was a Balaklava worker. He was a middle-aged man whom they knew under the name Mikheich.

From Mikheich they received information on the enemy that he had collected over some time. But after Burov's arrest, he had been unable to transmit it. It became clear from their conversation with Mikheich that someone had betrayed Burov. But who? This traitor had to be found and destroyed before he betrayed others. Mikheich was unable to answer questions as to whether Burov was alive and where he was being held. "Let's ask the chief of police!" Kalganov decided. But Mikheich told him the chief was not in Balaklava now; he had been summoned to Sevastopol. A deputy remained in his place—someone named N. [in the Soviet style, known but not named]. This man had recently been appointed to this position from the police ranks. He was young, about twenty-five. Mikheich said that he knew N. well, as many knew each other in Balaklava, a modest town, and could point out where N. lived.

"Well, let's pay this toady a visit!" said Kalganov.

At around midnight, Mikheich led the scouts in a roundabout way to a small stone building that stood deep in a courtyard not far from Balaklava's main street. On Kalganov's instruction, Mikheich knocked on the door.

"Who's there?" a male voice behind the door asked guardedly. Mikheich gave his name.

"Ah, it's you!" he said calmly from behind the door, and asked, "What's going on?"

"The Germans have shown up at the courtyard demanding something or other. An officer sent me to get you. He gave me a note to give to you."

The bolt slid back, and the door began to open.

Kalganov, who was standing next to Mikheich, flung the door open and brought up his pistol.

"Hands up!"

Globa and Chichilo rushed in behind Kalganov. Gurev was posted at the door as a lookout. They closed the door.

Kalganov's flashlight flickered in the darkness of the vestibule. The face of the man in a nightshirt and breeches, barefooted, standing up against the wall with raised arms, seemed especially pale in the white light. He was indeed young.

"Is this the man?" Kalganov asked Mikheich, who had accompanied the scouts into the building.

"It's him!"

"Search him!" Kalganov commanded. Globa patted down the policeman's breech pockets for weapons.

"Let's go!" Kalganov pointed his pistol in the direction of the door.

"Where are you taking him? Where!" a woman cried hysterically. "Where are you taking my son?" A rotund woman came out of the next room in a dress hastily thrown over her head. Right behind her was a seventeen-year-old girl, pressing her hand to her throat. Her frightened eyes shone in the probing light of Kalganov's flashlight, and she whispered softly:

"Brother!"

"Quiet!" Kalganov stopped the woman, drawing his pistol back. "If you don't want something bad to happen, don't tell anyone about us!" Then he commanded N., still standing with his hands raised, "Dress quickly. You are coming with us."

The sailors left the city with their prisoner several minutes later. Mikheich had pointed out the route to them as soon as they left the courtyard, and then they separated. Kalganov advised Mikheich to take his family and hide until our forces arrived, in case it should become known that he had helped the deputy chief of police.

Kalganov's group stopped far outside the city, in a gully thickly overgrown with vegetation. From their position they could see anyone who might be approaching. The first priority was to ascertain Burov's location. Kalganov had still not lost hope of finding and recovering him.

Kalganov began the interrogation:

"Where is Burov now?"

"He was sent to the Gestapo in Sevastopol," N. responded.

"You sent him?"

"No."

"Who have you personally arrested?"

"No one. I only recently came into this job." N. tried to vindicate himself. "On the contrary, I have done everything I could to decrease the number of arrests and deportations."

"If you're such a good and kind man, why are you serving in the police?"

"For the pay and the rations. There is no work in Balaklava, and we can't leave. I have an old mother and a teenage sister."

"My heart bleeds!" exclaimed Globa, who was sitting next to the commander. "Don't waste time with him, Comrade Senior Lieutenant!"

"A true statement!" Chichilo and Gura backed up Globa. "Shoot the police dog."

"There is one way to talk to a traitor—with a bullet!"

"Hold on!" Kalganov stopped his impatient subordinates. "We can always shoot him later. I want to have a little talk with him."

Even at the beginning, when Kalganov had just begun to conduct the interrogation, he had some intuition that this man did not have the malice in his spirit that was normally found in the traitors they captured, if they masked it.

Kalganov told the sailors to post a guard, then rest themselves. He led N. off to the side and began a detailed conversation with him. He wanted to find out what kind of person this was. Indeed, had he been forced by his circumstances into service to the occupiers, or was he a committed enemy artfully seeking a way out of his dilemma?

The conversation was long and frank. Kalganov drew the impression from it that N. served the occupiers only because of the weakness of his own character. But in Kalganov's opinion, this did not in any way diminish his guilt.

Having listened to N., Kalganov said to him:

"Perhaps you have indeed served the enemy without any special enthusiasm. But a fact remains a fact. You are a traitor and deserve death."

"I know." N.'s voice was frozen.

"But perhaps you can expiate your guilt."

"How?" N. asked with disbelief and a timid hope.

"If you return to Balaklava and carry out several of our instructions."

"Give me an order—I will do anything you ask!"

"Good!" Kalganov said. "But you must understand that if you think you can deceive us, you will not escape retribution. When they have to flee, the Germans will not take you with them. Our forces are coming, and there is no place to hide from their justice."

"I understand," N. whispered, and then finished, "Believe me!"

"Well, we'll see." Kalganov looked searchingly into N.'s face, still barely distinguishable in the darkness. "Okay, I will trust you. Now we will give you all the documents you need and you will return home. Your mother and sister will say nothing. You tell them in no uncertain terms on our behalf—not a word to anyone. In the morning, show up for work as if nothing had happened. Use any means to find out who turned over Burov. Find the traitor."

"And if I find him, what should I do?" N. asked in anticipation.

"When it gets dark, bring him here!" Kalganov decided after a moment's thought. He didn't want to risk going into Balaklava a second time.

"How will I get him to come?" N. asked with some bewilderment.

"Very simply. Won't he be working for the police? Order him. Tell him it's a secret mission."

"I'll try."

Kalganov detected both confusion and determination in N.'s voice. For a moment, he harbored some doubt. What if this man suddenly turned on us? Wouldn't it be simpler and more reliable to do as the sailors recommended and settle accounts with him for his service to the occupiers the same way they settled accounts with others—with a bullet? No. In the end, this man would not be able to escape justice. He himself now understood: if he deceived us, it would only increase his guilt, and if he carried out his instructions, it would diminish his guilt. So be it.

Kalganov and N. moved over toward the sailors who had been waiting close by. Kalganov informed them of his final decision.

"Scum! We should release this fish into the water!" Gura spoke involuntarily. Globa supported him.

"Exactly—he's scum!"

Chichilo suggested: "It'd be better if I led him off into the bushes!"

Kalganov took the sailors' opinions into consideration. He always consulted with them before he made a decision. This only strengthened his command authority, and the sailors always carried out his orders with zeal. The fact that now they expressed their disagreement with his instructions, counter to good order and discipline, distressed Kalganov. But he responded firmly:

"This decision is not subject to discussion."

N. left to go back into Balaklava.

By the following night, the scouts were again in the same thickly overgrown ravine. Kalganov took preventive measures in case N. had decided to trick them and a German cordon and search unit showed up in his place. Several scouts were positioned on the flank of the designated meeting site where they could immediately spot the enemy if he appeared.

The designated hour arrived. The scouts listened intently: was he coming? And with whom?

Then they heard the rustling of branches that were already adorned with young leaves. The voices of two men floated above the tops of the bushes in the semidarkness.

Caution is the mother of security. The scouts revealed themselves only after they had confirmed that just two men were coming into the gully, and there was no ambush nearby.

A short fat man in a long cape, with a large round head, on which was crammed a black *tyubeteyka,* stood next to N.

"Is this the man?" Kalganov asked, pointing to the fat man.

"This is the one," he heard in reply.

"Let's go!" Kalganov said to the fat man.

"Where? What for?" He obviously suspected something was wrong. "Mister Chief, who are these men?" He turned angrily to N.

"Keep your voice down!" Kalganov put a heavy hand on the fat man's shoulder and forced him to the ground. "And answer."

The stunned traitor, obviously not expecting that the "special mission" to which the deputy police chief had led him would end in this manner, was unable to utter a word for the first minutes. But then he was forced to provide answers.

The interrogation did not last long. The fat man, who was the owner of a fancy goods store in Balaklava, admitted that he had been a secret Gestapo agent for some time. In his store and in a cafe near the harbor, which he frequented often, he listened to conversations and questioned everyone possible concerning suspicious persons. He informed on these people and on those with whom they associated. He had suspected Burov for some time and recently had informed on him. He assured them that he knew of no other agents in Balaklava.

There was no further reason to interrogate him. Kalganov summoned Chichilo and pointed him toward the spy-haberdasher, who already knew what lay ahead for him.

"Take him away!"

"Get a move on!" Chichilo shoved the traitor, who was sitting helplessly on the ground. He got up slowly.

A minute later, a single shot rang out in the bushes not far away. Justice was done.[2]

Several minutes later, no one remained in the dark thicket. The scouts hurried away because the shot that put an end to the traitor could have attracted the enemy's attention. Kalganov sent N. back to Balaklava, instructing him to remain at his post as deputy chief of police until the very end, until Balaklava was liberated, and to do everything in his power to prevent the Germans from evacuating the population with them. In addition, Kalganov required N. to bring daily reports, at night, of anything new that he might have learned about the German forces operating in and around Balaklava, about German vessels stopping at Balaklava harbor, and about new instructions from the German command. N. was to leave notes containing these reports at a clandestine drop, under a rock not far from the road on the outskirts of the city. Each night, the runner sent out by Kalganov brought in the notes he found under the rock, which contained new information from N. about the enemy.

Kalganov, dressed in civilian clothes, went himself into Balaklava several times and met there with N. With his assistance, Kalganov obtained additional intelligence data.

Soon N. was carrying out another mission. One night he arrived at a barn that was guarded by his policeman in which fifteen local citizens were detained who had been arrested on suspicion of contact with partisans and were slated to be sent to the Gestapo in Sevastopol. N. ordered his policeman to open the barn, and he went in to talk to the detainees. Several minutes later, the barn was empty, and in the morning N. reported to his chief that the detainees had killed the guard and fled.

The Germans were driven from Balaklava several days later. Kalganov and several of the sailors of his detachment were among the first of our fighting men to enter the city. Kalganov immediately sought out N. and gave him a new assignment: go into German-occupied Sevastopol, present himself to his police command structure, claim to have fled from Balaklava, and ask for a new job. In Sevastopol, as in Balaklava, N. was to busy himself collecting information about the enemy. He was also to determine if the arrested Burov and the underground members of Revyakin's group were still alive, where they were being held, and if it was possible to rescue them.

To get into Sevastopol, N. needed to pass through the front line. He had to accomplish this in such a way as not to arouse the suspicion of the Germans. Kalganov, who had made an arrangement with the command of one of our army units that occupied positions between Sevastopol and Balaklava, arrived there with N. early in the morning. N. had all his documents that verified his service with the police. They led N. through the forward positions, and, according to the plan, he ran toward the German positions. Right behind him, the army unit opened fire with rifles and submachine guns, but in such a way as not to strike the fleeing man. Kalganov observed from the infantry's trenches. N. pulled a white kerchief out of his pocket and waved it as he was running through the neutral zone. The Germans did not fire at him. Then he jumped and disappeared into the ground—he had jumped down into a German trench. Everything was working!

Kalganov, who now constantly remained with his scouts near the forward edge, went alone into Balaklava on the following day to meet with several members of the underground. With their assistance, he hoped to reestablish communications with the Sevastopol underground that had been broken when Revyakin and his group were arrested.

On the way back, Kalganov dropped in at N.'s home, as he had promised, to report to N.'s mother and sister that he was alive and healthy and to calm them.

After talking with N.'s mother and sister, Kalganov left their house, intending to return to his sailors at the front-line unit. But after taking several steps down the street, he heard:

"Halt!"

Two soldiers, along with some civilians, ran up to him.

"Is this him?" the soldiers asked them.

"It's him, yes. It's him."

Not responding to Kalganov's questions, paying no heed to his strident protest, and not listening to his explanations, the soldiers disarmed him, searched him, and led him away. A noisy and ever-growing crowd of Balaklava citizens followed behind them, shouting:

"We found a German spy!"

"Aha! A vermin has been caught!"

Someone explained: "I saw him go away with the senior police-man with my own eyes! The policeman has fled, and this man is here. Something smells."

Someone suggested: "Comrade soldiers, why are you taking him away? Put him up against the wall, and we'll put a quick end to him!"

They brought Kalganov to an army *osobyy otdel*[3] that had just been established in Balaklava. At that moment, Kalganov had no way to prove who or what he was. As his work often required, he was dressed in civilian clothes and had no identification documents with him. No one in the *osobyy otdel* wanted to take his word, and worse, they knew nothing about a detachment of naval scouts. In fact, they could not have known because before this the scouts had been with the advancing army units and obviously had established no liaison with fleet intelligence.

Kalganov vigorously protested and demanded that they contact the intelligence department of the Black Sea Fleet to establish his identity. But the *osobyy otdel* tended to believe the local citizens more than Kalganov. They threw him into a solitary confinement cell.

Only when the heavy cell door closed did Kalganov understand that he might die from our own bullets for absolutely no reason. It was a front-line situation. They would not investigate long, and then they would shoot a spy delivered by the population. Would the *osobisti* [counterintelligence agents] not want further to clarify his identity, or would they be unable to do this for some reason?

Kalganov pounded on the iron-lined door and demanded that he be immediately presented to the officer in charge. But they ignored him.

Several agonizing hours passed. Finally, someone drew back the bolt, and in the open door stood an officer in a blue naval jacket. Kalganov immediately recognized him: a major from fleet intelligence, the same man who had seen him off several months ago before his parachute insertion into the Crimea! Kalganov joyfully embraced the major.

"Is this him?" they asked the major from behind the door.

"Yes, it's him!" Laughing, the major turned to the agents. "You don't know your own!"

N. returned from Sevastopol a week later, surreptitiously crossing through German lines one night. He reported to Kalganov that after he jumped down into the German trench, they held him while they checked his documents and then sent him to Sevastopol. "This means that I was in custody at about the same time as you!" Kalganov laughed to himself, recalling the time he had spent behind bars. N. recounted that they held him under lock for two days and then let him out, apparently having confirmed his identity.

He appeared at the Sevastopol police department and, explaining how he had miraculously escaped from the "Reds," asked for a position. But there were no openings. Besides him, there were many other policemen lounging about the city, who had fled from nearby Crimean towns from which the Germans had been driven. Just the same, N. remained at the Sevastopol police department, in reserve, as it were. He stayed there all day for days and had the opportunity to talk with many of his previous acquaintances in service and meet new ones. They related sympathetically to him, as to one who had suffered a misfortune.

All this helped N. to find out a great deal. He told Kalganov that after Revyakin's underground organization had been tracked down, the Gestapo had arrested almost all of its members; only a few had managed to hide. N. also reported that none of the arrested, including Burov, were in the Sevastopol jail. Perhaps they had already been shot. Of all the earlier arrested underground members held in the jail, only a man named Zavozil'skiy, who turned out to be a traitor, remained. With his assistance, the Gestapo hoped to regain the trail of the underground members still at large.

After reporting this news that was of little comfort, N. gave Kalganov new and very important information on the enemy's defensive fortifications and locations of artillery batteries in Sevastopol. Having passed on everything that he had learned, N. then requested:

"Send me back into Sevastopol. I can get still more information."

On the following night, N. again was sent through the forward edge but this time in such a way that the Germans didn't spot him.

N. did not succeed in returning before the decisive assault on Sevastopol began. The enemy defending the city was quickly defeated. Only pathetic remnants of the defeated German Seventeenth Army, pressed up against the sea at Cape Kherson and along several of the small bays near Sevastopol, continued to offer fierce resistance.

The scouts walked into Sevastopol, as into Balaklava, alongside our lead conventional units. Great was the scouts' joy when they finally saw their Black Sea Fleet capital free of the enemy! How they had dreamed about this during the difficult months of the war on the Caucasus coast and around Novorossiysk and Tuapse! This dream—to enter Sevastopol as victors—had helped them withstand unbelievable hardship and danger in the enemy rear, in the mountains around Yalta. How beautiful their native city seemed after a long absence, even though there now lay only piles of white stones in place of the white stone buildings that had once towered over the sea and the black smoke of fires rose up over the ruins into the clear spring sky. Firing could still be heard on the city's outskirts.

As soon as the scouts entered the city, they hurried to building number 46 on Laboratory Highway, where Revyakin lived. Spotting the sailors, Revyakin's neighbor Anastasia Pavlovna Lopochuk came out to meet them with her fourteen-year-old son Tolik.[4] In the garden between the stones of the fence, they showed the scouts a secret cache built by Revyakin that the Gestapo had never been able to find. In the cache were rubber stamps and seals of the underground organization, typeface, leaflets printed with this typeface, issues of the newspaper *Za Rodinu* [For the Motherland] published by the underground, and Revyakin's diary. Kalganov took all this to turn over to the command. Now these documents and items would become sacred relics of the heroic struggle of Soviet patriots.

Kalganov searched out N. in the first few hours after entering Sevastopol. In truth, they found each other—N. was also looking for Kalganov.

In the last days of the battle, N. had been among the Germans who, retreating from Sevastopol, were fighting their way toward the bays in the hope that they would be evacuated by sea. The deputy chief of the Balaklava police, who had sought safety among his erstwhile bosses, did not arouse any suspicion among them. Taking advantage of this trust, N. gathered a fair amount of good information about the German defenses on the approaches to these bays. This information could still turn out to be useful, and Kalganov quickly turned it over to their command. N. also told Kalganov that he had learned from one of his police acquaintances that Revyakin and other underground members had been shot and were buried in a field, in bomb craters. Only one of the underground members managed to avoid the bullets during the executions. As far as N. knew, on the last day, when the Germans were already fleeing Sevastopol, the Gestapo also shot the traitor Zavozil'skiy—they no longer needed him.

Later, when the battles around Sevastopol had finally concluded, Kalganov and his sailors visited the excavations of the graves of the underground heroes. They found the body of Gorlov, their Sevastopol contact. He was buried together with members of Revyakin's underground group.

N. eagerly agreed to return into the German positions—an area of the bay where they were continuing to fight. Kalganov gave him several instructions. Taking advantage of his documents concerning police service, N. was to take every possible measure to save those Sevastopol citizens the Germans had taken with them. In addition, N. was instructed to seek out the major who was chief of the Sevastopol Gestapo. N. was to capture him and, if that was not possible, kill him so that this murderer of many Sevastopol citizens and executioner of the underground would not avoid his just punishment.

N. headed off to accomplish his mission.

Battles with remnants of enemy troops pressed up against the sea lasted for four more days. The hopes of thousands of defeated Germans that ships would come to pick them off were in vain. The ships did not come. Those many that did appear were subjected to destructive strikes by our air forces and ships during their approach to the coast or after they had taken aboard full loads of German soldiers and officers.

At the end of the fourth day, when our forces were concluding the destruction of the remnants of enemy units on the shores of the bays, three automobiles with German markings darted along the road leading from the fighting area into Sevastopol. The cars stopped on the outskirts of the city, alongside a building that had been designated for meetings between Kalganov and N. Kalganov came out of the building. N., jumping out of one of the cars, hurried to meet him. Two other men walked behind him.

"These drivers are with me." N. pointed them out to Kalganov. "They are ours, forced by the Germans to work for them. Today they helped me steal these cars. We came out straight through the fighting."

Leading Kalganov to one of the cars, N. showed him officers' identification booklets, medals, and shoulder boards thrown on the seat.

"I didn't find the major. But in his place—three others." N. recounted, and both drivers affirmed, that he had shot three Gestapo officers along with their drivers. He had managed under various pretexts to lure them from their vehicles in an isolated sector of a coastal road along the overhanging cliffs. The drivers also confirmed that N., operating under the guise of a policeman, managed to save several tens of Sevastopol citizens whom the Germans were taking with them but in the end had decided to execute.

Having told all this to Kalganov, N. took him off to the side and asked:

"Do you have any other missions for me?"

"You are eager for assignments!" The senior lieutenant smiled. "Had I met with you earlier, and you didn't have the background you do, I would not have hesitated to take you into the detachment. So now—what kind of assignment? Not a single armed German remains in Sevastopol or outside it. As of today, I myself am unemployed."

"What am I to do now?" N.'s voice lingered.

"That about which we spoke earlier." Kalganov saw how sad N.'s face had become. "I will vouch for you, for how you expiated your guilt and then gave yourself up."

"I'm afraid."

"But to wait until they come for you would hardly be less frightening."

"More frightening. You will not leave me?"

"I already promised!" Kalganov put his hand on N.'s shoulder and looked him in the eye: "Believe me, your best move is to give yourself up. Don't drag it out. I'll go with you."

"What will be will be. But I ask you for one thing—I will give myself up in Balaklava, not here. I don't know what will become of me. I want to say my final good-bye to my mother and sister."

"Good," Kalganov agreed. "We will go to Balaklava in one of these cars that you 'liberated.' "

They were in Balaklava in an hour. Kalganov wanted to go straight to N.'s home, but N. asked him:

"Turn the car toward the shore. I want to be near the sea. I need to gather myself."

They sat together, talking, under the vertical Balaklava cliffs on a knob worn smooth by the waves, and watched as the low waves washed against the rocky coast. Kalganov tried to encourage N. He believed that N. would receive leniency. There, in N.'s presence, Kalganov wrote out a long declaration for the investigative organs, in which he laid out in great detail everything he knew about this man. He recounted the feats he had committed in expiation of his guilt and asked that his punishment be lightened. Then Kalganov and N. drove together to his home. Kalganov waited while N. said his good-byes to his mother and sister. Finally, they went together to the *osobisti*, to the people who just a short time ago had considered Kalganov himself to be a traitor.

But now they greeted Kalganov like an old acquaintance in the *osobyy otdel*. He presented N. to them, told them everything about his activities, and gave them his statement. Kalganov believed that his favorable recommendation would be taken into consideration in the course of the investigation. Encouraging N. not to lose faith in justice and courageously to face all the trials that he would have to withstand, Kalganov said good-bye to him.

Driving near N.'s home, Kalganov asked the driver to stop the car, and he dropped in one more time on N.'s mother. He found her crying. Kalganov had seen no small river of women's tears during the war, the tears of mothers and wives whose sons and men had perished, among them many of his comrades, from German bullets at the front lines, or who had been turned over by traitors and were shot by the police or tortured by the Gestapo. Now he saw crying the mother of his recent enemy, whom he had intended to shoot, but who managed to accomplish deeds that he would have not done except to save his own skin. The main thing was that she was a mother. What tears are more bitter than a mother's? And though he wished to comfort this woman, Kalganov said to her the only thing he could:

"Your son deserves leniency. Don't despair."

CHAPTER FIVE

"NORD"

After the Crimea was liberated, the scouts were recommended for awards. The commander of the Black Sea Fleet ordered the entire detachment to take six weeks' leave. The scouts exchanged their quilted jackets and pants that had become tattered during the winter in the mountains near Yalta for new jackets and blouses and traveled to Foros [on Crimea's southernmost shore]. A sanitarium had been set aside there especially for them.

But Kalganov could not sit in one place. He was pulled back to the site where he had spent the eighteen months before his insertion into Crimea. There, he paid with his own blood for the right to stand in the ranks of the party of the communists. He wanted once again to visit the Tuapse and Novorossiysk areas, where he and his combat comrades, each of whom he remembered to this moment, had walked in the mountains and forests: Sayfulla Yusupov, on whose grave the young spring grass was now turning green; Yunachev, Borisov, Krivda, and all the others. He regretted that wartime fate had separated him from them after he left the hospital. Where were these comrades of difficult marches and dangerous patrols now?

Kalganov wanted to visit many memorable places. But he wanted first of all to see a small village alongside Magra sanitarium, near Tuapse. Picking up a travel voucher, he boarded a ship going to the Caucasus coast.

On a clear July [1944] morning, Kalganov hopped a ride on a passing truck. It turned down the road that led past the sanitarium village. The fighting had concluded in this area about a year before. The then prominent craters, now overgrown with grass, did not hit one in the face. It was quiet all around. The loud rumble of artillery cannonades did not echo through the mountains, and the heartrending wail of Junkers or Fokke Wolfs going into their bomb runs did not drop out of the serenely clear, sun-filled sky. The war was now far away to the west, beyond the Black Sea, already crossing the border.

Kalganov walked down the stony road alongside slopes now covered by bushes lightly yellowing in the sun, and his heart was full of the joy of anticipation.

He arrived in the familiar village. The white walls of the houses were streaked by soot—there were no roofs on many of them—and the charred trunks of trees showed up black from behind half-ruined stone fences. But fresh green young branches already shielded them here and there. In some yards, homeowners who had returned once again were making themselves at home. They were repairing their roofs and putting in windows. Just a bit more to travel, and he would reach a familiar house.

Kalganov increased his pace in anticipation. Then he stopped, frozen in his tracks. The house was not there—only gray stones and tiles growing brown and bits of grass poking up through the debris.

Kalganov removed his *furazhka* and scratched his head. It was as if the radiant summer day had become dark to him. He stood in disbelief. And in the vision of his memory he saw what had been here a year earlier, in 1943.

Our offensive was being prepared. Each evening, after the sun sank into the sea, the scouts went out into the mountains wrapped in twilight. They clambered the night through across the rocky slopes, overgrown with prickly underbrush, looking for German trenches and bunkers. They walked back out at dawn.

Returning from the night's search to their dugout, carved in the slope of a coastal ravine, they normally walked past the long abandoned white sanitarium buildings, past the settlement, then already half-ruined by bombing attacks. Just a few intact houses remained in this settlement, which almost the entire population had abandoned.

The house whose ruins Kalganov was now standing by was on the edge of the settlement. It was a white hut, devoid of a roof, which had been blown off by the shock wave of a bomb. The scouts dropped in on this hut fairly often—the mistress of the house, a middle-aged woman, had stayed here. The scouts knew that her husband, who worked as a locksmith at the sanitarium, had been killed by a German bomb. More than once they had advised her to evacuate the area: the forward edge was close, and new air raids and artillery strikes were possible. But the woman stubbornly refused to abandon her beloved nest.

Besides, the woman was not living in this half-destroyed hut by herself—she had a dog with her. It was a young but fully grown sheepdog named Nord [north]. Kalganov, who had long had a love for dogs, liked this animal. It was as if Nord was a kindred spirit with the young bearded sailor. Nord trustfully came to him and permitted Kalganov to pet him.

One time Kalganov asked the woman:

"Give me Nord. You have nothing to feed him. And I will care for him and train him."

"No!" The woman sighed. "My man took Nord when he was a little puppy and raised him. I can't give him up to a stranger now."

Days passed. In his free time, Kalganov frequently dropped in on the hut without a roof. Digging into his ration packet, he fed Nord. They became fast friends. Seeing this, the woman finally gave in to Kalganov's request. Nord willingly allowed a leash to be attached. But when Kalganov led him out of the yard, the dog sat down. He howled, whined, pulled back, and tugged at the leash. Kalganov managed to lead the dog to his hut only with difficulty.

But Nord quickly became accustomed to his new master. Kalganov made time to teach his pupil the basic dog skills: to obey his master, sit on command, get up, and retrieve. Kalganov was aided by his previous knowledge. As a teenager, he had dreamed of having a trained sheepdog and had studied books on dog training. Someone asked the soldiers of the neighboring unit if any of them had ever served on the border and had dealings with service dogs.[1] Kalganov wanted to train Nord so that he could take the dog on reconnaissance. Several weeks passed. Nord made striking progress. He was already able to carry out more than simple commands. Kalganov had taught him to jump up behind him into the back of a moving truck, to low-crawl, to sit for hours in ambush, to follow in someone's footsteps, and to carry reports. The sailors took an active role in Nord's training. They tied a loaded submachine gun or pistol in the hand of a scarecrow dressed in a German uniform or in a German poncho, and then tugged at the sleeve, which was connected to the trigger, thus firing shots. In this way they taught Nord not to fear gunfire, to throw himself at a firing enemy, and to bite the trigger hand. In the end, the dog was trained in all the finer points of reconnaissance that his dog's mind was capable of comprehending.

Finally the day arrived, or rather the evening, when they took Nord on reconnaissance for the first time. Nord passed the test with flying colors. From that time onward, he was an indispensable participant in every reconnaissance patrol.

One time, Kalganov went out with fourteen sailors to reconnoiter German positions around Two Brothers Hill. Here, as in many other sectors of the front along the coast, neither ours nor the German defenses were continuous. The mountainous terrain, overgrown with forests, intersected by ravines and gullies that drained down toward the sea, interfered with building a position. The German trenches and bunkers, camouflaged in the thickets and on separate hilltops, had to be found and marked on a map. The scouts went out into no-man's land under cover of the darkness of a June night. Habitually, as they had so many times, they crossed a ravine on a hanging bridge. By some miracle, this half-destroyed bridge remained suspended on two ropes above a boiling mountain stream that the scouts called Chertovym [the Devil's]. It was a short distance from the bridge to the enemy positions.

Normally, the scouts tried to return while it was still dark. Following their practice, they always returned from their missions by a different route so as not to give themselves away to enemy searches. But they always had to cross the Devil's stream using the bridge—there was nowhere else to cross the boiling stream.

On this occasion, the scouts had not succeeded in crossing the bridge before dawn. The summer night was short, and their search took more time than they had initially allocated. It was already light when they climbed down through the overgrown vegetation toward the bridge. The whitish night fog was falling away from the bushes down into the ravine, where the still invisible stream flowed.

A familiar path, long, long ago beaten out by the local inhabitants, led to the bridge. The scouts did not return along it but off to the flank.

Though the enemy positions were behind them, and their own positions were on the other side of the ravine, the scouts held their weapons at the ready and walked in a well-dispersed file. These were normal preventive measures in case the enemy, having discovered that the scouts were operating among their positions, had set an ambush to catch them on their return.

Everything was proceeding normally. It was quiet. Only the muffled gurgling of the stream and the infrequent short call of some awakening bird broke the silence. Already, the rocky ravine, the bridge hanging lopsidedly on two cables, and the path leading to it between the undergrowth could be seen through the bushes in the soft, somewhat rosy light of the beginning day on the slope below. They turned toward it. Kalganov, walking in front with Nord, stepped onto the path.

The chatter of automatic weapons split the morning quiet. Kalganov gave a quick order:

"To battle!"

In a second, not one of the scouts could be seen along the trail. They were lying in the bushes. Nord dropped to the ground next to Kalganov, turning his head and ears toward the direction of the firing.

German submachine guns intermittently swept the flanks of the bridge. Branches knocked down by the bullets rained down on the scouts' heads. "About a platoon!" Kalganov quickly determined the strength of the enemy by the intensity of the fire. "They outnumber us two to one."

He glanced to the right and left. Everyone was alive and intact. The Germans' lack of patience in not permitting the scouts to approach closer before they opened fire saved the scouts.

Only several seconds passed after the enemy opened fire before the commander made his decision.

"Stay here, fire, attract his attention to you, then rush to the bridge!" he ordered four sailors. Four submachine guns immediately opened up. "You," he ordered two others, "run across the path through the bushes and take the Germans in the rear! The rest of you—follow me!"

He jumped up and, crouching down, ran through the vegetation, skirting around the place where the enemy was lying. Nord stayed right with him in broad leaps. Eight sailors, dispersed in a file, ran nearby.

Kalganov had a goal: while the four who remained near the path attracted the enemy fire to themselves and two others were taking him in the rear, he with the remaining scouts would strike from the flank and drive them away from the bridge. The most important thing now was to prevent the enemy from blocking their sole path of withdrawal.

On the run, Kalganov detected that the voices of two additional submachine guns had been added to the uncoordinated firing. These were the sailors who had been sent around the Germans' rear, opening fire. Now they reached the edge of the ravine.

Kalganov and his scouts lay under the bushes near the trail, not far from the approach to the bridge. Nine submachine guns fired at the same time. In a few minutes, an additional four joined them, then still two more. It was clear by the sounds of the firing that the commander was where he needed to be and had brought together the sailors who had been left behind to draw enemy fire with those who had struck the enemy from the rear.

The Germans were confused. Several moments before, they thought they had taken the scouts unawares. Now, it turned out, the Russians had found their flank and rear!

Fearing they would be caught in a trap, the Germans, firing on the move, began to run from the bridge along the path toward the hill. Now the scouts could break contact with the enemy.

"One at a time—get to the other side!" Kalganov commanded. "When you get to the other side, cover the withdrawal of the others. I'll come last."

The Devil's bridge shook on its suspension cables when, one behind the other, the sailors ran across it. Once on the other side, they fell down behind the rocks or bushes and fired across the ravine with their submachine guns. Their commander remained at his previous position. He lay behind the mossy debris of the slopes, firing short bursts. Next to him lay Nord, guardedly glancing at his master.

Without taking his finger off the trigger, Kalganov looked around. Half of his sailors were already on the other side of the bridge. Their submachine guns were firing from behind rocks and from the scrub vegetation that hung over the edge of the ravine. In several more minutes, the remainder would be on that side. They could then hurry back to their own lines.

But what was this? To the right, in the bushes, they glimpsed crouching figures in spotted ponchos. The commander understood. Having spotted the sailors racing across the bridge from the slope above, the Germans had decided to cut off the path of the rest of them. The scouts' fire weakened for a few moments. One was running across the bridge; the others, having already run across, were still looking for a good firing position, and their hesitation encouraged the enemy.

Those who had not yet managed to cross the bridge fired furiously into the bushes along the edge of the ravine. Worst of all, the Germans were not visible in the thick vegetation. Taking advantage of the concealment available to them, they were moving closer and closer. Nord, who was lying next to Kalganov, looked around impatiently. Then a nearby bush rustled, and a flat-sided, gray-covered helmet bobbed between the branches.

"Throw grenades!" Without getting up, the commander threw the first grenade.

The brown smoke of the explosions cloaked the bushes. Broken branches flew up into the air; shredded leaves flew in all directions. Some Germans went to ground; others were forced back.

"Across the bridge!" Kalganov ordered the three sailors remaining with him.

"What about you?" one of them asked. "Are you coming with us, Comrade Senior Lieutenant?"

"Across the bridge!" Kalganov repeated. "Nord and I will cover you!"

The sailors got up and ran toward the bridge. Several submachine-gun bursts spewed out of the bushes, through the thick leaves. Kalganov fired a long burst into the bushes, emptying the entire disk. He looked around. Three sailors were already running across the shaky planking. Now was his time. He couldn't delay for a second! He got up, and Nord jumped up behind him. Both rushed toward the bridge.

"*Offizier! Offizier* [Officer, officer]!" A frantic shout was heard close behind him. "*Nicht schiessen* [don't shoot]!"

Kalganov looked back on the run. Five Germans in flapping camouflage smocks, brandishing their submachine guns, were running behind him and catching up.

"They aren't firing, they want to take me alive! What can I do? I've emptied my disk."

"Nord, face!"

Growling, the sheepdog leaped and threw himself on the enemy. Running on the bridge planking that was swaying under his feet, Kalganov glanced behind him without stopping. Nord had sunk his teeth into one German and was rushing at another, and the remaining enemy were momentarily taken aback.

While his master was running toward the opposite end of the bridge, the sheepdog continued fiercely to attack the pursuers, now totally surprised and confused. But this could only last for several seconds. One of the Germans would come to his senses and kill the dog with a burst of submachine gun fire.

"Nord, come!" Kalganov shouted, and, running off the end of the bridge, threw himself on the ground.

He replaced his empty disk with a full one, then saw Nord bounding across the bridge in broad leaps, with German submachine guns spitting out bullets behind him. Kalganov pulled back the bolt and took aim in the direction from which the bullets were flying at Nord.

Through the resonant clatter of his own submachine gun, he heard other submachine guns chattering somewhere nearby. The sailors were covering Nord with fire along with him.

There was an explosion somewhere in the middle of the bridge, and Nord was tossed in the air. "Did they kill him?" Kalganov was afraid for his dog.

No, he was alive!

Nord scampered across the bridge and, with a dog's nose for scent, determined where his master was and ran to him.

The Germans did not risk exposing themselves near the bridge, let alone go out onto it. They again lay in the bushes above the ravine and let loose with a torrent of submachine gun fire. But their bullets were no longer feared. The scouts had moved off into the thick woods, far away from the Devil's bridge, toward their own positions. Nord ran alongside his master. Listening to how his sheepdog was plaintively whimpering, Kalganov asked him:

"What's the matter, Nord?" Only then did he see that a bullet had passed through the dog's tail. Kalganov performed a surgical operation on the march. He took out his knife and cut off the broken tailpiece, then wrapped up the wound using his individual bandage. Thus Nord became a bob-tailed sheepdog.

Kalganov became even more attached to Nord after this incident. With good reason, he considered the sheepdog his lifesaver in the engagement at the Devil's bridge. Now the faithful Nord accompanied him on every patrol. The sheepdog became a genuine combat auxiliary of the scouts, and all the sailors loved him.

Several months passed. Winter came. Kalganov received the mission to fly to Crimea with several scouts to be dropped by parachute into the enemy rear, near Yalta. He decided to take Nord with him and prepared a special parachute and harness for him.

A twilight November day was coming to a close. A fleet air forces bomber, employed as a transport aircraft for this mission, stood ready at a coastal airfield. The aircraft was supposed to lift off while it was still light so as to reach the drop zone in the middle of the night. Everything was ready. All that remained was to load Nord. Kalganov strapped him into his harness, took the dog in his arms, and lifted him toward the open hatch. But Nord did not want to go through the hatch; he was afraid of the unknown. No matter what he tried, Kalganov could not push Nord through the hatch. "I should have trained him ahead of time!" Kalganov acknowledged his own error. But there was no time to train him now. The aircraft commander, impatiently glancing at his watch, was concerned about the flight. Cursing himself for his oversight, Kalganov abandoned his attempt to load Nord. He put him down on the ground and unharnessed his parachute. To one of his comrades, who took charge of the dog, he said:

"Take Nord back to his previous owner. Give her all my money. Let her feed and look after him. When I return, I will take him back."

All the scouts were already seated in the aircraft. Kalganov shook hands with those staying behind, looking at the clearly agitated Nord. Then he grasped the edge of the hatch, scrambled aboard the aircraft, and immediately pushed his way toward a porthole window in the fuselage. He spotted Nord anxiously running alongside the plane.

The motors revved up. The aircraft roared down the runway, which ended at the water's edge. Kalganov saw that Nord, as if trying to atone for his stubbornness, ran along behind.

The aircraft lifted off and headed out over the sea. Kalganov managed one look back. Nord had run into the water up to his chest, stopped, and raised his head in sadness, his glance following the disappearing aircraft.

All this he recalled now, as he stood with his hat in hand and looked at the ruins of the hut. But perhaps the woman, this kind, unfortunate woman, now lived somewhere in the village, in another house? Perhaps Nord was also here? Kalganov had to ask. Perhaps he could find them.

Putting his hat back on, Kalganov walked down the path. He stopped at the first yard where he saw people. They told him. During the last battle, when the Germans were being driven out of the area, their aircraft bombed the village. One of the bombs fell on the house at the outskirts, where the woman lived with the dog, and killed both of them.

Perhaps no one was in the house when the bomb fell? He stopped at the next house and then at another. Everywhere he stopped, they told him the same story. They had died.

From that time, Kalganov never again owned a dog.

CHAPTER SIX

GREETINGS, SAILORS!

Have you ever had occasion to sail the Danube on a steamer? The smooth surface of this great river is immensely broad—one can hardly see one bank from the other. Oceangoing cargo ships of great draft and tugboats with river barges travel uninterrupted along this great water highway, which extends from the Alps to the Black Sea, through the territories of eight countries. Passenger ships sail majestically, like white swans. One can see the flags of other seafaring nations on these vessels as well because, after the war, the socialist governments developed trade relations with the world.

This international water route remains fully active even on the darkest, most impenetrable night. White and red buoy markers, riverbank lighthouses, and alignment lights mark the way. The lights of the ships move, reflecting in the transitory mirror of the water. The lights of villages and towns on the banks twinkle with a scattering of golden sparks.

But the Danube did not appear this way in the severe wartime nights of the fall of 1944, when Soviet forces, hurriedly attacking along the river, pushed westward, liberating the countries along the Danube one after the other from the German yoke.

There were no lights on the banks or in the channel. The Danube was deserted where the front line crossed it at the juncture of three borders—Romania, Bulgaria, and Yugoslavia.

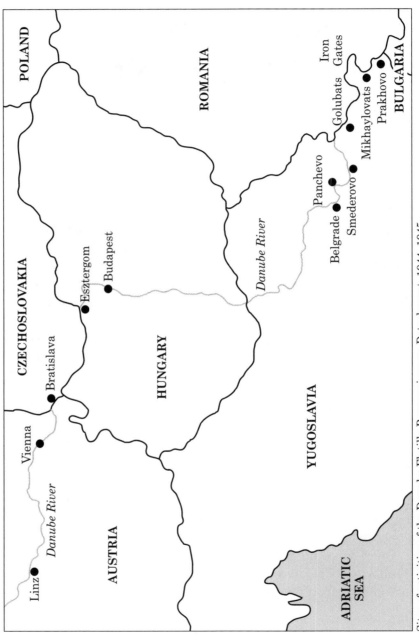

Sites of activities of the Danube Flotilla Reconnaissance Detachment, 1944–1945.

Somewhere on the banks, concealed by the darkness, German batteries pointed at the river. At this night hour, who would risk moving from the lower reaches, from the direction of Soviet forces?

But what is this? The engine of a vessel murmurs barely audibly, the ship moving against the current in the middle of the river. The night darkness hides it. And, probably, the rumble of the motor is not heard by German listening posts—it is a long way to the bank.

What if they hear it? What if they hear it and fire illumination rockets? In the merciless white light would be seen a small cutter with a low superstructure, with a Soviet navy flag flapping in the river breeze. This flag has not been seen in these parts of the Danube's waters. This small, not military looking cutter is the first to carry the flag here.

This cutter belongs to the scouts commanded by Senior Lieutenant Kalganov. Not too long ago, these sailors exchanged the ribbons on their *beskozyrki,*[1] and now the still untarnished gold letters spelling "Danube Flotilla" shine in place of the letters "Black Sea Fleet." Not so long ago, they sang:

Farewell, Black Sea,
We are saying good-bye to you.
Tomorrow we are going to the Danube,
To reconnaissance and into battle.

Kalganov's detachment was now the reconnaissance detachment of the reestablished Danube Flotilla.[2] They jokingly called the cutter on which the scouts sailed on this dark autumn night near enemy-occupied shores their flagship. There was no name stenciled on its side. But already the entire flotilla knew it under the name *Zhuchka* [House dog]. The scouts themselves nicknamed the cutter for its modest size and good maneuverability and because on it they could easily slip in everywhere.

The *Zhuchka* was a trophy cutter,[3] captured in the port of Galats, where the scouts first fought on the Danube, hot on the heels of the hurriedly retreating enemy. Before this, some had sailed on rubber boats and tiny plywood cutters, and some had moved on shore—on foot and on trucks.

The scouts had much urgent work to accomplish beginning on 24 August, when the flotilla's first combat vessels entered the Danube, attacking together with the Third Ukrainian *Front*.[4] Carrying out the missions of the flotilla headquarters, they searched for the safest route up the river for the armored cutters; they determined, by talking to the local inhabitants, whether the channel was mined; they searched along the banks for enemy shore batteries; they reconnoitered the best sites for amphibious landings; and they captured "tongues" on the banks. They had already covered hundreds of kilometers along the Danube. Ismail, Braila, Rushchuk, and all of Bulgaria were behind them. The *front* relentlessly fought westward along the Danube. Together with the forces, the ships sailed against the current. Their path was toward Belgrade, still more than one hundred kilometers ahead. And, feeling their way along this path, moving in the dark and cold autumn night up the Danube on the *Zhuchka*, the scouts sailed into the unknown. They were the first.

Where was the *Zhuchka* sneaking off to this night? It was going to the Yugoslavian village of Raduyevats. Somewhere in the vicinity of this village, on the far approaches to Belgrade, the enemy had created strong defensive lines.

The flotilla commander, Rear Admiral Sergey Georgievich Gorshkov, had given the detachment the mission to reconnoiter the enemy's shore positions near Raduyevats and to take "tongues."

It was after midnight. Rain clouds filled the sky, and a light autumn rain was falling. The *Zhuchka* quietly approached the low riverbank, overgrown with alders, not far from Raduyevats. Four men jumped from the deck onto the bank and immediately took cover in the wet, bare shrubbery. Turning sharply around, the *Zhuchka* moved off and disappeared into the darkness.

The first of the four men to move into the slippery alder thicket did not belong to the detachment. He was a Yugoslav partisan by the name of Radule. He led three scouts: Chichilo, Globa, and

Morozov—the senior scout and leader of the group. When the scouts had passed through the riverbank vegetation, they came out in a cornfield, where cornstalks stood that had long ago given up their ears of grain and then dropped their dry leaves. Radule, who spoke a bit of Russian, said in low tones:

"The village is nearby. There is a partisan safe house there. We will put on civilian clothes, find out as much as we can there, and take a guide beyond that point."

"You lead, Radule!" Morozov agreed.

Radule led the scouts straight through the cornfield. Their boots were sucked into the soil soaked by the autumn rain. The wet, rough cornstalks and leaves, invisible in the darkness, slapped their hands and faces.

They entered a village not along the road but through the gardens. When the walls of a hut began to show dimly white between the black trunks of the fruit trees, Radule told the scouts to wait and went forward by himself. They could hear through the rustling of the rain on the bare branches as Radule cautiously tapped on the window and then as it opened with a squeak.

Radule looked back at them and called quietly:

"Come on."

In the hut they met the head of the house—a black-mustachioed middle-aged man, in a canvas shirt that showed white out from under a sheepskin jacket. Shaking everyone's hand, he anxiously whispered:

"Welcome, Soviet friends! Greetings, sailors! You are the first Soviets we have seen!"

The window in the hut was completely covered. The wick of the oil lamp gave off a rosy glow.

Bustling about, the host pulled out an earthenware jug encased in braided straw from somewhere, with a corncob stopper:

"For you, liberators! For our victory!"

But Morozov stopped him.

"Thank you, friend, but we can't drink now."

The host gave a sigh of regret, then put the jug away. He animatedly discussed something with Radule, then crawled up onto the stove and looked into the corner, shut off by a multicolored curtain. He ran out into the vestibule, then returned carrying some clothes.

Some time passed. Out of the hut walked a quartet of men in peasant leather and canvas jackets like the local fishermen wore. Their weapons were not visible: pistols and grenades were concealed under their clothes. The host left the hut last. Quietly closing the door, he moved around in front of the four men and led them away.

The three scouts and Radule moved behind their guide through the gardens, then along the wet stubble of the harvested field, under light raindrops falling from the dark night sky. The escort stopped in a vineyard, where knotted vines sprinkled with leaves showed up darkly among the high stakes with wire stretched between them, and whispered something to Radule.

After listening, he passed the words on to the scouts:

"The highway from Belgrade to Raduyevats is near here. The Germans travel along this road. This is a good spot."

"Fine," Morozov agreed.

Having said his farewells, the guide left.

They sat in the vineyard along the side of the road. The rain rustled monotonously as before. The scouts listened: is anyone moving on the road? But the road that vanished into the darkness was empty. Apparently, the Yugoslav partisans had taught the Germans not to drive at night. They would have to wait until dawn.

Morning approached. The rain gradually diminished, then stopped entirely. Just a short time ago, the scouts, who were chilled to the bone and had not closed their eyes all night, wanted to get warm and get a few moments' sleep. But now, when the sky was beginning to whiten, they did not notice their tiredness. They watched the road impatiently. Far off down the road, they heard a muffled rumble that was growing louder. A column of trucks was coming from the direction of Belgrade toward Raduyevats.

The enormous vehicles with canvas-covered tops passed by, splashing and throwing up mud. With the skilled eye of a scout,

Morozov noted that they were loaded with crates, by all appearances containing ammunition. He committed the divisional markings on the sides of the vehicles to memory. A bit later, several more trucks went by, going in the same direction. Three large prime movers passed by, deafeningly laying tracks, towing cannons. Morozov noted this also.

The scouts sat near the roadside for a long time, observing this movement. By how many and what kind of vehicles passed by, it was possible tentatively to establish what kind of forces the enemy was bringing forward to reinforce the Raduyevats defensive lines.

The vehicles were moving in groups and quickly. As if out of spite, no Germans appeared on foot or traveling in horse-drawn wagons. It became more and more obvious that they would hardly be able to capture a "tongue" here, on the highway, the more so during daylight. But just the same, Morozov decided to wait a while in case a sudden opportunity appeared. Meanwhile, he had Radule go and reconnoiter a safer way to travel to Raduyevats, where there were no doubt many Germans. It would be easier to capture a "tongue" and gather information on the enemy there, in the rear, where the enemy was less careful, than here on a front-line road.

Radule left.

Sitting with Globa and Chichilo in ambush along the road, Morozov thought about Radule with concern: Would he accomplish his mission? When would he return? Meanwhile, Radule cautiously walked toward Raduyevats, a bit off to the side of the road. Before he entered the village, he wanted to talk with someone who lived in the village and ask questions about the enemy.

The fields and vineyards were deserted on this gray autumn day. Small wooden structures normally used to store tools and implements were scattered about.

Radule noticed a wisp of smoke floating up into the still morning air from alongside one of these sheds. Hiding behind wet vines, he moved closer and watched. In front of the door was a tripod, with a fire flickering beneath it, licking a smoke-blackened pot. Next to the fire sat a black-haired twelve-year-old girl, stirring the pot with a large wooden spoon. He heard a chopping noise from inside the shed—either someone was making kindling or clapping. Certainly, there were no Germans here.

No longer hiding, Radule walked toward the fire.

"Greetings, pretty young girl!"

The girl was silent, looking at him in surprise but without particular fear.

"Who is here besides you?" Radule asked.

Before the girl could answer, an old man came out of the shed. He was gray-haired, with long, graying mustache hairs that hung down toward his clean-shaven chin. His face was lined, as if etched by time, and he was wearing an open old cloth jacket. He held an ax in his hand.

The old man, who turned out to be an inhabitant of a village near Raduyevats, guardedly offered to help. He told Radule that approximately a battalion of Germans, who had arrived two days before, were in his village, but he did not know if there were any Germans in neighboring villages. But his granddaughter—he pointed at the young girl—could go around the nearby villages and find out everything he wanted to know. It would be easier for her to do it because the Germans would pay her no particular attention.

In response to Radule's questions about the Germans in Raduyevats, the old man replied: "I heard that there were many there, but I have not been in Raduyevats myself." The old man revealed that his longtime friend, Iosip Kovachevich, lived off to the right on the outskirts near the village entrance. Radule could bring his Soviet comrades to Iosip, and he could assist them.

The old man advised him to go to Raduyevats in the evening, when the local inhabitants normally returned from their work in the fields. His granddaughter would also have returned by that time.

Having agreed with the old man that he would wait for the Russians in the village, Radule returned to the scouts. He found them right where he left them, next to the road. When the short autumn day had come to a close and it began to darken, Radule,

Morozov, Chichilo, and Globa moved to the shed. The young girl had already returned. Radule questioned her. She told him everything she had seen in detail: how many Germans were in which village, where they were digging trenches, and where their guns were positioned.

When Radule translated the young girl's responses to Morozov, he said:

"Thank the young girl and her grandfather and tell them we must leave now."

Ensuring once again that their pistols and grenades were concealed under their clothes, each of the scouts picked up a large bundle of hay that the old man had prepared for them. Saying their farewells, they headed toward Raduyevats on the field path he pointed out to them.

Without raising anyone's suspicion, they entered the village through a small perimeter lane, the path the old man had talked about, still before nightfall. They found the desired hut, approached it through the backyard, dropped their bundles of hay, and then knocked on the door.

Seeing unfamiliar faces, Iosip Kovachevich was frightened at first. But, having learned from Radule who sent them, he became very receptive. He told them in some detail how many Germans were in Raduyevats, where their ammunition dumps were located, and where their shore batteries were aimed at the Danube. He also informed them that there were some German sailors in Raduyevats. The German command had ordered them to sink their boats somewhere not too far away. The sailors had then been placed in the shore defenses.

"We absolutely must capture a 'tongue' from among the sailors!" Morozov said to his comrades. "This is the kind of 'tongue' we most need. He will be able to tell us where mines have been laid in the river and where the sunken vessels block the channel."

They asked Iosip if the German sailors appeared on the streets.

"They loaf about!" the old man said with anger. "These cursed swabbies demand wine, suet—give them everything! For free!"

"If someone would drop in here now," said Chichilo, "we could grab him."

"It's hardly likely now," Iosip responded, when Radule translated Chichilo's words for him. "The sailors are more likely to be out and about in the evening, after supper."

The scouts consulted with Iosip on how best to operate so as to capture a "tongue." They decided to split up into two pairs: Morozov and Radule in one and Chichilo and Globa in the other, each pair to operate separately, to double the chances of success. They agreed that all should return to the old man's shed by midnight.

Meanwhile, it grew dark. It was time to begin. They decided that Chichilo and Globa would leave the hut first and head toward the waterfront. Iosip said that an acquaintance of his lived not far from the waterfront. Like all the villagers, this man was hostile toward the German sailors and would help his Russian brothers with great pleasure.

"We will go there!" Chichilo hurried Globa. "Perhaps we can select a drunk. We can all take a look at what's happening on the dock." He asked Radule, "Tell our host to lead us to his friend."

When Iosip returned from guiding Chichilo and Globa, Morozov said to him:

"All three of us will go out. We will wait for some German sailor to show up."

The gray autumn twilight already enshrouded the street. At this evening hour, as usual, people came out of their yards to take in the fresh air and gossip with their neighbors. It would have looked very much like peacetime had there not been German soldiers in the village. They strutted along the streets in twos and threes, and sometime singly, not hurrying, accompanied by hostile glances. It seems that these unwelcome guests greatly perturbed the peasants.

Radule, Morozov, and Iosip stood alongside the house. Radule's fisherman's jacket and the tattered look of Morozov's jacket could not have aroused suspicion. Radule conducted a quiet conversation with their host in their native Serb language, and Morozov gave the appearance that he was participating in this leisurely peasant conversation.

Morozov attentively watched everyone who appeared on the street. He already had noticed that among the Germans lounging about the street in this evening hour were some in gray army greatcoats and others in black sailors' uniforms.

Three Germans in naval blouses, with numerous unclasped buttons in the two rows and their *beskozyrkas* with tailless ribbons, turned toward the building opposite the scouts. They boldly pushed open the gate and spilled into the yard, where they were met by a barking dog. In a demanding tone they conversed with the woman who ran out of the hut. She began to explain something to them, gesturing with her hands. One of the Germans cursed loudly, then all three turned toward the gate and went out into the street, arguing. Two went on, and the third, having seen Radule, Morozov, and Iosip, headed toward them with resolute step.

"Guten abend [Good evening]." Radule pleasantly exchanged greetings with the German.

"Gut, Gut!" The German broke out in a smile. *"Verstehen Sie deutsch?* [Do you understand German]?" The German had been taken by surprise.

"Yes, I understand," Radule answered in German. "When I was young, I served as a sailor on Danube steamers and visited Germany. The Germans are a good people."

"Oh, yes!" the German exclaimed in delight. "You are also a sailor? You look like a good man, for a Slav!"

While Radule and the German conducted this mutually flattering conversation, Morozov was inspecting his prey. He was a hefty chap. On his jacket were shoulder boards with bars—he was a petty officer. He was worth taking! Morozov gave a covert sign to Radule.

Meanwhile, the German was complaining:

"What swines! We went to five houses and found nothing to drink! My comrades have lost hope. But not me. Could some wine perhaps be found in this house?"

"Of course!" Radule said cordially. "I am a sailor, and you are a sailor. Sailors treat each other right! Let's go in, *kamrad!*"

They led the long-awaited "guest" into the house. As soon as the door closed, Radule pulled his pistol out from under his shirt and said:

"Quiet! And for you—here is your wine!" He thrust the pistol directly into the startled German's face.

"And this is to snack on!" Morozov pulled out his own pistol.

"If you make a noise," Radule said in German, "you will receive this snack directly in the mouth."

The German was dumbfounded. He stood, looking straight ahead with fixed, wide eyes.

It was already completely dark outside the window. They pushed the prisoner through the door and led him out of the village by way of the gardens and back alley. In the darkness of the damp autumn night, Radule and Morozov took a route across the deserted fields toward the agreed-upon rally point—the shed where they were to meet with Chichilo and Globa. But no one was there. The shed was locked, the tripod trivet was folded up, and only lifeless coals showed black where the fire had been. The old man and his granddaughter had long ago gone home to their village. Chichilo and Globa were late. At first, this did not disturb Morozov much. Both of them were experienced scouts, and little could delay them in these circumstances.

But hour after hour passed. Morozov and Radule became more worried. What had happened to their comrades? The night was already half gone, and still they had not returned. Should they go out looking for them? Then what would they do with their "tongue"? Though he was tied up and sitting quietly, they could not risk leaving him. They had to return to the partisan rendezvous where they had changed clothes while it was dark. The man who would lead the scouts through the front line to their own positions was waiting for them there.

Morozov glanced up at the sky more and more impatiently and at the illuminated dial of his watch. Perhaps their comrades had already been killed, or worse.

Morozov recalled Gennadiy Konshin and the partisans' story about how they found his body, mutilated by the Germans. No, he did not want to believe that such a thing could happen to Globa and Chichilo! But not more than two hours remained until dawn. There was just enough time! To move in daylight was a great risk. They might not be able to deliver their "tongue." What should they do?

The sky was noticeably showing light on the horizon. Morozov breathed heavily and looked Radule in the eyes. He nodded his head in understanding. Yes, it was time. "Well, should we leave?" Morozov wanted to say. But then they heard approaching foot-falls. Had the Germans found them? Peering into the darkness, Morozov and Radule prepared their weapons just in case.

Then they could make out three men walking through the vine-yard toward the shed. How could they not recognize Chichilo among them with his great height and his waddling step!

Chichilo and Globa also were leading a "tongue"—a corporal from the 1st Alpine Division, who had been patrolling on one of the streets near the waterfront. But they had had to wait a long time for the right moment. Chichilo and Globa recounted that they had been unable to seize the "tongue" without a commotion. The Germans raised the alarm, and the scouts had barely escaped pursuit with their prize. They also had managed to learn a great deal with the help of the man to whom Iosip had sent them. Now the scouts could report to the command information on the disposition of enemy firing positions on the waterfront in Raduyevats, and near it, they could indicate the site most favorable for the approach of vessels and landing of an assault force. Certainly, they would also obtain valuable information from the "tongue." Now they could set out on their return journey. It was already light when the scouts said farewell to Radule in the thick oak grove, with dried leaves still hanging on the branches, that bordered our for-ward positions.

"Thank you, friend!"

"My thanks to you!" Radule responded. "From all of us, we await you, liberators."

CHAPTER SEVEN

A SECOND LİNE

Once again, the *Zhuchka* moved against the current in the dark autumn night. The close Romanian shore could barely be discerned on the right. The Yugoslav bank was lost in the dark in the opposite direction. Somewhere in that direction, the Germans were waiting in their defenses. But they could hardly hear the *Zhuchka*—the Danube was wide here.

The muffled engine was growling, creating a foamy wave around the modest bow, raising a steep, whitening lather in the darkness. It seemed that the cutter was moving ahead rapidly. But it only seemed so. The *Zhuchka*'s speed was not great because it had to overcome the strength of the current.

The fighting for Raduyevats had concluded three days before.[1] The enemy had been driven from the town by the combined attacks of forces of the Third Ukrainian *Front* and the vessels of the Danube Flotilla, which had landed an amphibious force and supported it by fire. This fire was extremely precise. On the eve, the scouts on the *Zhuchka* and rubber boats had moved near the enemy's shore battery positions, obtained a fix on their location, and then, boarding the armored cutters, directed their fire. The information brought from Raduyevats by Morozov, Chichilo, and Globa and obtained from the two "tongues" they had brought in— the corporal and the petty officer—contributed much to the success.

The petty officer gave important information. Tens of vessels lay on the bottom farther up the river, beyond Raduyevats, intentionally sunk on order of the German command to block the route of the Soviet combat vessels.

Not waiting for Raduyevats to be taken, the scouts moved past it against the current at night in two rubber boats toward the river village of Prakhovo to confirm what the "tongue" had reported. The captured sailor had not lied. The scouts indeed spotted masts and wheelhouses of many vessels sticking out of the water in the channel at Prakhovo and reported this upon their return.

The enemy forces that had been driven from Raduyevats had fallen in on previously prepared defensive lines around Prakhovo. The armored cutter unit received the mission to assist the attacking ground forces by taking shore positions near Prakhovo under fire and landing an assault force there. But there was an underwater obstacle on the route. Could the armored cutters pass through it somewhere?

This was the task of those on board the *Zhuchka* on this night—Kalganov, Morozov, Chichilo, Veretenik, Globa, Bura, Andreev, and Kotsar. The only rookie on board—he was standing at the wheel and had thin, still adolescent facial features—was not quite eighteen years old. This was Aleksey Chkheidze, a young lad from Tbilisi.[2] He had been fighting for more than a year already, having gone to the navy through the Komsomol at age sixteen. He had trained as a helmsman but was impatient to engage the enemy face to face, and he requested assignment to the naval infantry. He had been in the detachment for only several days. Having heard of Aleksey's burning desire when the young man had encountered some scouts in one of the river towns, Kalganov took a liking to him and requested his transfer from the naval infantry battalion. The senior lieutenant liked this very young man who wanted to become a scout. Kalganov found out that he had already distinguished himself with courage and daring. Not long ago, at the beginning of the battles on the Danube, Aleksey Chkheidze had captured a German general—a division commander—along with two staff officers.

It was getting on toward midnight. The *Zhuchka* proceeded, holding toward the right bank of the river. So far the channel was clear. But then, turning toward Kalganov, who was standing near the wheelhouse, Chkheidze reported:

"I see it!"

Something showed black on the water dead ahead of the *Zhuchka*. The cutter cautiously approached at reduced speed. The scouts held their submachine guns at the ready. Would they be needed?

Nine pairs of eyes looked intently ahead into the darkness. Something angular sticking up out of the water became more clearly visible. It was a superstructure. Not far ahead was another, with a broad smokestack nearby. Masts. A round hull protruding at an angle out of the water. More masts.

The *Zhuchka,* at the slowest speed, its motor barely turning over, cautiously moved closer. Now they could see. The vessels were lying close to each other, forming an uneven, dense row that extended from the right, from the Romanian shore, toward the middle of the river. And thirty to forty meters upstream, parallel to this obstacle, was a second, also visible by the stacks, masts, hatches, and handrails of boat deck structures. A second line. They could not pass toward Prakhovo along the Romanian shore. What about the middle of the river?

"Left rudder!" Kalganov gave the command to Aleksey Chkheidze. The *Zhuchka* slowly moved away from the shore along the obstacle. Now it was in the middle of the river, and the end of the obstacle was not in sight. The *Zhuchka* moved more carefully. The enemy-occupied Yugoslav shore was already close by on the left.

The blinding white light of a German illumination rocket noiselessly arched up into the sky and illuminated the deck of the *Zhuchka,* lighting up the alarmed faces of the scouts. The Danube waters, rocking in rapid motion, reflected steel blue in the light's cold radiance, and the stacks and masts that were sticking up out of the water were especially sharply outlined, like the trunks of dead trees that had long ago lost their leaves.

At the same moment, a machine-gun burst rushed by above the *Zhuchka* with an intermittent scream. They had been spotted!

"Hard to starboard! Full ahead!" Kalganov commanded. Chkheidze sharply turned the *Zhuchka,* now fully bathed in the white, sinisterly flickering light. Machine guns chattered, chasing after it from the Yugoslav shore, which was now astern. Behind it, the white lightning of the enemy rockets turned the water a silvery color.

The *Zhuchka* was out of danger now. The rockets sputtered out, and the firing stopped.

Making a large circle, the *Zhuchka* returned. They had to find out if the obstacle they had detected extended to the Yugoslav shore.

But hardly had the cutter reached the middle of the river when, from the left, from the shore, German illumination rockets again flew upward. The machine guns again fired. Mortar rounds fell close, sending up water and spray. Shrapnel whistled past and tinkled against the cutter. With a muffled knock, fragments struck the hull and the superstructure. They had to withdraw.

Enemy rockets, exposing the cutter in the darkness, made it a visible target. But they also provided a service. In their light, the scouts were able to see that the double row of sunken ships extended right up to the Yugoslav shore.

Returning to base, Kalganov reported that the enemy held the approaches to the Prakhovo obstacle under fire.

"At whatever cost, you must find a passage lane during the night!" was the order he immediately received. The flotilla could not fall behind the advancing ground forces, who needed the vessels for fire support from the river and to transport the assault force. Once again, the *Zhuchka* departed upstream.

Now the scouts acted with more stealth. If the enemy was alert and attentively listening to every sound on the river, the *Zhuchka* would not find a passage. Even the low sound of a slowly running engine could interfere with the success of the mission.

Kalganov decided to proceed toward the obstacle in launches. It was difficult and dangerous but offered a greater chance of not being detected by the enemy.

So as not to attract the enemy's attention, the *Zhuchka* stopped near the Romanian shore just short of the underwater obstacle. They climbed down into fishing boats, which before this had been tied astern of the *Zhuchka*. Kalganov, Gura, Globa, Chkheidze, Andreev, and Kotsar got into the larger boat. Morozov and Chichilo boarded the small boat.

Throwing themselves into the oars, the scouts immediately steered their boats along the first line of sunken ships, toward the middle of the channel, to determine whether the Germans had left a lane for their own ships in the most navigable portion of the river.

It became even darker toward midnight. Rain began to fall. Picked up by the raw river wind, the cold drops beat tirelessly into their faces, penetrating their thick leather storm gear. But the scouts, it seemed, noticed neither the cold nor the wind. They slowly moved their boats from one sunken ship to another. They held their boats in the current with difficulty while inspecting and measuring with boat hooks and ropes—could an armored cutter pass through here? But the boats had been sunk right up against or so close to each other that it would have been impossible for a vessel to pass between them.

Was there a place where the armored cutters[3] could pass over the top of the sunken ships? Measurements indicated that this also was not possible. There was insufficient draft.

The search continued.

The boat on which Kalganov and the five sailors sat probed in the darkness from one ship to another, ever closer to the middle of the river. The boat had already passed over tens of vessels under the Danube's churning waters. Here were barges, passenger ferries, tugboats, trawlers, dredges, and lighters. By the fading inscriptions on the stacks and on the life preserver rings that hung on some of the deckhouses sticking out of the water, it was clear that the Germans had collected here the vessels of various

Danube countries—Romania, Bulgaria, and Yugoslavia. They had not hesitated to sink many of their own ships as well.

Kalganov reached the middle of the river. Here the water was deeper than along the banks, and fewer superstructures, masts, and pipes were visible on the water's surface.

Kalganov gave instructions to tie the boat up to a barge deck-house that barely protruded above the water. The deckhouse was about two meters high. The draft of the armored cutters was less than two meters. Perhaps an armored cutter could pass over the top of this barge?

With boat hooks, they secured the boat to the deckhouse, its top splashed by the waves. The boiling Danube waters pulled angrily, trying to carry the boat away. But the sailors firmly held on to their boat hooks.

They measured the depth with a pole by probing for the barge's deck beneath the water. The depth was sufficient. But what if there were something down below that could cut into the bottom of an armored cutter? They had to check.

"Who will go into the water first?" Kalganov asked.

Globa and Kotsar undressed quickly. The night autumn rain beat on their naked bodies. One after the other they jumped from the side of the boat into the dark, rushing water. It was so cold it took their breath away. The current dragged and pulled at them. They could barely hang on to the side of the boat—their comrades in the boat assisted them.

They dived and groped under the water with their bare feet and hands for the deck and the outline of the sides. It appeared that the Germans had blown the barge up before they sank it.

Shaking from the cold, Globa and Kotsar scrambled back into the boat and began hurriedly to dress. They moved their boat to the next sunken ship. Three other scouts lowered themselves into the water.

Meanwhile, the enemy on the shore was undisturbed. The six scouts moved their boat along the underwater obstruction, making frequent measurements. This was dangerous work, in the darkness, and still more so under the water; they could not see where they were going or where the current was carrying them. And the river, as if out of spite, was striving to capsize them or drive them into something. The Danube waters had already drawn first blood: when he dived, Kotsar was cut on the side by a piece of sharp metal.

The night came to an end, and a passage lane had not been found. The scouts were tired and frozen. Each of them had plunged into the cold autumn water many times, and there was no place to get warm. The persistent rain continued to fall.

During all this time, Morozov and Chichilo on their boat, which they, of course, in the naval tradition, called a launch, proceeded along the first line of ships far from the middle of the river in the direction of the Yugoslav bank. They made measurements and dived many times, probing to determine what obstacles for ships were hidden under the dark, rushing waters. But they too were unable to find a passage lane. Something more than two hundred meters remained to the enemy-occupied bank. Could the sunken ships be laid against each other any farther?

The sky was beginning to show light. Soon it would be dawn. In just a little time, the enemy would be able to see the tiny launch scurrying about between the sunken ships.

But the boat was probing directly toward the shore. The closer it came, the more exposed above the water in the fading darkness were the hulls of the sunken ships, and the easier it was to discern how they lay on the bottom. The Germans had attempted to place each ship on the bottom perpendicular to the current, with bows and sterns of adjoining ships touching each other. But during the minutes when the vessels were going down, the current turned some of them, and some free space remained between them. Now, toward morning, when the night darkness was not so thick, it was easier to make out where the ships were not contiguous.

Now some 150 meters from the dimly black shore, Morozov and Chichilo found one of these places. They measured with staffs—it was sufficiently deep that an armored cutter could pass. But what if there was a cable was stretched between the ships, or a collapsed mast, or something else under the water? The cutter could snag its hull on such an obstacle, impale itself, and block the passage for the remaining vessels. This would disrupt the entire operation, and the scouts would be to blame. No, they had to check carefully!

Morozov took off his clothes and jumped into the water. Chichilo held the boat in place, tying it off to the top of a mast protruding from the water.

Morozov's head went under the water several times and again showed itself in the first light of dawn. Finally, he swam toward the boat and grabbed the side. Chichilo helped him climb in. Morozov was shaking so badly from the cold that his teeth were chattering. His hands trembled, making it difficult for him to dress.

"Well, how about it?" Chichilo asked.

"I checked," Morozov replied, pulling on his *tel'nyashka*. "It's sort of clear."

"Sort of? I will check it out, just to be sure!" decided Chichilo. He took off his own clothes, and the water was already splashing next to the boat, giving way to his large body.

Chichilo spent more time in the water than Morozov. When he crawled out, his fingers were unable to grasp the side of the boat, and Morozov managed to drag his heavy comrade into it with difficulty.

Now there was no doubt that a passage had been found fully suitable for the armored cutters. Of course, it would have been better had it been farther from the enemy-occupied shore. But there was no choice.

Overcoming the current with difficulty, the two scouts proceeded in their boat a short distance upstream from the passage, toward the second line of obstacles. They found a probable site, measured the depth, and confirmed that the armored cutters could pass through there also.

It was possible that the Germans had left these passages near their occupied shore for their own ships in the hope that Soviet vessels would not risk using them because of the danger of coming under fire. But the passage would have been discovered—and it was not the first time the armored cutters would proceed under fire.

Morozov, pulling a notepad from his pocket and straining his vision—it was just beginning to get light—drew a crude sketch of the positions of the sunken ships and marked the discovered passage lane. They had to hurry and deliver this information to the command.

"We will get warmed up!" said Morozov.

Both put their weight to the oars. They had made several oar strokes when from their left the water was thrown up in low fountains that skipped across the water toward them. The hurried beat of machine gun fire sounded behind them.

"They're firing at us!" Morozov glanced around. "They have discovered us! To the left, toward the barge!"

They threw themselves into the oars with all their strength and in several seconds managed to make it to a large barge. The upper portion of the high side of the barge, which had listed upon sinking, stood above the water and covered the boat from enemy eyes. The machine gun on the shore fired a bit longer, then fell silent.

The darkness had almost dissipated. The rain stopped. All around—both the sky and the water—it was not black as it had been thirty minutes earlier but gray.

"Well, we didn't make back it in the dark!" Morozov complained. "But we can't sit it out here." He suggested, "Let's press on. Perhaps we can make it to the next cover."

"Let's give it a try!" Chichilo agreed.

But hardly had they poked the nose of their boat out from behind the barge when again the machine guns chattered from the bank. It was less than five hundred meters from the shore to the barge, and the enemy observers and machine gunners now, in the light of approaching morning, were well able to spot the boat as soon as it showed from behind the cover.

Morozov and Chichilo saw the small fountains made by the bullets in the water and heard the bullets strike the steel sheeting on the side of the barge above, over their heads. Then it became quiet again. They rowed their boat to the edge of the barge opposite from where they attempted to move the last time. Perhaps they could deceive the enemy?

The boat had just begun to move into the open space when a machine gun burst ripped the water right in front of the bow.

"They are guarding that flank, too!" Morozov said with fury. "Go back!"

Pressed by the current toward the inclined side of the barge, the boat stood in place. It was quiet. Only the water, flowing around the half-sunken barge, seethed and boiled. The Germans did not fire any more. Perhaps they realized that the machine gun could not reach behind the barge. But one thing was clear: the enemy was on the alert and would not let them pass. Certainly they would be trying to guess why this boat was here.

What should they do? Continue to wait?

But the command was waiting for the scouts' return. They had to do something.

Several anxious minutes passed.

A heavy mass of water and spray rained down on the heads and shoulders of Morozov and Chichilo and poured into the boat. They had not recovered from that shock when a new column of water rose up alongside their boat. Above them, shrapnel rattled off the steel side of the barge as though it was thrown by the handful.

"Let's give them the boat to shoot at, and we will swim!" Morozov blurted out his idea.

The German shells crashed closer and closer.

Holding his notebook with the sketch of the hard-won passage lane in his teeth, Morozov quickly threw off his clothing, keeping on only his underwear. Chichilo also undressed. They pushed the boat out into the current and swam, trying to stay close to each other. Morozov held his head up high while he swam to try to keep the notebook with the sketch dry.

German shells were striking the water behind them. They were firing at the moving boat from the bank. Several shells whistled through the air from the Romanian side. This was our artillery opening fire across the Danube on the German guns, which had given away their position by firing.

Morozov and Chichilo were happy for the artillery exchange that had begun. It distracted the enemy.

Swimming from one sunken ship to another and taking short

rests where it was possible to hang onto something protruding out of the water, Morozov and Chichilo, exhausted from their effort and feeling the cramps that took over their arms and legs, finally swam almost to the opposite bank. If they, like all the scouts, had not been outstanding trained swimmers, they would not have made it.

They were stopped for their last minute of rest, hanging on to a barely visible edge of the side of a sunken barge. Some distance remained to the Romanian shore. The artillery exchange had ended. In the gloomy morning light, the water's surface had become dull silver; the sky was growing white with a dense shroud of clouds. And if they had looked, the far-off bank, where the enemy sat, was now clearly visible.

They started swimming again. Weakened and chilled to the bone, they were swept away from the line of sunken ships by the rapid current. Now the bank was a stone's throw away. It was already visible: a sandy strip and gray autumn-bare bushes above it.

The churning, turbulent water hid the shoreline. Shrapnel rattled over their heads. A piece burrowed into the water between Morozov and Chichilo.

Apparently, German observers spotted the two scouts when the current carried them into an open place. Shell after shell fell into the water, and shrapnel plowed into the water all around them.

Morozov and Chichilo swam. What else could they do?

An explosion, a second, then a third.

Finally, their legs touched the bottom. Run! But this was not so easy. The bottom was mushy and pulled at their legs. Shells were falling into the water behind them and onto the bank in front of them, throwing up fountains of sand.

With their last strength, greedily sucking in air, both men, in clinging, wet underwear, one of them with a notebook in his teeth, ran across the sand and threw themselves into the bushes. At the same instant, somewhere close by two explosions rang out, one after the other.

Morozov and Chichilo, both at the same time, fell into some springy, slippery branches.

"*Kamrad!* Comrade!" they heard.

"Ah, ally!" Morozov finally spit the notebook out of his mouth.

A Romanian soldier ran up to them, one of those who occupied the defense on this bank, alongside our units.

It turned out that the Romanians had for some time been observing the two scouts as they worked their way away from the enemy-occupied shore. When the German guns began to fire at their unseaworthy craft, the Romanians immediately reported the events to our artillerymen, and they opened return fire.

Morozov and Chichilo warmed up some in the Romanian dugout, and the Romanians supplied them with some clothes. But they could not find boots of size forty-five for Morozov, who had to remain barefooted.

Morozov and Chichilo quickly rejoined their comrades who had been looking for a passage in the large boat. Proceeding along the obstacle from the Romanian bank to the middle of the river and back, painstakingly sounding the water alongside each ship, after extended effort they found still another passage lane in the first and second lines.

Early in the day, the scouts returned to base on the *Zhuchka*. Kalganov reported to the flotilla chief of staff on the accomplishment of the mission. He immediately inquired with some concern:

"How are the sailors? Is everyone all right? Was anyone wounded or did anyone become ill?"

Only after he heard the response to these questions did the chief of staff inspect the sketch of the passage lanes that Kalganov carried with him. The longer the chief of staff studied the sketch, the more he knitted his brow. Then, still looking at the sketch, he anxiously said:

"The passage lanes are narrow. Just a little bit to the side, and we have an accident. If something happens with one armored cutter, the path is blocked for all the others."

"Let the *Zhuchka* go first!" Kalganov suggested. "We will lead them precisely. All they have to do is stay in our wake."

"And if they fire at you?" the chief of staff asked. "How many shells can the *Zhuchka* absorb? It will only take one."

"It is better to risk losing the *Zhuchka* than the success of the entire operation!"

The chief of staff did not accept Kalganov's suggestion right off. The *Zhuchka* carried no armor plate as the armored cutters did. But, finally, having given it some thought, he said:

"Okay. You go ahead of the column. But I will give instructions that the armored cutters are to cover you."

When the haze of the early autumn twilight began to cover the Danube expanse, a long column of armored cutters proceeding upstream appeared on the river. On the vessels of the forward portion of the column, soldiers in gray ponchos and black sailors' pea jackets could be seen sitting packed tightly on the decks, behind the gun turrets, and behind the commanders' wheelhouses. Small antitank guns also stood on the decks. These armored cutters were carrying an assault force.

The decks of the armored cutters sailing in the rear of the column were deserted. These were the artillery support cutters. The *Zhuchka* jauntily sailed in front of the column of armored cutters. Its position in the formation of combat vessels had been specified by an "order from headquarters." The scouts who had participated in the night search were aboard the *Zhuchka*. They were to lead the armored cutters through the passages they had reconnoitered.

It was still not quite dark when the small, defenseless *Zhuchka* boldly approached the passage lane in the first line of underwater obstacles. Its stern light, hidden from the enemy's eyes, was a reference point for the armored cutters.

The *Zhuchka* had not yet entered the lane when a cannon roared from the enemy shore. It would have gone badly for the *Zhuchka* had not the artillery support cutters opened fire an instant later on the German batteries, whose muzzle flashes were clearly visible. The enemy batteries ceased fire on the *Zhuchka*—they hurried to direct their fire on the still barely visible armored cutters. Taking advantage of this diversion, the *Zhuchka* safely entered the passage lane of the first line, then the second. Staying close behind it, the lead armored cutter proceeded through the double obstacle line. The remaining armored cutters moved forward behind it, maintaining their formation astern. The enemy batteries again shifted their fire to the head of the column, to the *Zhuchka*. But one of the armored cutters was now covering it.

The enemy's hope that the obstacles of sunken ships would prevent our vessels from proceeding toward Prakhovo was not realized. The ships sailed through. Prakhovo was captured in a combined assault, unexpected by the enemy, of amphibious forces and units attacking on land. The Germans fled, leaving behind guns, ammunition, vehicles, and much other equipment.

One more node of the enemy's defenses on the road to Belgrade had ceased to exist.

Night was falling when the *Zhuchka,* having received several bullet holes, proceeded into the port of Prakhovo along with the armored cutters and tied up at the dock. The scouts, exhausted after an unbelievably intense two sleepless nights, dropped where they stood into heavy sleep.

But hardly had dawn begun to glimmer when a runner came aboard the *Zhuchka* and announced:

"Senior Lieutenant Kalganov, report to the formation commander!"

Several minutes later, Kalganov was on the flagship armored cutter.

"Did you get a chance to rest?" sympathetically asked the commander of the formation, Hero of the Soviet Union Captain Second Rank Pavel Ivanovich Derzhavin,[4] glancing at the scout commander's sleepy face. "Well, what's a man to do?" Derzhavin looked on with some feeling. "Another day is gone, Beard [Kalganov's nickname]. You must go out on reconnaissance once again. Belgrade awaits our arrival."

"We are ready," Kalganov replied.

CHAPTER EIGHT

REiNFORCEMENTS HAVE ARRiVED

The quiet autumn night lay over the river and the bank. Blacked out, without a single light showing, armored cutters were pressed up against the shore. All the portholes and hatches were tightly sealed; the covers had been placed over the barrels of the guns, and the decks were deserted. Only the figures of the duty machine gunners loomed in their turrets, alongside twin-mounted machine guns pointed into the air.

Next to the armored cutters, alongside the riverbank, were several small boats of various hues. The scouts proudly referred to them as their own boats. There was the unprepossessing *Zhuchka,* loved by all, and several rubber boats. On these craft, and particularly on the *Zhuchka,* the scouts had done their glorious deeds in the recent battle for Prakhovo and had expended much effort to reconnoiter the route farther upstream.

On this day, certainly not long before the receipt of a new mission, the armored cutters and the reconnaissance detachment that sailed in front of them all the time had stopped here by a small Serbian village, one of many river villages, towns, and cities on the route toward Belgrade, still more than two hundred kilometers up ahead by river.

Fierce battles were being waged up ahead. The enemy was

112

resisting stubbornly, trying to take back the initiative from the advancing Soviet forces by counterattacks.

But the rumble of the continuously moving battle was not heard here. It was possible to rest. After many sleepless nights, the scouts were sleeping in the confined crew spaces of the *Zhuchka.*

A sailor leisurely walked along the deck of the *Zhuchka,* shivering from the night cold that had penetrated through his pea jacket. His replacement would come on soon.

But what was that? The watch heard something that sounded like cannon fire. Again, then again and again. Yes, they could be clearly distinguished. Cannons were firing.

"Do you hear it?" he called over to the watch on a nearby armored cutter.

"I hear it," the other watch responded in an anxious voice. "I can't quite make it out. The front is far ahead, and our forces are advancing. But these sounds are getting closer."

"Perhaps the Germans have broken through?"

"Who knows."

"I'm going to wake up my commander."

"Me too."

The watch climbed the steep ladder into the dark crew compartment of the *Zhuchka,* where Kalganov slept in one of the bunks, his long legs hanging over the end. He gingerly shook Kalganov by the shoulder.

"Comrade Senior Lieutenant."

Kalganov got up, put a greatcoat around his shoulders, and went up on deck to stand and listen with the watch. The cannons spoke more distinctly with each passing minute. Now they could be made out clearly. The battle was several kilometers to the north, perhaps on the same side of the river as the ships were now anchored. The lower edge of the black night sky was lit up for a second by a dull purple light in the direction from which the firing was heard. Was this rockets or the reflection of artillery fires? Had the enemy broken through to the Danube? The situation had to be clarified. Their rest was over!

Several minutes later, a rubber boat, breaking the night calm with the throb of its motor, set off from the bank and moved at full speed upstream against the current. Kalganov, Morozov, and several sailors were aboard.

The farther upstream the rubber boat sailed, the more distinctly was heard the roar of a battle up ahead. On the port side, the white, crimson, and greenish flashes of rockets and bullet and shell tracer streams were more and more distinguishable above the darkened, diffused outline of the bank. It was clear from all these fires and the sounds of firing that a bitter battle was being fought close to the river.

Suddenly, several dull fires intersected their path—a line of tracers extended across the river. Could this mean that the enemy had already reached the bank?

Kalganov pulled out his map. Bent over from the wind that was beating at his face with the boat at full speed, Kalganov shone the flashlight on the map, hiding the light so that it could not be seen from shore. The village of Mikhaylovats was several kilometers ahead, on their port side. This village, and the entire bank of the Danube in its vicinity, had already been bypassed by our advancing units. But the reflected lights of the battle were all but in Mikhaylovats itself. Could they proceed in the channel straight to Mikhaylovats? Perhaps the enemy was already there? They had to bypass it.

Kalganov ordered his helmsman to go to starboard, toward the opposite bank.

Several minutes later, a narrow, black strip of land began to show in front of them in the darkness of the night. But Kalganov did not order the helmsman to port. He knew that they were approaching the large Mare Island, which extended several kilometers along the Danube. There was a narrow channel between the island and the east bank. They could proceed along this channel, covered by the island. [This locale is a short distance upstream from the Bulgarian-Yugoslav border.]

Reducing speed somewhat, the rubber boat entered the channel. Kalganov planned to proceed along the channel between the bank and the island to a position upstream of Mikhaylovats, determine if the enemy had reached the bank near the village, and then turn downstream, pass toward Mikhaylovats itself, make contact with the defending units, and definitively ascertain the situation.

The rubber boat proceeded a long time in the dark, narrow, twisting channel, so narrow that the rhythmic lapping of waves along the edges of the low shores, overgrown with vines, could be heard from both sides.

Then, dead ahead it became a bit lighter—the channel was ending.

"Be alert!" Kalganov suddenly exclaimed.

To port, at the end of the island, right up against its bushy shore, the silhouette of a military vessel could be seen, barely distinguishable against the backdrop of the night sky. The wheelhouse could be made out, a short gun on the bow deck, and its steep side. With his experienced eye, Kalganov immediately determined that it was an armored cutter. Whose? It was not ours, of course. None of our vessels had sailed up here.

There was no time for contemplation. Without doubt, those aboard the armored cutter had already heard the rubber boat's motor. One round from the cutter's gun would be sufficient to blow this inner tube to pieces. Kalganov made a lightning decision:

"Submachine guns—get ready! Full ahead!"

Responding to the command, the helmsman increased speed. The rubber boat surged toward the armored cutter.

"Fire a warning burst over their heads!" the senior lieutenant ordered a sailor with a light machine gun. He quickly executed the order.

They could see several dark figures rushing about on the deck of the armored cutter. To the gun? The rubber boat flew toward the vessel's stern.

"Board!" Kalganov shouted, and lightly jumped onto the armored cutter's stern. Morozov and two sailors leaped up onto the deck.

But the scouts did not meet any resistance. The silhouette of a man with upraised hands separated itself from the wheelhouse. They heard a worried voice:

"*Rus, Rus!* Don't shoot, don't shoot!"

"Put down your hands!" the senior lieutenant ordered with a gesture, realizing that it was not a German standing before him but a Romanian.

The Romanian presented himself to Kalganov. He was a lieutenant, the commander of the armored cutter.

It turned out that the entire crew consisted of Romanian military sailors. Their vessel was part of the Romanian Danube Flotilla. Retreating, the Germans had forced the crew to hijack their ship. But the Romanian sailors were not keen to serve Hitler. Their people had already turned their guns against him. Knowing that the Soviet army was advancing along the Danube, the sailors had decided to wait for it. At one of the anchorages, the lieutenant alleged an engine breakdown, and the armored cutter remained behind while the other vessels departed upstream on German orders.

On this night, the lieutenant and his crew were taking their vessel downstream, hoping to encounter Soviet forces. But on the approach to Mikhaylovats, they heard an ongoing battle and decided to wait in the channel.

Kalganov, who understood some Romanian, said to the lieutenant:

"Form your crew up on the deck."

"I can't get them all." The lieutenant threw up his hands.

"Why not?"

"When you began your attack, many of my sailors fled to the shore. Now they do not know what has happened and are afraid."

"We will go gather them up!" Kalganov suggested to the lieutenant and turned to Morozov.

"While we are gone, conduct a political session with the sailors that remain on the cutter. Explain to them that they are now our allies and not prisoners."

Kalganov went ashore with the lieutenant. They gathered up all the sailors and returned to the ship. Along the way, Kalganov managed to question the Romanian lieutenant about the situation and learned that there were enemy positions north of Mikhaylovats on the bank. They did not fire on the armored cutter when it moved past because the Germans, of course, considered the ship theirs.

"And what if we were to approach Mikhaylovats on the armored cutter?" Kalganov had considered this idea before he went ashore. "If we start back toward our own positions, the Germans will certainly fire on us. How many rounds can our rubber boat take? But this armor will cover us if something should happen."

Kalganov asked the Romanian lieutenant to talk to his sailors about what purpose their cutter could now serve. He was not sure that the Romanians would readily agree to risk their boat again. From the very beginning of the conversation, the lieutenant had been primarily interested in the safe passage of his boat into the Romanian rear.

The Romanian sailors assured him, however, that they were prepared to help and, if it was necessary, to fight. The Russians and Romanians now had a common enemy.

Sending the rubber boat back with a report, Kalganov and Morozov remained on the Romanian vessel. The crew went to their stations. The engines were quickly fired up, and the cutter moved out of the narrow channel in reverse, then turned and went upstream.

Kalganov decided to proceed some distance upstream on the river, holding to the right bank to remain undetected as long as possible from the German positions on the opposite shore. Then he intended to turn sharply and sail toward Mikhaylovats, now downstream, past the enemy positions. The Germans, if they even noticed the armored cutter, at first would certainly take it for their own, proceeding to the battle site near Mikhaylovats. And while the Germans were sorting this out, they would slip past.

The supposition proved correct. They safely passed the German positions above Mikhaylovats. It seemed that the Germans indeed took the cutter as their own—how else could it have come from upstream?

The closer they approached to Mikhaylovats, still unseen on the dark shore, the more they heard the sounds of battle. The flashes of explosions and fired rounds came closer and closer under the dark sky. The fires of the tracers flickered. Kalganov now understood how important it was to ascertain the situation of our units defending Mikhaylovats, where the fighting was going on. Perhaps the flotilla could help them with an amphibious landing or artillery fire support from the armored cutters that stood at anchor several kilometers downstream.

Kalganov attentively studied the direction of the tracer streams over the bank of the river. This would permit him to determine more precisely where the line of the defense passed, where it would be safer to approach Mikhaylovats.

On Kalganov's command, the Romanian helmsman turned the armored cutter sharply toward the shore. Bullets struck the armor with a staccato beat. Shells flew above the cutter and exploded behind it.

"Our troops have mistaken us for the enemy because we are coming from upstream!" But Kalganov did not panic. He shouted to Morozov:

"Get a sheet from the Romanians in the crew compartment and raise it on the gaff! It's no disgrace to show it to our own troops!"

A minute later, a broad white sheet was flapping in the wind above the cutter.

"Light it up!" Kalganov ordered.

The beam of the cutter's searchlight shone directly on the sheet hanging on the halyard. Certainly it was clearly visible from the bank. And one could presume that our troops realized that some German cutter, having come under fire, had decided to surrender. The firing stopped.

The bank—high, steep, covered with black clumps and indistinct silhouettes of trees—stood out more and more sharply against the backdrop of the night sky. Kalganov ordered the helmsman to reduce speed.

Its motors shut off, the armored cutter, now moving only on inertia, softly nudged its bow into the sand.

"The bank!"

Coming out of the wheelhouse, Kalganov and Morozov peered into the darkness. Had they come ashore in the right place? What if the enemy was here and not our own forces? Anything was possible. As they had upstream, they could hear machine gun firing echoing above the bank.

"Let's go!" the senior lieutenant said to Morozov. "We have to find our troops!"

Cautioning the Romanians to wait there for them, the two scouts jumped down onto the soft riverbank sand. Out of the darkness they heard a shout:

"Halt! Who goes there?"

"The Danube Flotilla!" Kalganov replied loudly in the darkness.

His boots rustling in the wet grass, someone was almost running to meet them. Now they could make him out. It was a soldier with a submachine gun, wearing a poncho. He stopped abruptly and looked with amazement, as much as the darkness would allow, at the two unidentified figures in naval uniforms standing below him.

"Are you sailors?"

"We are indeed!" Kalganov laughed.

The soldier spun around and shouted to someone up above:

"Hey, guys. Reinforcements have arrived! It's the navy!"

Kalganov and Morozov requested and were quickly led to the command post of the division that was defending Mikhaylovats,[1] in the cellar of a large stone building.

They were happy to see the sailors at the command post. The colonel told them that his division had been advancing on Belgrade, but several hours earlier the enemy had launched a powerful counterattack in his sector. The Germans had pressed the division back toward Mikhaylovats, cut them off from adjacent units, and, by throwing in more and more fresh forces, were trying to drive the division into the Danube and seize Mikhaylovats. Division artillery had expended its ammunition, and the defending infantry sorely needed fire support.

"We will attempt to help!" Kalganov said to the division commander. "Our armored cutters are anchored not far away. They can reach the Germans with their cannons. Do you have radio communications gear?"

"Yes," the division commander replied. "But we do not know your flotilla call signs."

"I will give you all the information you need to communicate with our formation commander. You designate the targets, and the ships will commence firing."

The relieved division commander immediately instructed his radio operators to make contact with the armored cutter formation headquarters. His deputy for political affairs, who had arrived at the command post, said:

"We must inform everyone in the forward positions that the sailors have come to our aid! Every soldier should know. It will bolster their morale."

After radio communications had been established with the armored cutter formation, Kalganov asked the division commander to give him a runner who could lead him to the artillery unit forward observer's position.

Kalganov and Morozov, now seeing with their own eyes from where and how the enemy was conducting his night attack, quickly prepared the request for fire. The division radio operators transmitted this request to the armored cutter formation headquarters without delay. And quickly howling crimson fires rippled through the blackness of the night sky in waves. They flew over Mikhaylovats, over the positions at the forward edge, where the division's soldiers were holding on, fending off the enemy's attacks. They flew on and, dropping sharply, fell where the enemy was attacking. Immense flashing fountains of crimson fire erupted in the dark. These were the explosions of rockets from *katyushas,* launched from the armored cutters.[2] The shells of 76mm guns fired from the cutters were simultaneously crashing into the enemy positions.

But the enemy was stubborn. It seems the command of the German units attacking Mikhaylovats had been ordered to throw the Russians into the Danube at any price. Despite their losses suffered from our naval gunfire, the Germans rose in the attack again and again, but each time the explosions of rounds fired by the armored cutters blocked their path.

The battle for Mikhaylovats was still being fought two days after the scouts had landed at the village. And all the while it lasted, Kalganov and Morozov, remaining at the division artillery forward observation post, coordinated the naval gunfire by radio.

By the end of the second day, having suffered great losses and having failed to break the resistance of the defenders, who were encouraged by the sailors' support, the enemy was forced to abandon his intent to seize Mikhaylovats. The division, coordinating with adjacent units, went over to the offensive itself against the enemy, who had exhausted himself in fruitless attacks. The army soldiers pressed the hands of Kalganov and Morozov and said to them:

"If you had not shown up in time, we would have been in dire straits."

The division commander, saying farewell to Kalganov, said:

"I will be happy, senior lieutenant, to meet with you again."

"I hope we can meet again!" Kalganov replied. "We are always happy to fight side by side with the infantry."

CHAPTER NINE

İRON GATES

The Danube is wild and severe in its middle course, between the Romanian towns of Orshova and Turnu-Severin. The Balkan Range extends fully up to the right [west] bank on the Yugoslav side, and the Carpathian Range extends to the left [east] bank on the Romanian side. It is as if two powerful mountain ranges attempted to merge here. They reach out to meet each other from opposite banks. The gray cliffs, overgrown with moss and vegetation, extend upward toward the clouds. The two ranges come together and block the path of the Danube—the river narrows to approximately 150 to 200 meters wide from shore to shore.

For a distance of about twenty kilometers, the Danube is squeezed into a narrow, sheer-sided gorge. This gorge is called the Iron Gates. Its banks are unpopulated. Only mountain eagles live in the high, rocky cliffs, eroded through the centuries by the wind and water, that overhang the river. Snakes and lizards have built their nests in the crevices of its cliffs and in the ruins of its castles, which can be seen in places on the tops of the moss-covered cliffs.

If one is sailing along the Danube toward the Iron Gates, he will hear them long before he sees them. The water roars furiously, passing through countless rapids and shoals, between the rocks that protrude from the water like fangs concealed in the lower jaws of gigantic beasts. The incessant noise of the river, which boils among the rocks, is carried far into the surrounding area. The spray of water dashing against the sheer cliffs continuously drifts into the air, and rainbows shimmer above the water in this mist on a sunny day.

The old Danube rages. It flows freely for almost its entire three-thousand-kilometer length, up to the Iron Gates and beyond, in many places for kilometers through valleys. But here, it is compressed and funneled. It roars through the confines of the Iron Gates with violent strength, as if racing to the Black Sea. Any ship that attempts passage directly through the Iron Gates risks catastrophe. The current, which has enormous speed here, will throw it on the rocks, capsize it, or turn it. There is no safe route through here.

The Iron Gates are thus impassable. They are literally a stone barricade in the middle of the great Danube route.

To allow ships to pass through this area, at the end of the last century a canal was dug that bypassed the Iron Gates along the right bank. The speed of the current in this canal is significantly lower than in the main channel because of a breakwater that limits the entry of water into the channel. But even in the canal, the current is so strong that only ships that have powerful engines can negotiate it against the current. Special skill is required of the helmsman, or the current will push the vessel off course and against the bank of the canal. So that ships can move upstream against the current, a railroad track was laid alongside the canal, and steam engines are used to tow the vessels.

It was a rainy autumn day, 2 October 1944. A rubber boat was proceeding from Turnu-Severin toward the Iron Gates. A Soviet navy flag flapped in the wind behind it. The small, gray-blue, low-sided boat would have been almost invisible from the shore had it not been for the steep white "ears" that extended widely to the sides from its nose-high bow. The motor was working at full speed to overcome the boiling current. They were in a hurry. Armored cutters were twenty or thirty kilometers behind them, on a course for Belgrade. The scouts had to reconnoiter their route, the path through the Iron Gates, locate the enemy shore positions, determine whether the channel was mined, whether the bypass canal was passable, whether the towing steam engines could be used, whether the Germans had destroyed the railroad track during their withdrawal, and whether they had remained at the canal.

There were five men in the rubber boat—Senior Lieutenant Kalganov, Chief Petty Officer Shchepkin, old enough to be the father of the rest of the scouts, Petty Officer Second Class Globa, and at the helm, Seaman Monaykin. The fifth was a lean man, thirty years of age, with thin, energetic facial features. He was dressed in a gray jacket adorned with a badge. On his head was a *pilotka* with a five-pointed star. This was Lyubisha Zhorzhevich, a Yugoslav communist. He was a ferry pilot by profession, and he knew the channel in the area of the Iron Gates well, along with all the rest of the Danube. He had piloted tens of ships along the river.

Not too long ago, Zhorzhevich had been a fighter in a Yugoslav partisan brigade. The badge on his jacket was awarded only to those who had been partisans since the very beginning of the war. Before this trip toward the Iron Gates on a rubber boat, the Yugoslav partisan command had sent Lyubisha so that this experienced river pilot could help lead the flotilla's combat ships through the most difficult sector of the Danube. Lyubisha could converse in many languages—Romanian, Hungarian, German, French, and Spanish. Kalganov was happy with this situation. If something happened, Lyubisha could be his interpreter.

The banks crowded in. The roar of the water rushing through the rapids and shoals became increasingly louder. The Iron Gates were already close by. The polished rocks showed noticeably black in the foamy water more and more frequently. Lyubisha warned the helmsman:

"Hold to the left! Otherwise, the current will throw us onto the rocks."

Ahead, and left of the route, a flat yellow strip extended along the shore, under the overhanging gloomy cliffs shaggy with bushes.

"The breakwater!" Lyubisha pointed at the strip. "Go there."

Monaykin steered the rubber boat toward the breakwater that enclosed the exit from the canal.

Five pairs of eyes peered intensely at the breakwater and at the gray and black fissured slopes above it. Perhaps the enemy had control of the breakwater? Perhaps he already had them in his sights?

The scouts' hands reached for their submachine guns. Monaykin grasped the rudder tightly. Would he have to make a sudden, sharp turnaround or go straight in to shore, as the commander had ordered?

A fountain of water erupted to the right, another fountain to the left. A third shell passed overhead with a jingling whistle and plunged into the water behind them. A frothy spray rained down on the plywood planking of the rubber boat and on their heads.

The outcome was determined in seconds.

"Forward!" Kalganov shouted to the helmsman. "Toward the breakwater!"

Skirting the breakwater, the rubber boat departed the main channel into the canal at full speed. The howl of shells and their muffled explosions in the water ceased. Apparently they had slipped through. Reducing speed somewhat, the rubber boat proceeded up the canal. It was not at all wide—ten meters. The sloping banks were lined with stones. There was not a soul in sight.

Kalganov was intending to tell Monaykin to turn toward the bank. But at that moment, a shell furrowed into the slope of the bank, a second directly into the canal, a short distance behind them.

Turn back? They couldn't withdraw without conducting their reconnaissance.

The rubber boat raced along the canal. Two broad bow waves ran from it toward the banks, struck the evenly placed stones, and sprayed over them. The shells burst over and over. After a minute or two, the explosions were behind them. It grew quiet. The enemy had apparently lost sight of the scouts. The stone mass of the bank hanging over the canal hid them. But were the Germans on the canal itself? Perhaps they were still guarding it? But they saw no one.

"Go to shore!" Kalganov ordered. The rubber boat went toward the shore of the canal. They tied it up to an iron mooring ring mounted in a rock to prevent it from being carried away by the current. The scouts jumped to the shore and, holding their submachine guns at the ready, cautiously moved close to the water along the flat, rock-lined slope, attentively inspecting the area.

The opposite end of the canal was not far away. A second breakwater was on that end, outlining the entrance to the river. On the bank, at the foot of the cliff and near the breakwater, was a small hut of gray stones, covered by darkened tiles. Alongside it were two boats that had been dragged up on land, several buoys, and branches and poles leaning up against the wall of the hut. Not far from the breakwater was a tall striped pole with a cross-beam. Judging by everything, this was the buoy keeper's hut. Perhaps there was someone in the hut?

The scouts approached the hut and knocked on the door. It came open. A frightened face with a gray mustache looked out.

"Lyubisha, question him!" Kalganov turned to Zhorzhevich.

The fright on the old man's face changed to happiness when he saw that Russians were standing in front of him. The old man indeed was the buoy keeper, a Romanian.

Zhorzhevich quickly conversed with him in his native tongue. The buoy keeper said that he had hidden in his hut when he heard the explosions of the shells, but in general it had been quiet on the canal. The last German tugboats, pulling heavily loaded barges, had gone up-stream through the canal yesterday. Since that time, no more German ships had appeared.

Why had the enemy left the canal untouched? Had they hoped to be still using it? Were they unable because they had hurriedly withdrawn? Or were they confident that they could prevent the advancing forces from using it by fire? Perhaps the Germans had mined the canal and, at the place where the rubber boat, with its minimal draft, had slipped through unhindered, they were planning to blow up the first armored cutter?

To the questions put to him by Zhorzhevich, the old buoy keeper replied that the Germans had not planted mines after the passage of their last ships, and the route was safe. He also indicated that, besides him, the engineers of the towing locomotive lived here. They could be found in another hut on the other side of the railroad track, near the foot of the cliff that screened its entrance.

The scouts climbed up the bank toward the railroad grade that ran parallel to the bank and saw a steam engine standing motionless. They looked into its cab. It was empty, the firebox tightly closed. Kalganov placed his hand on the boiler.

"It's cold."

This troubled him. Of course, the armored cutters, with their powerful motors, might be able to overcome the current by themselves and negotiate the canal. But the minesweepers, the other vessels, and the *Zhuchka*? Without this steam engine, they could not make it. They had to ask the engineers to bring up the steam if the locomotive was operable.

It did not take long to find the engineers. Hardly had the scouts crossed the rails and turned up the path leading to the white hut at the cliff when they saw two men in coveralls quickly coming to meet them, waving their arms in greeting. Like the buoy keeper, they were Romanians. With the help of Zhorzhevich, the engineers talked with the great ardor of those who carry out the responsibility of towing. In recent days they had had to tow many Romanian, Bulgarian, and Yugoslav vessels commandeered by the Germans with their locomotive. Yesterday, after a routine convoy was passed, the modest German guard force that was stationed at the canal left with the last steamer. In the end, the officer who commanded the guard force warned the engineers to keep their locomotive under steam. More tugboats and barges should be moving upstream from Turnu-Severin. But as soon as the steamer carrying away the German guard force disappeared, the engineers let the fire go out and released the steam. Now no one could force them to serve the Germans! Fearing that the Germans might return and settle scores with them, the engineers hid not far away in the bushes near the foot of the cliff to wait for the Russians. Hearing the explosions and seeing that a small cutter was racing upstream against the current, they did not immediately come out of their hiding place because they could not determine if this was the last German cutter or the first Russians.

Kalganov knew that the Germans no longer needed the canal. They had been unable to move their last ships from Turnu-Severin. He also understood that the hurriedly retreating Germans, who now were occupying positions on the banks somewhere upstream, could suddenly remember to dispatch sappers to blow up the railroad track or stop up the canal by placing bottom mines or sinking a vessel brought downstream in the canal. He and his men had to hurry. They had to warn their forces about the German mortars and show them the route into the canal. They had to lead the ships through it as quickly as possible, before the enemy took steps to correct the blunders committed in his hurried retreat.

"Tell them," Kalganov instructed Zhorzhevich, pointing at the engineers, "to fire up the locomotive. And wait for our ships."

Lyubisha translated. The engineers guardedly agreed but expressed concern for their safety. What if the Germans suddenly appeared again?

"I don't know what to do," Kalganov thought to himself. "If only there were more of us."

He could not leave any of the four sailors who were with him for security. They could not avoid running the gauntlet of mortar fire on the return trip. The enemy had now been warned. Anything could happen to any one of them. Without fail, the results of the reconnaissance had to be reported as quickly as possible.

"Give us some kind of weapon!" the engineers asked. "We will protect our steam engines from the Germans ourselves."

Kalganov gave the engineers his submachine gun and two spare drums and showed them how to operate the weapon.

Accompanied by the friendly engineers, the scouts returned to their rubber boat.

"Return quickly! We will be waiting for you!" one of the engineers shouted from the bank.

The tiny rubber boat turned easily in the narrow canal and, pushed along by the swift current, set off on the return course.

"Give it full throttle!" Kalganov ordered Monaykin. "Speed is our armor."

Their hearts were beating more anxiously with each second. Just a little farther and the rubber boat would pass into the part of the canal accessible to enemy observation, where they had fired on the scouts on the way here.

And so it was again!

The first shell, falling steeply, came in with a howl that grieved the spirit. The water thrown up by the explosion was hurled forward, surging over the bow of the rubber boat.

The scouts bent their heads down. Monaykin fell on the tiller. Forward! Forward, as fast as possible!

A second shell fell, then a third and a fourth. The enemy was firing well this time. There was an explosion next to the boat. The rubber boat was buffeted by a water shock wave. Monaykin, feverishly turning the tiller, corrected the course.

Another shell, then another. They were breaking through! The rubber boat was approaching the exit from the canal at full speed. The helmsman had to be careful. The current here flowed strongly at the side of the boat. Could the plywood shell take it?

A tremor ran through the hull. Kalganov felt water under his legs. It was coming in quickly. Had a seam been broken? There was a leak in the lower part of the right side. The water was coming into the unseaworthy hull in a thin stream.

The water was already up to their ankles.

Kalganov and Globa tried to hold the tear closed, but in vain. The breach grew in size. The hull was already half filled with water. Monaykin, holding on to the tiller, anxiously listened to the motor. It was sputtering.

Zhorzhevich, taking off his *pilotka*, feverishly began bailing water. Old Shchepkin did the same with his *michmanka* [warrant officer cap]. The boat settled deeper into the water. The motor went dead. The hull was now full of water, and the current violently threw the boat, turning it.

"Everyone in the water!" Kalganov commanded. He went out last.

He slid off into the water and looked around. The rubber boat had already disappeared beneath the surface. Where were his comrades? Were they uninjured? The water was extremely cold. It was October—hardly summer. He started cramping up. Shchepkin was old; could he stand up to this?

Kalganov worked his arms and legs vigorously to prevent the cramping from overwhelming him. He looked around in alarm. One, two, three, four wet heads glistened not far away among the turbid gray waves. Everyone was all right!

The current carried the swimmers into the river's channel. The severe cold began to take over his body. His wet clothing pinned his arms and dragged him down. Kalganov maneuvered his way out of his leather coat, boots, and trousers. It was sufficient to undo the buttons of his blouse and spread his arms back. He did not throw off his blouse—his medals were pinned to it and his party card was in the pocket.

How long could he swim in the frozen autumn water? Still some, though his arms and legs were severely cramped.

He wanted to swim over to the shore and there await the vessels moving upstream. They had to report the results of their reconnaissance as quickly as possible. But the roaring current carried Kalganov and his four comrades away from the shore, farther and farther into the middle of the channel and away from the rocks lining the banks where the water crashed and sprayed. The wild, steep shore protruded outward, then withdrew. He would not collide with the rocks.

"I hope one of us survives this!" thought Kalganov. "There has to be at least one left to show the ships the way."

He could hardly keep his own head above water and could see that the others were also swimming with difficulty. How far had they already been carried? A kilometer, two, five? How much longer could they hold on? Was this where it would end?

"Armored cutters!" Suddenly he heard a happy shout nearby. "They're ours!"

Indeed, far up ahead he could barely make out the low, gray silhouette of an armored cutter that grew larger each second. The vessel was moving to intersect the swimmers, overcoming the current with some difficulty. The high foamy "ears" at the bow attested to this. A second armored cutter was spotted astern of the first, then another and still another came into view. These were the armored cutters for which Kalganov and his men were reconnoitering.

They dragged Kalganov in his underwear and blouse and all the remaining scouts aboard the lead armored cutter.

"Comrade *Boroda* [beard]!" the boat commander greeted Kalganov, recognizing him. "We've been looking for you for some time. Where's your rubber boat?"

"The Danube ate it!" Kalganov joked sardonically.

Following the route indicated by the scouts, the lead cutter sailed into the canal. The German mortars were silent this time. Our army units advancing on land looked after this problem.

When the armored cutter was passing through the canal, Kalganov and the sailors waved greetings to their engineer acquaintances, looking out the window of the cab of their locomotive, now standing ready with steam up. Ships with less powerful engines were sailing behind the armored cutters. The locomotive would give them a hand.

The Iron Gates were now behind them. The flotilla's ships continued up the river toward Belgrade, staying on line with advancing ground forces. And once again, the scouts were moving up the Danube in front of the rest.

From that time forward, every time Kalganov opened up his party card, the crinkled pages and ink in the pay column smeared from the Danube waters brought back memories to him of reconnaissance at the Iron Gates.

CHAPTER TEN

GHOSTS OF THE DANUBE

The stationary night fog, normal for the Danube in the autumn, covered the river with an impenetrable veil. It seemed that the river under the fog was also immobile. Only the murmuring of the water as it slid past the clay banks indicated its movement.

The observers in German shore positions east of the Yugoslav town of Smederevo, where the German command had succeeded in creating yet another defensive node on the approaches to Belgrade, were unconcerned on this foggy October night. Soviet forces had come up against heavily reinforced German positions and for several days now had not attempted any further advance.

The German observers would not have been so calm had they managed to distinguish the barely audible rhythmic puttering of a motor in the fast-rolling Danube waters. A small boat, one of the reconnaissance detachment's rubber boats, was sliding along the middle of the channel, not visible to their eyes. It would have been difficult to hear a rubber boat on the river from the bank. Its hull was submerged in the water to the degree that the end of the exhaust pipe was in the water, and therefore the motor was working almost noiselessly.

Seven men armed with submachine guns sat in the rubber boat, tightly filling it. Five of them were wearing oilskin storm

132

hats, like cutter sailors wore: Senior Lieutenant Kalganov, sailors Chkheidze, Monaykin, Shchepkin, and at the tiller, Yaragin. Two men in *pilotkas* sat with the sailors: one who now was a regular in the detachment, Lyubisha Zhorzhevich, and a partisan liaison from the Yugoslav partisan escort group. This group had been formed in the following manner. When the *Zhuchka,* first of all the flotilla ships, approached the shore near any Yugoslav village, there were always people who wanted to assist the Soviet sailors. They not only reported everything that they knew about the enemy but expressed a desire to go out and reconnoiter the unknown. Kalganov accepted such assistance with joy—it permitted them to conduct reconnaissance more rapidly and over a larger area. In the end, these voluntary informants, who requested and received weapons from the scouts, were organized into a standing force—a shore reconnaissance escort group. It became, as it were, an auxiliary unit of the detachment.

The *Zhuchka,* also with muffled exhaust, sailed right behind the rubber boat. A second group of scouts was aboard, led by Andreev: Kotsar, Gura, Globa, Maksimenko, Chichilo, and one of the new men in the detachment—powerful in the shoulder and tall Nikulin. As on the rubber boat, there was one of the Yugoslav partisans for liaison.

The night before, seamen Nikulin and Globa had gone out on reconnaissance with their Yugoslav comrades from the auxiliary group. They returned and reported that, based on information obtained from local inhabitants, there were Vlasovtsy—a unit of the ROA [*rossiyskaya osvoboditel'naya armiya*]—the so-called Russian Liberation Army,[1] created by the Germans from various riffraff and traitors, in the large river village Golubats, on the way toward Smederevo, in the enemy's rear. Their headquarters was in Golubats. [Golubats is about one hundred kilometers straight-line distance east of Belgrade on the Danube River. Smederevo is also on the river, about forty kilometers southeast of Belgrade.]

Having heard about the enemy that Nikulin and Globa had discovered, their comrades decided: "We must crush the reptile before it can crawl away!" They burned with greater hatred toward these traitors than toward the Germans.

Kalganov shared his sailors' desire. Therefore, when he reported the results of Nikulin's and Globa's reconnaissance to the command, he requested: "Let us conduct a raid on this headquarters."

The scouts' initiative was approved. The detachment received the mission to penetrate beyond the enemy's forward edge, into Golubats, and capture documents and "tongues" in the Vlasovtsy headquarters. It was important to the command to receive reports about the structure of the "army" of the Vlasovtsy and for what purpose its units had been sent to this sector of the front. The preparation for this operation was particularly serious. As he did before each difficult mission, Kalganov consulted with the communists. Who should go? Of course, they decided to send themselves first of all. Of this group, Kalganov selected Andreev, Gura, Globa, Maksimenko, Shchepkin, and Yaragin. Before departing, they pledged: "We will seek revenge against the traitors!" Maksimenko uttered these words with special passion. During the occupation, the police had visited much grief on his relatives.

The banks were hidden in the night fog. The enemy was on both of them. Somewhere in this area the forward edge passed perpendicular to the river.

Several more minutes of movement. By the scouts' reckoning, the enemy's forward positions were now behind them. Zhorzhevich, as usual filling the role of pilot, warned:

"Now we will come to some small islets, and beyond them— Moldova Island."

Zhorzhevich guided the rubber boat more on memory than on visible features, indicating to Yaragin when to move the tiller. An experienced Danube pilot, Zhorzhevich remembered where the islets lay on the way to Golubats. Now these islets were covered by fog. Before long they should run into them. They passed through the islets, then barely made out the long, low shore of Moldova in the fog.

"Right rudder!" Zhorzhevich instructed Yaragin. On the left, invisible on the bank because of the fog, was Golubats. It was better to pass by it not in the middle of the channel but holding closer to the island's empty shore. This gave greater assurance that the enemy would not hear them.

They went past Golubats. The rubber boat turned sharply and crossed the Danube. Up ahead, a dark horizontal belt emerged through the fog. Zhorzhevich, after consulting with the partisan guide, motioned to Yaragin:

"Go in there!"

Hardly had the rubber boat, guided by the experienced hand of the helmsman, touched its pliant nose into the soft soil when Kalganov waved his arm and carefully, so as not to make the smallest noise, jumped onto the shore. The rest followed behind him. Only Yaragin and Shchepkin remained behind. Mounting a light machine gun just in case, they stayed to await the arrival of the *Zhuchka*.

The three scouts and two guides carefully clambered up along the bank. Their hands and feet slipped on the clay, wet from the autumn rains. Without warning, the ground could give way under the weight of their bodies, they could slide back down, and, if the enemy heard the noise, their mission was compromised.

Lyubisha Zhorzhevich and the partisan liaison from the escort group reached the top of the bank first. Grasping the wet grass growing at the edge of the bank, they peered into the gray pre-dawn darkness. Up ahead they could make out a small cornfield. It had been harvested long ago. But here and there stood the straight, tall stalks with large, drooping leaves. Close on the other side of the field, draped in fog, was a swampy stream that flowed into the Danube not far from the place where the scouts had come ashore. A wooden bridge crossed the stream. Farther beyond it were the dim white walls of buildings, with drooping roofs, barely visible against the background of the not yet light sky.

"We came in at the right place!" the partisan happily said to Zhorzhevich, pointing ahead. "Golubats!"

"Let's go!" Kalganov commanded in a whisper. He reached the top of the bank and, pulling himself over the edge with his hands, easily rolled over the crest. The rest of the group noiselessly climbed the bank.

The group that landed from the rubber boat was not the only one headed for Golubats. Andreev's group was being delivered by the just-arrived *Zhuchka*.

They crossed the cornfield and forded the stream. They turned off into the gardens behind the white buildings and approached the town through the wet willow bushes.

The damp bushes did not crackle, and the branches did not stir. The scouts, noiseless as ghosts, followed their Yugoslav guide in a file. So far, everything was going according to plan.

Golubats was a large village, more than two hundred peasant houses on a single street that stretched along the bank of the river. The village hall, where the Vlasovtsy had established their headquarters, was in the center. The remainder of the Vlasovtsy were dispersed on the outskirts of the village, beyond the spot where the scouts had landed. Patrols walked along the street throughout the village.

Kalganov's group was to move unseen toward the headquarters and take a position near it in the garden off the side yard. Andreev's group, divided into two subgroups, set up an ambush near the headquarters on the street, in case it was needed to cover the withdrawal by fire. The partisans of the escort group, who had arrived at the village earlier and for the time being were hiding on the outskirts in the gardens near the houses where the Vlasovtsy were quartered, were to cause panic by their fire and attract attention to themselves. The partisans would open fire as soon as their liaison with the scouts reported that the sailors were in position. Two partisans had earlier positioned themselves in the attic of one of the huts and set up a light machine gun in the dormer window. This machine gun was aimed along the street in the direction of the houses in which the Vlasovtsy were quartered. Kalganov's group would conduct the raid on the headquarters.

It was about thirty paces from where Kalganov and his group were camouflaged in the deep shade of the trees to the headquarters. The scouts could see the entire yard well. A sentry with a carbine in a *kubanka* [a flat, round fur hat] and long German cape walked past the porch, past the dimly lit window, from which was strung some black wire. A motorcycle was leaned up against the white wall under the window.

All the scouts were at their designated positions. All were ready. The operation could commence. Kalganov turned toward Chkheidze, who was sitting nearby, and gave him a hand motion. Understanding the nod, he brought the stock of his submachine gun up to his shoulder.

A short burst of fire broke the early morning calm. The sentry fell, dropping his carbine and losing his *kubanka*. There was the tinkle of broken glass and the thump of an explosion inside the house. The debris of the window frame whipped through the branches of the trees in the garden. At that same moment, there were more explosions inside the house. The scouts were throwing grenades through the windows, interspersed with bursts of submachine-gun fire.

"Forward!" Kalganov jumped up and rushed the porch. On the run he heard the muffled sound of machine-gun fire behind the houses, from the direction of the river. As if in reply, a machine gun chattered somewhere on the outskirts. In accordance with the plan, the scouts on the rubber boat and the *Zhuchka* had opened fire on Golubats with their machine guns. They were firing over the rooftops so as not to harm the civilians but at the same time to sow panic among the enemy. The partisan machine gun in the attack began to fire at the same time at the houses in which a minute ago the Vlasovtsy had been sleeping their quiet, rear-area sleep.

Running up onto the porch, Kalganov watched as the grenade explosions flashed in the window. The sailors fired bursts from their submachine guns, and then rushed into the building. Chichilo followed his commander up the steps of the porch and then ran past him.

The whitish light of the early morning barely penetrated into the building. The smoke from the grenade explosions streamed through the doorways. Kalganov, who was still standing in the hallway, saw a half-dressed figure in a far room through the smoke and through two open doors. Dodging around overturned tables, firing his pistol at the window on the move, the Vlasovets ran for the exit, straight toward Kalganov and Chichilo. Apparently, he had not yet spotted them.

So as not to scare away this prize who was running right into their hands, Kalganov stepped behind the door casing. But Chichilo, pushing him out of the way with his large body, rushed toward the door, shouldering his submachine gun. Kalganov, managing to throw his hand at the receiver of Chichilo's weapon, shouted a warning at him:

"Alive!"

Brandishing his pistol, breathing hoarsely, the Vlasovets in the disheveled uniform with officer shoulder boards dashed across the room, hurrying toward the exit. But before he reached it, he sprawled on the floor: Chichilo had hit him lightly with the butt-stock on the back of the head. The Vlasovets came to quickly and tried to get up. But Kalganov and Chichilo had already grabbed him and taken away his pistol. Other sailors rushed to their assistance. Cursing in despair, the Vlasovets tried to break free. They tied his hands. Throwing hateful stares at the scouts, he cried:

"If you hadn't taken me so soon, I would have ripped the hide off of you!"

"Shut up, you low-life scum!" Chichilo grabbed the traitor by the collar with his enormous hand and with his other fist smartly planted a punch in the prisoner's curse-spewing mouth. Kalganov pulled documents from the Vlasovets's uniform pocket. He glanced at his identification booklet:

"Ah, Your Honor, Mister Second Lieutenant!"[2]

In those seconds, while they were subduing the second lieutenant, the rest of the enemy in the house were finished off. None of the staff personnel got away. The acrid smell of gunpowder hung in the rooms. Between the tables and chairs scattered about by the grenade detonations, on the floor, amid the debris of papers, broken window glass, and empty bottles—they clearly had been drinking in the headquarters just before the raid—lay bodies in uniforms with the distinguishing patch of the Vlasov army—a shield with a slanting cross—on the right sleeve. Globa and Nikulin led still another captured traitor, a noncommissioned officer, in from the street. He was undressed, in a long shirt, and blood was dripping from his hand. They had captured him when he jumped out a window. The prisoner's teeth were chattering. His fleeting glance stopped at Kalganov's beard, then moved to the strapping figure of Nikulin, then he glanced at Chichilo and, it seemed, could not tear his gaze from this warrior. The prisoner looked dejectedly around at those surrounding him, as though he could not believe his eyes. All were in black storm caps, pea jackets with broad, unbuttoned lapels, behind which the blue and white stripes of their tel'nyashkas were visible, and bell-bottomed trousers tucked into their boots. To him, apparently, it was difficult to believe that Soviet sailors could suddenly appear here, several kilometers behind the front line.

The noncommissioned officer flinched, then ran his hands across his eyes as if to wipe away his vision. Then he suddenly, imploringly cried, "I am from Krasnodar!" (This city lies about seventy-five kilometers east of Novorossiysk, on the Black Sea's east coast.)

"You are now from Berlin!" Chichilo snapped back.

"Search him!" Kalganov ordered. "Then we will talk."

"Why talk with him, with a Jew?"[3] Chichilo brandished his submachine gun. "Give him one bullet, and be done with him. This 'tongue' is enough!" He threw a glance to the side at the bound, already subdued second lieutenant sitting on the floor.

"No. This one is also useful. You will answer for his safety!" Kalganov warned.

"Fine!" Chichilo conceded.

There were no more prisoners. The Vlasovtsy were shown no kindness. The sailors spared none of them.[4]

On the outside, not too far away, bursts of submachine guns signaled an engagement. Did this mean that Andreev's group had already been forced to open fire? Had the awakened Vlasovtsy, perhaps, already come to their senses, pressed past the partisans, and now were putting pressure on Andreev's group?

There was not a second to spare!

Quickly running across the room, Kalganov and the sailors gathered up papers, maps, and folders. They found a small portable safe in one of the rooms. It was an iron box with handles and was locked. It probably contained the most important classified papers and documents. Should they search for the key? Should they blow it up? It would take too long. There was no time. They tried to pick it up—it was heavy. One of the sailors dragged it out into the street. Kalganov tipped it up and placed a submachine gun under it, then deftly pried the top with a crowbar. The metal groaned, and the top popped open loudly. The safe turned out to be full of folders with the words *Geheim* [secret] in German and *Sekretno* [classified] in Russian written on the corner of each.

"Take it all!" Kalganov ordered.

They began to fill an empty pouch such as the Germans used for their military mail with the folders, papers, and maps. It had an enormous black stencil of an eagle, clasping a fascist swastika in its claws. They filled the pouch and tied it off.

The firing outside grew louder and more worrisome. Submachine guns stuttered, and machine guns were firing long, muffled bursts. The firing grew closer. The Vlasovtsy were hurrying to relieve the headquarters.

The pouch was tied tightly. They shook it—it was heavy!

"Carry it!" Kalganov said to the warrior Chichilo. He picked up the sack. One hand was insufficient, it took two.

"How will I be able to fire? My hands are full." Chichilo looked at the second lieutenant, with hope in his eyes at hearing the ever-approaching firing.

"Let this vermin carry the papers himself!"

"Give it to him!" Kalganov agreed.

Chichilo untied the second lieutenant's hands and pointed at the sack.

Gritting his teeth, the second lieutenant put the pouch on his back.

"Lead the 'tongues' down to the river, through the backyards!" Kalganov instructed Chichilo. "The rest of you—also go to the river, quickly! I will go to Andreev! Then I will catch up with you."

Thirty seconds later, there was no one in the destroyed head-quarters. Through the yards and gardens, pushing the second lieutenant, lugging the sack full of documents, and the noncom-missioned officer, holding his wounded hand, in front of them, the scouts of Kalganov's group hurried to where the *Zhuchka* and the rubber boat awaited them. Firing spread throughout Golubats.

Kalganov found Andreev and the sailors of his group where they had been since the very beginning, in a farmstead adjoin-ing the headquarters. Having settled in behind a stone fence, the scouts were firing their submachine guns, in short bursts to con-serve ammunition, along the street toward the far end. There, still poorly visible in the gray light of the slowly dawning morn-ing, the figures of the Vlasovtsy could be seen fleetingly, moving toward the headquarters building.

"Withdraw!" Kalganov shouted to Andreev.

"Did you take any?" Andreev asked.

"We took two!" Kalganov prodded him. "Quickly, don't delay!"

Firing several more bursts to delay the enemy, Andreev and his entire group hurried off toward the river.

Before he set off after them, Kalganov pulled a flare from the shell holder of his flare pistol and fired it. A bright green light arched into the sky.

The green flare that Kalganov fired was a signal for the parti-sans, who were still continuing to attract the attention of the enemy to themselves. Upon seeing the rocket, they were to with-draw into the nearby forest. At the same time, the rocket was a signal for those who had remained at the rubber boat and on the *Zhuchka*. They were to cover the withdrawal with fire.

Now the houses on the outskirts of Golubats were behind them. They again ran across the swampy stream. They were near the bank of the Danube. The face of the second lieutenant, who was loaded down with the weight of the document bag, was wet with sweat and purple from the strain. But Chichilo was pushing him hard:

"Move, move, Your Honor!"

Bullets were whistling behind the scouts. If they had looked around, they could have seen tens of Vlasovtsy in *kubankas* and baggy capes running behind them straight through the yards and gardens, spread out in an uneven line. Some of them were shouldering their submachine guns and rifles on the move and firing. Now they were emboldened, seeing that there were all of fifteen sailors.

An additional twenty to thirty Vlasovtsy showed up from behind the houses on the outskirts of the village, ran across the bridge over the stream, and with all their energy were moving along the stream to cut off the scouts' path toward the Danube's shore.

The scouts laid down and fired short bursts at the Vlasovtsy running to cut them off. Some of the enemy veered off to the side, some laid down, and others stopped.

But the scouts could not delay the enemy with this fire long—it meant that they would be delayed themselves. They had to hurry. Still more Vlasovtsy would be rushing out of the village in several minutes, and it would be more difficult to break off from the pursuit.

The scouts hurried toward the safety of the bank. It took only several seconds for one and then the other to move back, covered by his comrades' fire. But now they were low on ammunition. They had expended too much in the village.

The shore! Chichilo pushed the second lieutenant, who had stopped onto the edge of the riverbank.

"Jump! There's nothing you can do by looking back at your friends. You can't help them!"

The second lieutenant, without dropping the pouch, went down the clay bank on his buttocks. The noncommissioned officer, holding his wounded hand, slid down right behind him, followed by Chichilo.

Alongside the bank, two to three meters from the water's edge—it couldn't come in closer—stood the *Zhuchka*. Its engine was idling and only needed throttle. Two sailors were standing ready behind tripod-mounted heavy machine guns on the bow and stern. They opened fire on the enemy as soon as they appeared at the top of the bank.

The rubber boat with its bow up on shore was a short distance from the *Zhuchka*. Yaragin and Shchepkin were at their light machine gun, also ready to open fire.

Pushing his worn-out captives, right behind them in water up to his knees, Chichilo waded toward the side of the *Zhuchka,* shouting:

"Take this baggage!"

Sailors' hands grabbed the document pouch from the shoulder of "His Honor." The second lieutenant guardedly gave up his load. But he was slow in climbing aboard. Apparently encouraged by the firing that was now close, he kept looking around: would they come to help him?

Chichilo gave him a shove:

"Climb up!" and asked his comrades aboard the ship: "Give 'His Honor' a hand!"

Several strong sailors' hands pulled the second lieutenant aboard. Chichilo pushed the noncommissioned officer:

"You hurry up, too, former *Krasnodarskiy* [resident of Krasnodar]." When he had climbed up onto the cutter, Chichilo went aboard himself.

Firing their submachine guns along the side of the ship, the rest of the scouts climbed aboard the *Zhuchka*.

"Cast off!" Kalganov shouted from the shore.

The *Zhuchka*'s motor gave a throaty roar. It quickly backed off and turned around in the current.

"There they are!" Chichilo, standing at full height on the deck of the *Zhuchka,* pointed in the direction of the shore.

The Vlasovtsy were almost at the edge of the bank. Shouldering his submachine gun, Chichilo fired a long burst at them, emptying his last drum. His comrades' submachine guns and the bow and stern machine guns on the *Zhuchka* joined in.

The whistle of enemy bullets, carrying over the deck, went unheard in the noise of the firing. Leaving behind a boiling, foamy wake, the *Zhuchka* moved into the current at full speed.

The rubber boat had still not pulled away. They were waiting for the last of the scouts, who were sliding down the steep bank. The enemy was close, running along the edge of the bank, clearly visible from the rubber boat. Shchepkin, pulling the buttstock of the Degtyarev [7.62mm light machine gun] to his shoulder, fired a burst. Yaragin nervously grasped the tiller in his hands, prepared to accelerate his craft as soon as his passengers climbed aboard.

Almost all the remaining scouts—there were five, including Kalganov—were sliding down the bank and running across the sand along the water's edge toward the rubber boat. Only Kotsar and Globa remained up above. They were covering the withdrawal. Kotsar and Globa were lying in the yellowing wet grass at the edge of the bank and firing short but frequent bursts. In the lulls between bursts, first Kotsar and then Globa glanced around. Were all their comrades on board? Yes, all! Kalganov was raising his hand to signal them back.

Firing yet another burst in succession, Kotsar and then Globa jumped down onto the packed wet sand. The rubber boat had already backed off the shore and was moving in the shallow water to meet the running Kotsar and Globa.

"Get in! Get in!" their comrades shouted to them.

Splashing with their boots in the water, Kotsar and Globa jumped into the rubber boat. At that same instant, its motor accelerating, the boat turned toward the middle of the river and hurried to catch up with the *Zhuchka*. Up above, at the edge of the embankment, at that same place where the two sailors had laid only a minute ago, the Vlasovtsy appeared. Shchepkin's Degtyarev and the submachine guns of the others fired at them. They could hear the machine guns of the distant *Zhuchka* firing also. The Vlasovtsy immediately backed off.

The firing from the *Zhuchka* and the rubber boat continued for several minutes. But then the steep bank of Golubats was almost invisible in the dissipating morning fog. And, certainly, the enemy, running toward the embankment after firing ceased from the river, looked into this fog with disbelief and fear. The Soviet sailors had appeared from the fog like ghosts and now had disappeared into it like ghosts. They had appeared and disappeared with stunning speed. From the moment when the first burst of submachine gun fire that cut down the sentry at the headquarters broke the premorning quiet until the firing of the green rocket over Golubats—the withdrawal signal—fifteen minutes had passed. Fifteen minutes, that was all.

CHAPTER ELEVEN

A BRİDGE NEAR BELGRADE

It was a gray October day in a small town, its white houses stretched out on the slope of a forested hill along the Danube's bank. From the other side of the hill, the muffled thunder of a cannonade was heard from time to time. This was the battle for Belgrade, which was now quite near.

There were lively voices at the town's small dock. Farewell embraces were being exchanged. Friends in sailor uniforms were slapping each other on the shoulders. Some gave the appearance of having been around a while; others, with dark-complected faces, were wearing new uniforms without shoulder boards. By the noise and happy talk, one could immediately conclude that these were friends parting.

The *Zhuchka* stood near the low, dockside wall, its side tied up to it. Fresh bullet holes were visible in its planking, in the wheelhouse, and in the stern superstructure. It had received this damage recently, in the battle for Smederevo, which was now behind them.

Yugoslav volunteers who comprised the shore reconnaissance escort group had helped the scouts in many of their patrols. The Yugoslav friends, who had arrived during the night, had taken part in a joint operation for the last time. They had helped capture an important "tongue," a German colonel, who was headed toward his headquarters in Belgrade by car, on a highway that ran along the river in the enemy rear. This day, when it had become known that forces of the People's Liberation Army of Yugoslavia were already operating close by, these Yugoslavs had decided to take their entire group, which now had grown to a platoon, over to their own army and take part in the assault on the capital.

So here were the sailors with their Yugoslav comrades in arms. Each of the partisans had been given a trophy [i.e., German] pistol and a sailor uniform. They had already changed into the uniforms.

"Good luck in battle, until our common victory!" were the last words heard.

The Yugoslav comrades departed, and the sailors assembled to depart for points farther upstream on the Danube.

The scouts had just received the mission to proceed to a railroad bridge that connected Belgrade to the suburb of Panchevo, which lay on the opposite bank of the Danube [several kilometers east of Belgrade].[1] They were to reconnoiter to determine whether armored cutters could navigate the river upstream beyond the bridge, toward the center of Belgrade, where our advancing units needed their artillery support.

By all reports, enemy forces still held the banks near the bridge. It would have been safer to conduct this reconnaissance at night. But there was no time. Our guards infantry and soldiers of the First Proletarian Corps of the Yugoslav National Liberation Army were already fighting in the streets of Belgrade, working their way toward the city's river district. Now they were in particular need of assistance from the river.

Instantly picking up speed, the rubber boat rushed like an arrow against the current. In the boat together with Kalganov were Andreev, Globa, Chichilo, and Nikulin. They crossed the Danube, then proceeded upstream along the left [north] bank. By Kalganov's calculations, this route was safer. There were more German gun positions on the opposite, Belgrade, bank, where furious fighting was going on. The Germans, of course, were watching the river closely. On their left, perhaps, there were fewer Germans—the forces of the Second Ukrainian *Front* were attacking there.

The rubber boat flew along, cutting the Danube's surface. The shore ran past alongside, low, with sandy stretches. A sprinkling of white houses of suburban villages showed through the bare tree branches. On the left, the other side of the river, the city was visible on the hills. Though it was still far off, dim gray and white patches defined its sections that extended down toward the Danube. Broken layers of smoke swirled on the wind, mixing with low-hanging clouds above the city. The cannonades of artillery firing could be heard more distinctly through the rhythmically puttering motor of the rubber boat and the whispering of the water past its hull.

The battle for Belgrade was in full swing.

They were coming up on the bridge, closing on it with each passing second. "More to the right!" Kalganov instructed the helmsman.

The rubber boat proceeded all of several meters from the water's edge. If they had looked around, they would have seen how their bow wave ran up onto the sand at an angle. The bridge was close. Its massive pilings were planted like towers at intervals across the river. The delicate iron spans, dropped from the supports by demolitions, protruded obliquely from the water between them. The Germans had rushed to destroy the Panchevo bridge, to prevent the advancing Soviet forces from using it and at the same time to block the path of Soviet vessels moving toward Belgrade on the river.

Kalganov, bringing his binoculars up to his eyes, peered intently at the bank. They were about two hundred meters from the bridge. Had the enemy spotted them? Where was he on the bank? Would they reach the bridge?

A machine-gun burst carried across the water with intermittent whistles. Everyone involuntarily ducked. "Full ahead!" Kalganov commanded Andreev, who was sitting at the tiller.

A machine-gun burst again punctured the water alongside the boat. Where were they firing from? The rubber boat flew at top speed into the space between the bank and the bridge pier closest to it.

"Stop!" Kalganov commanded.

The scouts were now in relative safety. The very wide turret of the closest pier, constructed of gray stones, was covering them. The scouts had been able to determine that they were being fired upon not from the bank but from the third pier. But now they could not be seen from there. It seems that the Germans had placed a machine gun and crew directly on the bridge, just in case our ships attempted to sail underneath it.

What should they do? They had to take a look around.

The latticed heap of the span, held on one end to an abutment, with the other end deep in the water, hung obliquely over the scouts' heads. The water churned and swirled between the twisted iron girders.

Its motor working quietly to hold it in the current, the rubber boat held its position. The Germans on the bridge could not see it behind the wide bridge pier.

Several Germans with a machine gun on the third pier were not a threat to the armored cutters. One or two rounds were sufficient to deal with them. But before the armored cutters reached this location, a safe passage had to be found between or over the top of the latticed span that had been dropped into the water. And the enemy machine gunners were interfering with this task.

But, perhaps, there was a passage lane here, between the bank and the last pier? The scouts attentively inspected the sector of the river from the pier to the bank, taking measurements with poles. The wreckage of the bridge floor structure was alongside the pier, in the water, and the bridge's superstructure was hanging down closer to the shore. No, an armored cutter could not pass through here. This meant that they had to search farther, even if under fire.

On Kalganov's command, the rubber boat, turning sharply around, darted from behind the last pier and, going around it, entered the space between it and the second pier. They maneuvered so quickly that the Germans on the third pier were unable to fire at the boat.

Circling between the first and second pilings, the scouts made several measurements and found a suitable passage for the armored cutters under a destroyed bridge section, slanted with one end on the bottom. The Germans positioned nearby did not fire. Although they undoubtedly heard the sound of the rubber boat's motor as it scurried about between the bridge spans, either they could not see it or did not want to expend ammunition in vain.

The scouts needed to find one additional passage—a reserve—for the many ships. But to find a second passage, they had to come out from behind the reliable rock cover, directly under the fire of the enemy, toward the third piling.

"We are going to make a dash for the third piling, and everyone fire at it!" Kalganov ordered the scouts.

The rubber boat raced toward the third piling at full speed, leaving a twisting, sharp wake of foamy water behind it. Four submachine guns fired simultaneously from the move at the upper part of the piling, where several flat-sided helmets loomed behind the thick iron girders of the collapsed superstructure, one end still fastened to it.

The Germans did not open fire immediately. Certainly, they did not suppose that the Soviet sailors in a rubber and plywood boat, which any bullet could penetrate, would risk attacking them.

The enemy's confusion lasted several seconds. But these seconds were crucial. Stitched by bullets, three enemy soldiers fell into the water. The remaining enemy fired several wild bursts and then ceased firing. The scouts were able to fire at the Germans from several angles from the rubber boat, which they maneuvered past the piling. For the Germans to fire back, they had to run under fire from one edge of the piling to another.

"Cease fire!" Kalganov gave the command, sensing that no shots were now being fired from the third piling.

Reducing speed, the rubber boat went past the piling several times, each time moving closer. The scouts hugged its side, holding their submachine guns at the ready.

When they had passed near the base of the piling, Kalganov shouted up in German:

"Hands up! Throw down your weapons!"

In response, a submachine gun plunged into the water and a second right behind it. The figures of two German soldiers, standing at full height and holding their arms over their heads, appeared on the top of the piling.

"Wait for us!" Kalganov shouted at them in German.

Now, when the firefight had been successfully completed, they could search for the second, alternate, passage. They passed between the second and third pilings several times. They measured with poles—an armored cutter could pass over the bridge span lying in the water, but it had to proceed very carefully so as not to snag it.

Now they could return for the prisoners. They went right up to the piling, to the place where iron rungs fixed in the stone led upward, one above the other.

"Climb down!" Kalganov commanded the Germans waiting up above. Voluntarily they deftly climbed down. Kalganov seated them in the rubber boat, which now was low in the water. It was designed for four persons and now was carrying six. When the prisoners had been brought aboard, Kalganov instructed Nikulin to climb up the iron rungs and look around to see if the Germans had left anything of special interest.

From the top of the piling, Nikulin shouted:

"There's a machine gun up here, with ammunition!"

"Drop it into the water!" Kalganov ordered. "We have no room to take back trophies."

The light machine gun, the metal ammunition cans, and the ammunition containers fell heavily into the swirling waters at the base of the piling.

Nikulin began to climb down, moving his arms and feet on the iron rungs. An oblong metal container, painted a dark green color, hung off his shoulder on a belt.

"What's that? Drop it!" Kalganov said.

"It's a radio!" replied Nikulin, continuing to climb down. "Perhaps we can set it up on the *Zhuchka*?"

"Well, all right!" Kalganov agreed. "Apparently you will be bored without your toy."

Kalganov knew. Before he came to the scouts, Nikulin had been a radio operator. He had studied radio subjects even before the war, in a *tekhnikum* [vocational school] that prepared specialists for the fishing fleet. By the fate of military service, Nikulin had become a scout. But he had maintained his skill in his earlier specialty.

They loaded the radio into the boat. The rubber boat raced downstream with the current from the bridge toward their own forces at full speed.

Already quite far from the bridge, they suddenly fell under heavy machine-gun fire from the Belgrade bank. In another minute or two, the boat would have been punctured by the bullets. But the scouts managed to hide behind a low, bush-covered islet that extended along the shore. Their presence of mind and the ability to adapt quickly to the situation protected them as well. Concealed behind the islet, they proceeded out from under the fire.

Two hours later, the armored cutters were headed toward the Panchevo bridge. The scouts were on the lead cutter. All the armored cutters sailed safely through the passages indicated by the scouts. Taking cover behind Ratno Island, positioned opposite the central portion of the city, the armored cutters commenced fire on enemy strongpoints, thus aiding our attacking infantry.

The battle for Belgrade lasted three days. These were intense days for the scouts. Landing on the bank of the river west of Belgrade, alongside the suburb of Zemun, they reconnoitered the enemy's firing positions and artillery positions along the river and found many targets for the armored cutters' artillery. They were among the first to burst into Belgrade's old Kalemegdan fortress that stood on the bank of the river, the walls of which the Germans defended particularly stubbornly. In fierce hand-to-hand combat, the sailors broke into the very center of the fortress and captured five enemy officers, among them staff officers. They seized particularly valuable diagrams and maps indicating the obstacle plan on the river upstream from Belgrade. This would later help them make the way safe for ships and crossing assets on the subsequent path of the offensive.

Belgrade was liberated on 20 October 1944. Once again, the battle-scarred *Zhuchka* sailed far in front of the flotilla's ships, now reconnoitering the way to Budapest.

CHAPTER TWELVE

OPERATION "FLOUR"

After the conduct of this operation, none of the scouts were rec-ommended for any award. As a result of it, they did not deliver a "tongue" or any reports concerning the enemy. It was not recorded in staff summaries of the reconnaissance detachment's activities. Just the same, all the scouts who were able to participate in it recall it with pride to this day, more than fifteen years later.

No one ordered the scouts to conduct this operation. They could have avoided it, and no one would have asked why. Just the same, they went. They went out and executed it with the same zeal as they would any other mission.

After Belgrade, the path lay toward Budapest. In the Hungarian town of Ilok, in the center of an enemy fortified area, the scouts spirited a female agent, who had been trained for insertion into our rear, and a German intelligence officer away from a German headquarters. On the approaches to Budapest, they searched for the place where the enemy had cunningly placed explosive obsta-cles under the water, intending to blow up our ships. The scouts determined what kind of antiship and antipontoon mines of new construction the enemy was using and how he employed them. Penetrating far into the rear of enemy forward units, the scouts established the location of his artillery batteries and supply dumps on Chepel' Island, where the majority of Budapest's factories were concentrated.

But the operation conducted in December 1944 in Budafok, on the outskirts of Budapest, had a wholly different purpose. It was the first and only operation of its type.

A group consisting of Nikulin, Maksimenko, Neverov, and two others—the rookies Malakhov and Veretenik[1]— led by Kalganov had returned one evening from a routine patrol in the enemy rear. Warming by the hearth in one of the huts they had earlier chosen for their base for rest, the scouts were talking about their just completed mission. But the discussion was not about the nature of the enemy's defenses, the disposition of his forces, or how they had operated. The patrol had differed little from many others. Two times they had crossed no-man's land that stretched across a railroad track, past track-side warehouses and vacant lots, passed undetected by the enemy through his forward edge, and brought back intelligence data. No, the conversation was not about these activities.

The conversation was about a burning warehouse between our and the Germans' forward positions. The scouts had passed this warehouse, one of many near the railroad line, on their return trip.

Their attention had been drawn not to the fact that the warehouse was burning—they had seen many fires during the war. And it was barely burning at that, smoldering really, almost without flames. Only a thin wisp of smoke trailed out of the small windows near the roof and from the wide open doors. They were agitated that the entire warehouse was piled high with sacks. And in the sacks was flour. They had confirmed this by looking in the warehouse. It seems that the Germans had not anticipated having to abandon the territory where the warehouse was located so quickly, and they had not succeeded in evacuating it. Flour was already spilling out of some of the burning sacks. It was beautiful, white flour. It caught fire slowly, reluctantly. It would sooner rot than burn and only here and there was burning with flame and black smoke.

The conversation was about the flour.

Arkadiy Malakhov brought it up first. He had survived the most difficult first winter in blockaded Leningrad and had experienced hunger himself. Malakhov summarized his feelings:

"How much flour will go up in smoke, and in the town the people don't have a crust of bread."

"I looked into a cellar just a while ago," Veretenik recalled, "and besides the other people, it was full of kids there. I gave my sugar to one little girl—how she grabbed it! Her mother took it and began to divide it into three parts."

"I saw one of our teamsters' horses that had been killed by shrapnel," Nikulin recollected. "They just left the horse on the street, and the Magyars [Hungarians] butchered it on the spot. Only the tail was left. This is what Hitler has brought to these people!"

"They are starving. Why couldn't their authorities distribute that flour?"

"If they divided it, their pockets would burst! The Germans and their Salashisty[2] most likely didn't let anyone get near it, and when they began to clear out, they set it on fire."

"It's not burning from a shell?"

"Perhaps a shell started it. There's a mountain of potential bread, but right next to it, people are dying of hunger."

"What if we carried this flour out before it all burned and distributed it to the people?" Malakhov excitedly suggested. "The warehouse is in no-man's land, not in a German-controlled area."

"How would we get it out? The Germans are watching the road."

"What about the narrow lane across the vacant lot? Where we walked, a wagon can go."

"We'll set it up with volunteers!" Kalganov suggested. "They give us twelve hours' rest after a patrol. We'll use that time to feed the local population."

The scouts received the suggestion guardedly.

"Well, if everyone agrees, then we'll do it!" Kalganov issued instructions: "Lyubisha! Take Veretenik, Nikulin, and Malakhov. Go to the cellar where the people have taken shelter. Explain to them what we want to give them for their bread. Tell them where this flour is and how we can get it. Ask who wants to help. Tell them it will take strong men, who can pick up a sack. Choose ten men. And on the way back, drop in on our teamster soldiers. Ask them for one wagon for a while. Explain the purpose, and they won't refuse. Organize it!"

While Lyubisha Zhorzhevich—irreplaceable as an inter-preter—Nikulin, and Veretenik organized the loaders and the wagon, Kalganov went to the commander of the rifle company through whose front-line position he intended to lead his sailors and Magyars for the flour. Kalganov asked the company com-mander if his infantry would cover their retreat by fire in the event the enemy detected the "flour hunters." Surprised that they would undertake such a risky venture, the company commander agreed. Even more, he linked Kalganov up with the mortar pla-toon commander located at the same observation post, who promised support by fire if anything should happen.

The December night had already fallen when five scouts—Nikulin, Malakhov, Veretenik, Maksimenko, and Neverov, under Kalganov's command—crossed our forward edge along the streets of Budafok toward the adjoining railroad line. Behind them came a wagon drawn by a pair of horses and ten Magyar volunteers on foot.

It was dark and quiet. The scouts moved along the alleys and vacant lots, taking cover in the shadows of the buildings. They reached the burning warehouse safely, along with the Magyars and the wagon.

During the time that this expedition was being prepared, the fire had spread and had crept farther through the piles of bags. The flour was already burning strongly in some places, throwing tongues of smoky, heavy flame toward the warehouse ceiling. How much time remained until the whole warehouse burst into flames? Could they put it out? They had no equipment with which to fight the fire and no time.

They posted one man to watch for the enemy and concealed the wagon around the corner. The scouts and Magyars hurried into the warehouse. They picked up the heavy, hot—in places already smoldering—sacks, hoisted them to their backs, and hauled them to the wagon. As soon as they had loaded the wagon to the top, one of the scouts took the reins and drove it through the empty lots toward our front line, a distance of about two hundred meters. They piled the sacks in one of the courtyards immediately behind the forward edge, then drove the horses at a trot back to the warehouse.

They made several trips. A mountain of sacks grew in the courtyard. But when the empty wagon was coming out of the alley and quickly crossing a wide street, hurrying toward the warehouse, a long, intermittent whistle was heard overhead in the dark sky. A shell exploded on the paving stones not far from the wagon. The frightened horses took off at a gallop and pulled the wagon into an alley. Another shell and then another exploded behind them, on the street. Mortar bombs flew from our side in response.

Neither the horses nor the people who were accompanying the wagon were injured. But it became clear that they could no longer move the flour by the previous route. They could not take another road with the wagon.

What could they do? Cease work? But so many bags remained in the warehouse, and there were so many hungry people in Budafok.

Lyubisha Zhorzhevich suggested a way out. Rather, the Magyars with whom Lyubisha was speaking in their native tongue, who were loading the flour, informed him that they could reach the warehouse out of view of the enemy not by the alleys and streets but where the warehouse abutted the loading area of the railroad station. The wagon could not go through the crowded space, but a man could.

They decided to try the route suggested by the Magyars. Everyone picked up a sack and carried it to the fence, then through a gap in the fence to the loading area. The horses, unharnessed from the wagon, were waiting there. They threw two bags tied together on the horses' backs and led them through aisles between stacks of boxes and barrels, back to the forward edge.

After midnight, all the intact sacks were carried out of the warehouse and delivered to our forward edge.

In the courtyard, where the salvaged flour had been placed, the scouts assembled—tired, sweaty, with black stains of ashes and traces of flour on their faces and clothing— but very satisfied that they had executed their plan. Here also were Magyars, who had carried the flour with such zeal. Despite the late hour and the German shells falling nearby, a large number of other residents of nearby streets—men and women—gathered around them. More and more people were arriving. It seems a rumor that the Russians would distribute the flour had quickly spread through all the shelters where the hungry residents of Budafok had been hiding from the firing for a day.

Looking around at the growing crowd, Kalganov turned to Lyubisha: "Tell them to select several people, a committee or commission, to distribute the flour.[3] The children should be first in line!"

Later, Lyubisha heard many words of thanks that the residents asked him to pass on to his comrades in the detachment.

In the morning, the flotilla chief of staff, Captain First Rank Sverdlov, summoned Kalganov to give him a new mission.

When Kalganov appeared, Sverdlov asked him with some concern:

"Have you rested after yesterday's mission?"

"No," Kalganov replied. "There was no time."

"Why not?" Sverdlov was taken aback. "You were off."

"We were carrying out an operation."

"What kind of operation?"

"Operation 'Flour.' "

Kalganov began to recount the details of this operation. The captain first rank at first wanted to take him to task for his initiative, for taking an unnecessary risk. But having heard the whole story, he said:

"You did the right thing."

CHAPTER THIRTEEN

TEMPTATION

If you ever have the pleasure to visit Budapest, you must see Margit Island. It is a stone's throw from the center of the city, from Pest [east bank], halfway across the bridge that bears the same name as the island, one of six bridges across the Danube in Budapest. A small viaduct leads off this bridge to the island. The entire island, which extends along the river between Buda [west bank] and Pest, is a magnificent park. Ancient trees, their upper crowns joined, form a green canopy over the streets and lanes. Amid the thick greenery are countless restaurants and cafes, dancing and sports pavilions, and swimming pools in which people can swim not only in the summer but in the winter as well. Hot water is piped into them from a mineral spring more than three hundred meters deep. Wandering along the park roads and lanes, you will come to an enormous beach pavilion, Platinus, which can accommodate fifteen thousand people at one time. Near the beach, you will come upon a fantastic rose garden that houses more than two hundred varieties. You can visit one of the amphitheaters, opera or variety, that currently bears the name Mayakovskiy.

On this island park, your attention will be drawn to the plush ruins of an ancient monastery, the airy Grand Hotel building, the garden made of artificial cliffs, where thousands of flowers will greet your eyes, and a waterfall cascades from one of these cliffs into a pool of golden carp surrounded by old spreading trees. You can listen with delight to the Hungarian folk music coming from loudspeakers like smooth-flowing water. Walking around this picturesque park to the northern end of the island, under the second bridge across the Danube that crosses the island, Arpad Bridge, constructed after the war, you will come out at a gray stone breakwater that resembles the bow of a ship.

For the residents of Budapest, Margit Island is a favorite place to stroll and relax. They deservedly call it the "pearl of the Danube."

But this beautiful island had quite a different look in the severe days of January 1945, when fighting was going on in Budapest. For the Germans, pressed into Pest, but still firmly entrenched in Buda, Margit Island was like a forward fire base, from which they could easily look out over the river and Pest bank. The park was laced with trenches and with shell craters. Batteries of cannons and mortars were hidden among the snow-covered and in places shrapnel-riddled trees. Countless machine-gun nests lined the shore. Though the ice on the Danube had been hard for some time (this was an unusually severe winter for Hungary), it would be impossible to cross over from Pest to attack the island. The enemy closely watched all the approaches to Margit Island and kept them in his sights.

Separated from our positions by the ice field on the frozen river, the Germans on the island felt more secure than in other Budapest locales, where no-man's land passed through residential areas and in some places was so narrow that one could hurl a grenade across it. But regardless of how closely the Germans guarded the approaches to the island, the sailors of the reconnaissance detachment penetrated to Margit more than once.

On one occasion, Kalganov sent Lyubisha Zhorzhevich, Aleksey Chkheidze, and Vasiliy Globa on a patrol to the island. It was two days after New Year's Day, which the scouts had celebrated in a special way. Exactly at midnight, on their order, the salvos of several of our artillery battalions crashed down on the cabarets and restaurants where the officers of the German units encircled in Budapest were raising their goblets at New Year's banquets and wishing each other escape from the "pressure cooker" in the new year. Kalganov's detachment had reconnoitered these special New Year's targets.

In sending Zhorzhevich, Chkheidze, and Globa, placed in charge, to Margit Island, Kalganov gave them the mission to find the positions of large-caliber cannons that were shelling our positions in Pest daily. Data were needed on these guns so as to destroy them with precision artillery fire. Along the way, the three scouts were to establish the positions of other enemy forces on the island.

Globa, Chkheidze, and Zhorzhevich departed on their patrol early in the morning, when winter dawn was just slowly beginning. It was easier at that time to slip past enemy picket lines. At the beginning of the day, the Germans were less observant. They were changing their guard shifts and eating their breakfast.

Putting on white smocks, the scouts climbed down the Pest bank onto the ice exactly opposite the island and crawled toward it. The ice was uneven. Early in the winter, when it was thin, it had been broken up by the rapid current. More recently, artillery shells had landed on it, and it had refrozen in irregular mounds. The scouts in places crawled and in places ran from ice hummock to ice hummock, reaching the island safely. They inspected the shore and went up on the island where they believed the enemy would not be able to observe them.

They felt more at ease on the island, though on the ice they were separated from the enemy by greater distances. There was no place to hide on the ice if they were discovered. Here, in the event of danger, they could hide somewhere in the bare but thick bushes, behind trees, or in an empty building of one of the amusement park facilities. The three scouts walked about the island for some time, stealing from tree to tree and bush to bush, from one building to the next. They did this relatively freely in the enormous park, using the lanes and paths. They encountered few Germans. If the scouts spotted any enemy, they easily avoided them.

The scouts spent several hours on the island. They found trenches and machine gun nests along the shore, occupied by perhaps two German companies. Globa, Zhorzhevich, and Chkheidze finally found what they were looking for in a small glade in the heart of the park—the battery of 150mm guns aimed at Pest. The scouts registered the site and set off to return, their mission accomplished.

But even though his mission has been accomplished, a scout, while he is on the enemy side, continues to search, the more so because he always returns by a different route. Globa, Zhorzhevich, and Chkheidze attentively inspected the restaurant and cafe buildings they encountered along the way and carefully looked into several of them. Were there any Germans inside? But the buildings, mostly of light summer construction, were empty. The Germans were either staying warm in shelters they had constructed somewhere under the park's trees or were hunkered down in their trenches.

Almost at the shore, the scouts spotted a white, two-story building with many balconies on the facade, surrounded by precisely trimmed trees and hedges.

"Stop!" Chkheidze whispered to his comrades.

"What is it?" Globa asked.

"There's someone in that building. I heard voices."

"What kind of voices?" Globa looked toward the building. "Let's listen."

The scouts stood and listened.

"I don't hear any voices!" said Globa.

"But I did—like they were shouting." Chkheidze held his ground. "There are Germans in the building!"

"It's unlikely." Globa shook his head in doubt. "They would be freezing in there. Look, Aleksey, all the windows are broken out."

"Just the same, we have to look!" Chkheidze did not back down.

"All right, we'll look," Globa agreed.

"I'll go in alone, just in case," said Chkheidze, "and you wait here for me."

Zhorzhevich and Globa sat down under a powerful old oak tree, its branches covered with blackened, powdery snow, some twenty paces from the whitish building. On the wall facing the scouts was a wide door that at some time had glass in it from top to bottom. There were no tracks toward the porch onto which the door opened. The snow in front of it was unblemished.

Globa and Zhorzhevich watched Chkheidze as he crept along the shrubbery that edged the building. He paused for several seconds and observed, then quickly ran across a small open space that separated the shrubbery from the porch. Then he dashed up onto the porch and through the empty door frame and disappeared inside.

Hardly had Chkheidze entered the building when he pricked up his ears. It seemed to him that he could hear indistinct voices nearby. With his submachine gun at the ready, he pressed himself up against one of the walls and looked around. A semidark vestibule, broken glass on a snow-covered floor, an armchair with its legs sticking up in the air, doors to the right and left, a stairway leading upward—it looked like some kind of hotel. By all indications, there had been no one in the building since the battles for the city had begun. But what about the voices? Chkheidze could still hear them. It seemed like happy shouting, laughter. Who would be amusing themselves here, and why, here, in a thoroughly frozen building, in whose windows remained perhaps not a single unbroken pane of glass?

Hearing voices from up above, Chkheidze began to climb the stairs to the second floor. The voices were becoming more and more distinct. They were coming not only from above, as it had seemed earlier, but from below. What could this mean? From the top step of the stairway, where he stopped, Chkheidze could see that the entire second floor was a large square covered gallery, open in the center. Along the entire gallery were countless doors that certainly must lead into rooms. The inside portion of the gallery was lined with banister railings. There was no roof above the space that they guarded. The winter sky was gray overhead. There was no one visible on the gallery. Chkheidze crouched down, approached the railing, and looked down.

There, in a rectangle formed by the internal walls of the building, a light vapor wafting up under the open sky, was a large swimming pool, lined with light-colored stone. Nude people were splashing without a care in its greenish water. Two were swimming out in the middle, racing each other with flailing arms. Others were sitting around the sides of the pool, some completely naked, some half-dressed, and some in uniforms of the familiar hated dirty green, urging the swimmers on with shouts.

And, of course, none of the Germans even dreamed that the eyes of a Soviet scout were attentively following them from the gallery above. They could not have imagined it. They were in their own rear area, even though it was close to the front. Pressed up against the railing, Chkheidze watched the swimming Germans for some time. He was filled with anger and contempt for them. "We crawl around in the snow, and they set up swimming competitions! They act like they're in a spa!"

Aleksey wanted badly to fire a submachine-gun burst or throw a grenade into the middle of the pool, but he contained himself. A scout was not allowed to open fire if the enemy did not force him into it.

Chkheidze returned to his waiting comrades.

"Let's go and see for ourselves!" Globa decided after hearing Chkheidze's story. "Maybe we can capture a 'tongue'?"

Chkheidze led his comrades to the gallery by the same route that he had taken himself. Sitting in a secluded spot behind the railing of the gallery, all three stared intently at the swimming pool and consulted with each other in whispers. There was no point in trying to capture a "tongue!" There were forty Germans, all of them lumped together, and not one of them was standing off to the side.

"We need to leave!" Globa said in a whisper.

But Chkheidze, not holding back, asked:

"Let me drop a grenade on them!"

Globa objected:

"We don't have the right to take this risk!"

"What risk?" Looking around, Chkheidze pointed at the stairway that they had climbed up. "As soon as I throw the grenade,

I'll run down the stairs into the bushes. The Germans won't be using these steps."

"We have to do it!" Zhorzhevich unexpectedly supported Aleksey. "We raise a commotion in the Germans' rear, their attention is distracted from observation to this place, and during that time we head out across the ice."

"We draw off the enemy's eyes? It sounds good to me!" Globa agreed. "Let's do it, Lesha [diminutive for Lyubisha]! We'll add our submachine guns to his."

Pulling a grenade from the pocket of his pea jacket, he hurled it with a wide swing of his arm across the railing of the gallery into the pool. The scouts opened fire while the grenade was still in the air, extending their submachine guns through the banister railings. The explosion and the hammering of the submachine gun bursts engulfed the Germans. Hurrying behind Globa and Zhorzhevich toward the stairway, Chkheidze glanced back on the run. He saw the crazed bathers in the swimming pool down below, rushing about in all directions. Some were in their birthday suits, others with their uniforms and trousers in their hands, and still others trying to get dressed on the run.

Not two minutes after the explosion of Aleksey Chkheidze's grenade, the three scouts had left the building, burrowed through the bushes, run pushing their way through icy and brittle branches, and raced toward the shore facing Pest. Submachine guns rattled behind them, but they heard no bullets whistling overhead. The Germans were not firing at the scouts. They could only guess that the Germans who had been swimming in the pool were firing up into the gallery.

The scouts quickly climbed down onto the ice and again hurried across the Danube, running from hummock to hummock, skirting patches of open water made by shells. Not one shot was fired at them.

The trio returned safely to the detachment base. After hearing Globa's report and noting the location of the detected enemy battery and other positions on his own map, Kalganov would have liked to reprimand the scouts sternly for giving themselves away for no reason. But the commander was somewhat older than his sailors. He could easily put himself in Aleksey Chkheidze's place at the moment when he found the swimming pool with Germans relaxing in it. He did not lecture them, the more so because the patrol had been concluded safely. Kalganov understood how great was their temptation and doubted he would have acted any differently in the same circumstances.

"Well, all right!" he said. "All's well that ends well," and joked: "It's a pity, of course, that you didn't bring a freshly washed German back with you."

"How would we have led him?" Globa answered a joke with a joke. "Naked like that, everything would have frozen."

CHAPTER FOURTEEN

TWO MAPS

S low January twilights. Infrequent snowflakes were falling, curling in the air. A narrow street, like many others in Pest—the central part of the Hungarian capital. Gray building walls, in places black from soot. Burned-out windows looked like dead eye sockets. Rafters protruded from steep roofs, broken by bombardment. A sign riddled by shrapnel hung askew over a shop window, tightly curtained by iron shutters. Cannon shots thumped infrequently somewhere behind the buildings, and muffled machine-gun bursts were heard sporadically. It was quiet and deserted in this small street, behind the German defensive line, in their rear.

But whose tracks were these on the pavement in the fresh, powdery snow? Who had just passed by here? The tracks led along the pavement toward the arch of a gate, crossed the confined courtyard, disappeared into a gap in the wall of the building, then appeared on the other side and dodged among the ruins of the bombed-out buildings, courtyards, and vacant lots.

But two men were hurrying along the tracks, inspecting them. One was wearing a black cap pulled down over his ears and a long coat. The other was wearing a cloth peaked cap, a jacket with cord on his chest, and high military boots. Both had a three-colored band on their arms with a representation of four black crossed arrows. Hungarian fascists wore these armbands. Along with their German masters, they sat in defensive positions and patrolled in sectors of the city that lay behind the forward edge. They could steal and shoot on sight without fear of punishment. The residents of Budapest tried not to catch their eye.

These two were moving stealthily. Each had his right hand in his pocket. What was driving them? Who were they following?

The tracks that dodged across the vacant lots and courtyards led toward the front line. Five quickly marching people were leaving them. The one in the lead was tall and bearded, wearing a warm brown pile cap, an ample threadbare leather coat, and trousers outside his boots. This was Senior Lieutenant Kalganov. Following behind the commander, slightly stooping but taking long strides, was a young man in a yellowish jacket—Veretenik. Alongside him was a third—small, frail looking, with sharp facial features. He was dressed in a broad, dark cloak, clearly the wrong size, his pile cap tilted on the back of his head. This was Veretenik's bosom friend Malakhov. Behind them moved Maksimenko, cautiously looking toward the flanks from under thick black eyebrows; he had a small but very noticeable black mustache. He was wearing a cape of some indeterminate color. And last moved the large figure of Nikulin, dressed in a green raglan coat, who from time to time unhurriedly looked around.

All five had submachine guns concealed in their clothing. None of them had spotted the two fascist bloodhounds tracking them.

Where were these five scouts coming from? What mission were they executing in the enemy's rear this time?

Back in December, when the detachment had just began to operate in Budapest, the flotilla chief of staff, Captain First Rank Sverdlov, had summoned Kalganov. He gave Kalganov the mission to obtain information on where the enemy had placed mines and scuttled ships in the Danube above Budapest and what routes the enemy was using that were free of these dangers. This information was needed for the future, when the fighting in Budapest would be over, the Danube would be free of ice, and the flotilla's vessels would once again proceed upstream together with the attacking ground forces.

It seemed an impossible mission. The desired data were in documents or on maps, where the navigational situation was recorded. Where could these sources be found? In some enemy headquarters? But how could they determine in what headquarters and how to get there?

The scouts pondered long about how to accomplish the mission. Kalganov always kept in mind the suggestion given him by the chief of staff when he assigned the mission. Navigational documents could be in the directorate of Danube shipping because Hungarian ships, carrying out military movements for the Germans, moved along the Danube above Budapest while the river was not frozen.

From local residents, the scouts already knew that the shipping directorate was located in one of the central sections of Pest, well inside enemy lines. They decided initially to search for anyone who worked in the directorate. Taking advantage of Zhorzhevich's skill with the Magyar language, the scouts questioned local residents. They cautiously helped in the search. After long searches, they finally brought a shipping directorate employee to Kalganov. It turned out that he was a courier and knew nothing about navigational documents. But he said that, in his opinion, the documents might be secured in the classified section of the shipping directorate. And most important, the courier provided the name of one of the workers of this section. True, he couldn't say where this man lived—in the already liberated section of Budapest or in one of the sections of the city still occupied by the enemy.

Nonetheless, the scouts held the end of a thread in their hands. Now they needed to unravel the entire ball. A young woman named Mari, who lived in the building next to where the scouts were barracked, would help them do this.

This wide-eyed, pretty young woman was cordial toward the scouts and guardedly told them about herself. The scouts knew that she was a student at Budapest University, that she lived with her parents, and that her brother, also a student, had been arrested by the Salashisty. They had received no news of him since that moment. Mari talked with anger about how much she hated both the Salashisty and their German masters. After some hesitation and consultation with his comrades, Kalganov decided to enlist Mari for the search. When Zhorzhevich, at Kalganov's direction, asked Mari if she could find anyone who worked in the city information bureau, which everyone knew was in the already liberated section of the city, the young woman cautiously undertook to carry out the instructions.

She quickly brought in a heavyset man whom she recommended as an employee of the address bureau. Kalganov gave him the last name of the classified section clerk and asked him to find the man's address in his card file.

The address was found. It turned out that the clerk lived on one of the streets in our own rear area. That same day, Zhorzhevich and Chkheidze searched him out and brought him to Kalganov. But it seems that this man had an insignificant position in the classified section and knew nothing about navigational documents. Just the same, he was a lucky find. He provided the name and address of his section chief, a senior bureaucrat, who had access to the classified documents. His apartment was in the section of the city still in enemy hands. This meant they had to cross the forward edge.

Kalganov, Zhorzhevich, Chkheidze, Monaykin, and Neverov went out on the patrol. Mari went with them. They crossed over to the enemy's side during daylight, taking advantage of the fact that the enemy's attention was distracted by nearby street fighting.

The early winter dark had already fallen when they approached the building where this bureaucrat's apartment was located. The building looked empty, as did many Budapest buildings in these days. The residents were seeking shelter from shelling and bombing in the basements.

Leaving sailors in a concealed position to observe the streets, Kalganov went into the entryway with Mari and Zhorzhevich and climbed the stairs. Mari pointed to the door of one of the apartments.

The door was locked. As was expected, no one answered their knock. Kalganov asked Mari to attempt to search out the man in the shelter and tell him that his subordinate, the young worker, had come on instructions of the police and was waiting for him by his apartment door.

Kalganov and Zhorzhevich awaited the young woman's return with impatience and trepidation. Then they heard steps coming up the stairs from below, muffled in the quiet of the deserted building. Kalganov and Zhorzhevich could see from the landing. A portly man in glasses, dressed in a high-quality black coat and a black, tall, clipped-fur pile cap, such as well-heeled people wore in Hungary in the winter, was coming up the stairs with Mari. He peered at the two of them in disbelief, as if looking among them for his subordinate. But it was already dark on the landing, and their faces were difficult to make out.

Kalganov gave a signal to Lyubisha, and in a decisive tone, he said to the man:

"Let's go into your apartment. We have to talk to you."

The confused bureaucrat pulled a key out of his pocket with a trembling hand and opened the door. When everyone had entered the apartment and the door was locked, Kalganov said to Lyubisha:

"Explain to him who we are and what we want from him."

Hearing Russian speech, the bureaucrat shuddered and collapsed into a chair standing nearby. He looked at the unidentified men with wide eyes, and even in the dim light of the winter day, it was clear that his glasses had fogged over. The bureaucrat's lips quivered and his teeth chattered. It seemed that he did not understand what they were asking him about. For some time, he was unable to utter a single word. But he gradually recovered, calmed himself, and began to respond to questions.

The bureaucrat said that the shipping directorate had ceased to function after the battle for Budapest had begun, but everything in the directorate building had been left as it was, under guard. The most important documents from the classified section had been turned over to the German liaison officer, but directorate workers had secreted away several documents. The navigational charts for the Danube with annotations on the current situation were in the classified section's safe. Several other documents also remained in the safe and cabinets that specified what places in the channel were dangerous for sailing. But, the bureaucrat said, he did not have the keys for either the safe or the cabinets and did not know who did have them.

How could they get into the classified section? They had to know the layout of the directorate's facilities and how it was guarded. They understood from the responses of the bureaucrat that he himself could provide some information about the condition of the channel. But they needed more time to interrogate him in greater detail. After they questioned him, they could not release him—no one could know about this conversation.

Kalganov decided to take the bureaucrat with them. When he explained this to him through Lyubisha, the bureaucrat asked permission in a trembling voice to say good-bye to his family. Kalganov could not allow this. It was dangerous and could attract attention. But he allowed Lyubisha to tell the bureaucrat that he would be released later to come home. Kalganov sent Mari to the basement to tell the bureaucrat's wife that her husband would be gone for several days on important official business and not to worry.

Winter night had already fallen over the rooftops of Budapest, infrequently cut by the brilliant tracer shells and bullets, when the scouts led the bureaucrat out of the building. Mari went out with them.

The scouts made their way through courtyards and deserted vacant lots almost to the Germans' forward edge. When they approached it, darkness had fallen and curfew time had arrived. Now the German and Salashisty patrols would stop every pedestrian. They had to move stealthily. Not wanting to subject Mari to unnecessary risk, Kalganov suggested that she go ahead alone. Mari departed. If they detained her, she could talk her way out.

The scouts made their way between enemy front-line positions by gaps that they knew—through burned-out buildings, courtyards, and deserted trenches on streets and squares. The bureaucrat followed them obediently. Everything went smoothly. Only at the end of the route, when they had to cross the final street, did a German machine gun fire at the scouts. But they, and with them the bureaucrat, who of course wanted to live, made a dash, and several seconds later they were all safe. They quickly learned that Mari had safely avoided enemy positions and had already arrived.

Now it was possible to question the bureaucrat in greater detail. He told them everything he knew, sketched a plan of the layout of the shipping directorate building, and pointed out the approaches to the building and where they would likely encounter the guard.

While Kalganov and Zhorzhevich conducted all these discussions and were preparing for the patrol, the scouts—this was about a day after their return—received a new and important task: clarify how the Germans were defending the approaches to Erzhebetheid—a bridge located in their rear that linked Buda with a section of Pest they still controlled. The command needed this information to prepare an attack on the axis of the bridge.

This second mission, like the first, was urgent. Consulting with his sailors, Kalganov decided to accomplish both missions simultaneously, operating in two groups. Led by Maksimenko, the first group included Veretenik, Malakhov, and Nikulin. The second group, which was to obtain the documents from the shipping directorate building, consisted of Globa and Chkheidze, led by Kalganov. He carried several explosive charges and ignition fuses to blow the door off the safe.

When everything was ready, Kalganov and Maksimenko, who was fulfilling the duty position of party organizer, reminded everyone that successful accomplishment of both patrols would not only hasten victory but prevent many losses on our side. They were not to spare themselves but to be extremely careful.

At nightfall, both groups crossed through the enemy's forward positions undetected in the riverside sections of Pest and moved off into his rear. After moving a while, the groups split off. Maksimenko led his group toward the bridge and Kalganov his group toward the shipping directorate. Before they split up, they agreed to meet at the end of the night in the ruins of a multistory building that had been destroyed by a direct hit of an aviation bomb.

Nothing broke the night quiet. Even the rumble of battle was quiet, perhaps for just a short time. Holding in the shadows of buildings and fences, from doorway to doorway, from gate to gate, at times remaining concealed in them to observe, Kalganov, Chkheidze, and Globa made their way toward the shipping directorate building. Kalganov confidently led the sailors along unfamiliar streets. He had studied the city plan well and remembered everything the bureaucrat had told him. There was no reason to fear that the bureaucrat had deceived him. For the time being, he remained at the scouts' base and well understood what would happen to him if they discovered that he had knowingly provided false information.

According to the bureaucrat's report, the shipping directorate was located at the end of a street, the second building from the corner, four stories high. Patrols walked past it constantly—there were several other activities on the block.

The scouts had already reached the building that adjoined the shipping directorate and hidden in its doorway. They were deciding how best to enter the building. They couldn't go through the door—it was in plain view and appeared to be locked. The windows of the ground floor were high. But the corner of the building had been damaged by a bomb or shell, and there was a large hole in the wall.

Kalganov wanted to give Globa and Chkheidze the signal to enter through the hole, when behind them, on the street, they heard the rhythmical steps of an approaching person. The scouts hid. Two Salashisty with slung rifles leisurely walked past the entrance. It would not have been difficult for the three of them to deal with two enemy. But the disappearance of the patrol would be quickly noted. And it was not known how much time was needed to search out the documents.

The three scouts patiently waited while the patrol passed.

The patrol walked as far as the shipping directorate building, went past it, and stood on the corner. The scouts listened as someone walked up to them, apparently a meeting patrol. There was an unintelligible conversation, a flame was struck—they were smoking. And again they heard approaching steps, muffled by the snow sprinkled on the asphalt. The patrol was returning. The two Salashisty again passed by the dark entryway where the scouts were hiding.

As soon as the patrol's steps were silent, Kalganov, Globa, and Chkheidze quickly ran toward the building of the directorate and slid through the hole. It was impenetrably dark inside the building. But Kalganov did not take the risk of immediately using his flashlight. Someone outside might spot it. They moved by feel, recalling what the bureaucrat had told them about the layout of the corridors and rooms. They climbed the stairway to the second floor. They groped in the darkness at the end of the corridor for a door covered by soft leather. The bureaucrat said that this door led to the classified section. Picking the lock, they opened the door without difficulty and went in. They cautiously shined their flashlight. It was a modest room. In the middle was a square polished desk, and on the walls were large photographs under glass—steamers and views of the Danube. On the middle of the inside wall was a black iron door. The classified section was to be behind this door.

As one would imagine, the iron door was locked. How would they open it? It would be simplest to blow it open, and they had the explosives to do that. But they wanted to use them only if they could conceal the sound of the detonation in the roar of artillery fire. Otherwise, the explosion would unavoidably attract the attention of the patrols and raise an alarm. As luck would have it, the guns were silent on this night. And all the scouts' plans were based on blowing the door and safe under cover of an artillery barrage.

They decided to attempt to open the door without making any noise. Instructing Chkheidze to watch the streets from the window, Kalganov and Globa began to smash the door open. They fiddled with the lock for a long time, trying quietly to spring the lock with a pry bar they had brought with them. But the lock was too strong. The hours went by, and they made no progress. Kalganov's and Globa's hands were bloodied from working the unyielding metal, but the lock didn't budge.

The night was already over. It would soon begin to get light, and then it would be even more difficult to make their way back without attracting the attention of the patrols.

Convinced that they would be unable to force the door despite all their efforts, Kalganov reluctantly gave the order to withdraw. When they left the shipping directorate building, Kalganov left Globa and Chkheidze in a nearby empty building to observe until his return for any changes in the patrol routine or any other new danger.

Only a short time remained before dawn when Kalganov, as had been agreed, met with Maksimenko and the other scouts in the ruins of the bombed-out building. They also had bad luck. They had been unable to get near the Erzhebetheid bridge. The enemy was extremely vigilant during the quiet hours of the night.

"Well," said Kalganov after listening to Maksimenko, "you didn't succeed at night, so we'll have to do it during the day. I'll lead."

It was already light when the scouts, taking many detours through courtyards and vacant lots to bypass enemy positions, managed to get close to the bridge on the embankment. Hiding among the snow-covered rocks, where the embankment had been destroyed by artillery bombardment, over the course of several hours they conducted observation. Kalganov marked all the enemy positions on a map and noted where the guns that covered the approaches to the bridge were positioned.

The basic information was collected. But the scouts were not accustomed to being limited to the minimum in their achievements. They remained near the bridge to observe what forces and means the enemy was moving across it into Pest from Buda. Having made an arrangement with Maksimenko to meet at the agreed-upon site, Kalganov hurried back to the shipping directorate as soon as it began to get dark.

He found Chkheidze and Globa where he had left them. They reported that nothing had changed in the directorate's vicinity.

The patrols were being conducted by the previous regime.

Waiting until it became dark, Kalganov, Chkheidze, and Globa waited for the patrol to pass by and then slipped into the shipping directorate building by the same route as on the night before, through the hole in the corner of the building. Kalganov hoped that they would be able to use their explosives this night. Our batteries were firing on enemy positions in Pest somewhere not too far away. From time to time, they could hear the explosions of the shells.

Leaving Globa and Chkheidze below near the hole so they could provide timely warning of danger, Kalganov climbed the stairs to the second floor and went to the iron door. He had decided to blow it up himself. Kalganov had studied demolitions back in 1941, when he was being prepared to operate in the enemy's rear in the Moscow area.

Kalganov hung an explosive charge on the door's lock and lit the fuse, then quickly went down the stairs to where his sailors were waiting. There was a thunderous explosion upstairs. But, as if out of spite, there was not a single cannon shot or detonation of a shell at the moment of the explosion. As Kalganov had feared, the explosion drew the attention of the patrols, who apparently were nearby at that moment. The sailors, hiding near the hole, listened as two enemy soldiers ran up, stopped close by, stood silent, apparently to listen, and then conferred in alarmed voices.

"If they stick their noses in here, we'll have to cut them off," Kalganov thought uneasily, though a confrontation with the enemy now did not enter into his calculations.

The enemy patrol continued to talk and then calmed down. They probably concluded that a lost round had exploded somewhere nearby. Their regular gait was heard once again as they disappeared. Now Kalganov and Globa went back upstairs, and Chkheidze remained at his post below.

The explosives had done their work. The heavily damaged lock of the iron door was barely holding. They had no difficulty in prying it open. They easily opened a second door behind the iron door. And finally Kalganov and Globa entered the classified section. Turning on a flashlight, they saw a window covered by heavy curtains, high metal cabinets on the walls, and a massive safe set into the wall between them. While Globa pried at the doors of the cabinets with the pry bar, Kalganov began to attach demolitions to the safe. He did this with great care, trying not to repeat the mistake he made when he blew up his first safe. It was in the fall, in the Kalemegdan fortress at Belgrade, where the headquarters of the German naval forces on the Danube was located, and where the scouts had rushed in at the height of the battle for Belgrade. In his inexperience, Kalganov had attached the charges to the doors of the safe, and after the explosion, only scraps of paper remained in it. Now he attached the demolition charges to the edges of the safe, along the lock and hinges, so that the papers inside would remain intact.

By the time the preparations to blow the safe had been completed, Globa had pried open all the cabinet doors. Kalganov sent him downstairs to Chkheidze's position. Before he lit the fuse, Kalganov decided to gather the documents that might prove useful from the cabinets. In the light of his flashlight, he quickly inspected the papers. Although he knew almost nothing about the Magyar language, from the external appearance he was able with some precision to determine the nature of a document and whether it would be useful. Kalganov found a leather courier pouch in one of the cabinets and shoved into it orders of the German and Hungarian command, a listing of the condition markers on sectors of the channel, reports of the chiefs of ports and captains of ships concerning obstacles they had detected, orders and instructions on shipping, and ships' sailing instructions.

When Kalganov had taken everything from the cabinets that he thought was valuable and stuffed it into the courier's pouch, he lit the fuse and went down the stairs with the pouch to Globa and Chkheidze. They heard the explosion on the second floor.

Kalganov was hoping that this time there would be no serious suspicions on the part of the enemy patrols, the more so because this time the detonation occurred simultaneously with many shell detonations. But several seconds after the detonation, rapidly approaching steps were heard on the street. The scouts listened with alarm to these steps. They were Salashisty, several men, perhaps two patrols coming together, and they were conversing excitedly. They arrived, stood around, went toward the corner and stopped next to the opening, where they argued about something. An explosion in an empty building, if they heard it, could not help but alarm them. Had they come to determine the cause? The scouts waited, prepared for anything.

But in a sharp, demanding voice, the apparent senior among the enemy soldiers cut short the argument. The scouts saw crouching figures in pile caps with high peaks and carbines at port arms silhouetted in the hole in the wall, barely distinguishable in the night darkness. Several Salashisty, whispering to each other, were crawling through the hole into the building, quite near the scouts hiding in the shadows. Holding their breath, the scouts listened as the Salashisty moved past them in the corridor of the first floor, only two or three paces away, and stopped at the end of the corridor, next to the stairway leading upward. If the Salashisty had gone up the stairs, the scouts would have had to follow them and attack them when they reached the second floor landing.

But the enemy patrol, which stood next to the stairs and heard nothing suspicious, apparently was finally convinced that there was no one in the building and both explosions were detonations of lost rounds. How could the Salashisty seriously believe that there could be Russians so far from the forward positions? And why would Russians be in the shipping directorate?

Talking loudly and exchanging smiles, the Salashisty turned around and headed out, apparently now fearing nothing. Their voices and steps echoed loudly in the empty building. They again passed by the scouts and went out by the same path—through the hole in the wall.

As soon as the Salashisty's footfalls disappeared down the street, Kalganov, leaving Chkheidze and Globa near the hole just in case, hurried up the stairs to the safe. The safe door was damaged but still holding. Kalganov began to lever it with the pry bar, and he worked up a sweat before it fell to the floor with a loud thud.

Shining his flashlight into the safe, Kalganov saw a document pouch and papers stacked in neat piles. There was no time to inspect all of them to determine what was valuable and what was not. Kalganov remembered what the bureaucrat had told him: the situation map was in the safe. Therefore he gathered up everything that was in the safe and hurried down the stairs to his awaiting comrades.

The scouts stuffed all the safe's contents into the courier pouch and, taking advantage of the absence of the patrols at that moment, darted through the hole in the wall and ran into the nearest courtyard. There, in a secluded corner, they carefully used their flashlight and inspected everything they had taken from the safe. Among the papers they found a map of the Danube route with minefields and scuttled ships marked on it, done in the form of a ferry pilot's navigational chart. The bureaucrat had not lied. Kalganov secured the chart under his leather coat, considering it the most valuable item captured that night. Thanks to this navigational chart, in the spring, when the flotilla's combat vessels advanced in concert with the attacking forces, they would not be endangered by the mines and underwater obstacles noted on the map.

The senior lieutenant divided the remaining captured documents between Globa and Chkheidze and ordered them to return quickly, while it was still dark. Before he separated from the sailors, Kalganov explained to them the place where he intended to pass through the enemy's forward position with Maksimenko's group. He instructed them to warn our infantry unit so that they would not fire on the sailors. Globa and Chkheidze departed. The commander was confident that they would pass through the front line undetected by the enemy.

The senior lieutenant found Maksimenko at the agreed-upon location. They conducted reconnaissance for an additional day.

Around evening, Kalganov gave the command to return to Soviet lines. Both missions had been accomplished. The priceless pilot's navigational chart was in his breast pocket, along with a city plan of Budapest that contained detailed annotations of the German defense of the Erzhebetheid bridge area.

The scouts moved, avoiding open areas and observing all security measures. They had already gone some distance. When they had crossed a narrow courtyard, bordered on all sides by high walls, Nikulin, who had dropped back, caught up with the group and told the commander:

"There are two men following us!"

Kalganov gave a signal, and all five ran to the entrance of the nearest building. They saw two men in civilian clothes, with armbands, who had appeared out of nowhere. They were arguing about something, gesturing with their hands and looking around.

"Are these the ones?" Kalganov asked Nikulin.

"These are the ones."

How could they break off from this pursuit? Should they lie in wait for them and quietly take them out? This would take time. What if the Germans, to whom these spies had probably already reported seeing suspicious people, came running up? Fire a submachine-gun burst at them? And if the firing served as an alarm signal? Who knew how many Germans and Salashisty were nearby? They had to move undetected and get away as quickly as possible. They could not risk the valuable information they had gathered.

The scouts hurried from the entryway into the building, jumped out a broken window to the other side, and ran across a vacant lot.

Though the forward edge was not too far away, Kalganov led the scouts in the opposite direction, deeper into the enemy-occupied zone. Experience told him that the danger of running into the enemy was far greater near the forward edge. The most important thing now was to shake the pursuit.

Circling through courtyards, the scouts turned again toward the forward edge. They needed to pass through three or four buildings to reach it. Then they were at the last building, and friendly lines were across the street.

But the scouts made a mistake, believing that they were no longer being followed. They heard voices behind them, calling to each other in words of command, then the clatter of boots. The scouts immediately returned to the nearest gate. Hearing their pursuers were running close by, they wanted to continue their flight. But at that moment they again heard the clatter of boots on the pavement. The Germans were returning.

"Go that way!" The senior lieutenant pointed at a narrow passage between two adjacent buildings deep in the courtyard.

The scouts ran into the passage. Behind them, someone was shouting something from the gate. Kalganov looked around. German soldiers with submachine guns at port arms were running into the courtyard right behind their two spies.

The five scouts ran with all their strength, trying to break off from their pursuers, to lose them among the buildings and stone fences. But the Germans did not fall behind. Their tracks were easily followed in the freshly fallen snow. The enemy had not yet spotted the scouts but was gaining on them. Why had they not yet fired a single shot? Perhaps the Germans had been ordered to capture them?

On the run, Kalganov felt for the bulge of the two priceless maps. In another hundred or more paces they might be able to make a run, albeit under fire, for their own positions. But, no, they could not make it. The pursuers were gaining on them. Like it or not, Kalganov had to veer off.

"Into the building!" Kalganov ordered the sailors on the run. All five ran through the open door of the parade entrance of a multi-story gray building with a gold-lettered sign on the facade. They quickly pushed shut a massive, decorated door and pushed a heavy cabinet that lay on the floor amid discarded papers against it. They quickly looked around. It was some kind of directorate. It had a spacious vestibule. A door led off it to the right into a large hall, partitioned off by a wooden barrier, behind which were many writing desks. At the end of the hall were glass barriers with cashier cages. This building was like a bank. A stairway led upward, and beneath it was a door that led downward, into the cellar.

They dragged two large writing desks from the hall and pushed them toward the cellar door so that the enemy could not enter the building through it. Preparation for the defense did not last more than five minutes. Then the scouts took up positions near the windows in the rooms nearest to the vestibule, prepared for battle. The building was suitable for defense. It had a good view from the high first floor windows, which had thick grilles, and the stone walls were thick.

Looking through the window, Kalganov pondered. The building was located on the corner of Vats Street and a small boulevard, beyond which our own positions lay two hundred meters away at an angle in buildings on the opposite side of the street. It was annoying that they had been unable to reach them. They would hold on here, defeat the enemy, and then make their way across.

The Germans, who now had caught up with the scouts, did not make them wait long. Through the window Kalganov could see how many of them were coming toward the building, how they were forming a line and surrounding it.

"Fire!" Kalganov commanded.

Five submachine guns fired out the windows. German submachine guns chattered from all directions in response. Running from window to window, the sailors tried to fire so as to prevent the enemy from getting close to the building. But there were only five scouts and more than forty Germans. All of them were armed with submachine guns and were acting energetically and skillfully. While some conducted continuous fire at the windows, others ran closer toward the walls of the building under the cover of this fire.

The sailors had to change positions more often to fend off the enemy rushes, which now surrounded the building on all sides. But the sides were too unequal. Several minutes after the beginning of the engagement, it became clear that they could not hold on long.

Then Kalganov remembered his flare pistol. Loaded with a white flare cartridge, it was fastened to his belt just in case.

"If I fire a flare, perhaps help will come."

Raising his hand with the flare gun to the window frame, along the edges of which protruded fragments of glass, Kalganov pointed the gun straight up into the air and squeezed the trigger. A ball of blinding white light arched into the gray sky. Returning the flare gun to his belt, Kalganov again grabbed his submachine gun. Several Germans were running straight toward the window where he was standing.

Somewhere up above, on the roof or attic, was a sharp explosion. The entire building shook. Was it a shell? Whose? Another explosion rang out behind the wall. Something fell with a crash. Had the attackers called for artillery fire on the building? But then they would not be staying so close to it.

Shells fell in the street next to the building, in the path of the attackers. They were clearly visible from the window. These were our shells! Yes, it was Soviet artillery. Our artillery observers had spotted the white flare that flew out of the tall building on the corner of Vats Street. They had not seen that Germans were attacking the building and could not know that the rocket had been fired by our scouts. But they opened artillery fire on the building, over which the white flare flew, on the enemy side of the lines, because it had been decided that the enemy must be in the building, which was previously thought to be empty.

The shells, penetrating the roof, were exploding in the attic, shaking the building. Shrapnel of the shells that fell on the street near the building flew into the windows with a whistle, threatening to strike the scouts. But the artillery fire beyond the thick stone walls on the lower floor was less threatening to them than to the Germans outside. Without knowing it, our artillerymen were helping the besieged scouts. Fearing the shelling, the attacking enemy pulled back and took shelter. The scouts were encouraged. Now they had to seize the right moment to break out.

But the firing stopped just as suddenly as it had begun, and the Germans immediately surged toward the building. Firing at the first floor windows from tens of submachine guns, without allowing the defenders to respond, the Germans ran right up to the walls. They did not try to enter the building through the window. But the massive door of the parade entrance was already shaking under their pounding.

"Go upstairs!" Kalganov shouted, understanding that they could no longer hold the first floor.

All five hurried up the stairs that led from the vestibule to the second floor. Hardly had they reached the second floor landing when the entryway door caved in with a crash and the Germans burst into the vestibule.

Hiding in the doorways that led off the landing, the scouts dropped several grenades into the vestibule below. In the fiery smoke they could see several soldiers in green cloaks collapse as the others dashed to the sides. But there were many enemy, and they were particularly energetic in this case. Disregarding their losses, they surged toward the stairway. Nikulin had already received a chest wound. But he did not drop his submachine gun.

Submachine gun bursts and several more grenades dropped below somewhat dampened the Germans' enthusiasm. They stopped attempting to climb the stairs and were hiding behind the protruding walls of the vestibule, firing furiously. Their bullets caused little harm to the scouts, however, who had taken cover behind the doorjambs of the entrances to the second floor. Understanding this, the Germans ceased firing. There was a brief break in the fight.

Could they now break away from the enemy? Kalganov had not thought of a way when, behind them, at the end of the corridor, a submachine gun hurriedly fired a burst, its bullets coming in overhead, breaking up the ceiling plaster.

Now they had to fight off an attack from the rear. A fight broke out in the corridor. Firing broke out simultaneously from the Germans who remained below in the vestibule. Firing frequent but short bursts—they had to conserve ammunition—the scouts did not permit the Germans, who had penetrated into one room on the second floor, to get out into the corridor. But the Germans, poking out from behind the door, were able to fire along the corridor. How did the Germans reach the second floor if the scouts were defending the entrance to it from the vestibule so strongly? Apparently, they had used the fire escape that led up to the windows.

Now the five sailors were located between two fires. It would have been certain death to remain in the corridor. They could only withdraw upward, to the third and remaining floors. And Kalganov again gave the command:

"Go up!"

Firing, the sailors climbed the stairs to the third floor landing. Again they dropped several grenades on the Germans below and stopped them. But not for long. Leaving their dead on the steps and stepping over them, the Germans stubbornly crawled upward. There were many of them, and they pressed the five sailors higher and higher—to the next floor.

Nikolay Maksimenko was wounded in the shoulder. An explosive bullet had struck Malakhov in the leg, and he could not climb the stairs by himself. His comrades helped him, leaving a blood trail on the steps. But, like his wounded comrades, Malakhov, surmounting the pain, continued to fire, though he could barely stand and with each minute was growing weaker from loss of blood.

A burst reached Kalganov also. In the exchange of fire that broke out on the stairway, hardly had he fired a short burst at a fleeting figure in a green cape on the landing below when he felt a blow near his right elbow. His hand burned immediately. He felt with his other hand, and it came away wet. They pain had not yet reached him, but he knew he had been wounded.

"Blood?" asked Maksimenko, who was nearby. "We have to bandage it!"

"There is no time!" Kalganov brushed it off and, clumsily moving his wounded arm, which had now begun to hurt, again took up his submachine gun. In these difficult moments, he did not want the sailors to see that it was becoming more and more difficult for him to hold his weapon.

Now four of the five scouts were wounded. By some miracle, only Veretenik remained untouched.

The scouts retreated upward from one stair landing to the next, firing all the way. But now there was nowhere to retreat to. Several submachine guns rained fire on them from above. It seemed that the Germans had climbed the fire escape to the top floor.

"You'll get yours, Fritzes!" Veretenik shouted, and, struggling, threw his last grenade—an antitank grenade—upward, to the door that led to the top landing.

A heavy explosion shook the stairway, and acrid black smoke engulfed it for several seconds. Not hesitating while the smoke cleared, the scouts threw themselves upward, to where Veretenik's grenade had just exploded. The corpses of the Germans scattered by the shock wave, strewn with fallen plaster, were heaped in the doorways leading from the landing of the fourth floor into the corridor and beyond along the corridor. The scouts took up a new position here.[1]

But how long could they hold out, weakened from wounds, having fired almost all of their ammunition and thrown almost all of their grenades? How long could they hold on, when there were several enemy soldiers for each one of them, when the enemy had encircled the building and was above and below them inside the building? There was no way out. The could not break through to their own positions. All that remained for them was to fight to their last bullet, to their last breath. What about the intelligence information? The information, gained with such difficulty and risk. Would they not be able to deliver it to the command?

With these thoughts in mind, Kalganov took his good hand off the submachine gun and touched the tightly bound sheets of the two maps in his breast pocket. Then he grasped the stock of his weapon again with his fingers—he had to keep firing. He had only enough cartridges remaining for several minutes of fighting. What would happen when he emptied his last magazine? He still had his pistol with two clips. He would save the last bullet for himself.

Our artillery observers were not the only ones to spot the white flare that burned in the gray dusk sky. Those same scouts who were anxiously awaiting the return of their comrades spotted it. Chkheidze and Globa, who for several hours had stood next to a window of a two-story building occupied by our infantry and who knew approximately where Kalganov and the remaining scouts should cross the front line, spotted it. Chkheidze and Globa knew that five of their comrades were trying to cross to our side without the smallest noise, undetected by the enemy. And when they saw that a flare had been fired over a corner building on the enemy side, not from the place where they intended to cross, and heard submachine guns exchange bursts in a firefight, they surmised that their comrades had been forced into a fight. Hardly had the first shots been fired near the corner building when Globa and Chkheidze hurried headlong down the half-destroyed stairs.

"Where is your commander?" they asked the soldiers.

"He's over there, near the window, the battalion commander!" they pointed, and then asked, "Why do you want him, sailors?"

"You can barely hear it—the Germans' firing," replied the sailors. "They've caught our comrades. We have to help them."

"We will always help our sailors," the soldiers said in readiness. "We only need our commander's order."

The major who commanded the battalion, having already noticed the firing in the corner building on the German forward edge, listened to Chkheidze and Globa, then said:

"I'll send up a company. We will ask the artillerymen for fire support."

Several minutes later, they heard the reports of cannons and the chattering of submachine guns. The smoke of explosions curled from the windows of the building on the opposite side of Vats Street, which the Germans were defending. Taking advantage of the fact that the enemy ceased firing under the artillery barrage, the infantry crossed the street in small groups in rushes and ran to the entryways of the buildings and to the courtyards, preparing for a fight. But the Germans did not engage them. Even before our artillery pounded them, they had heard firing behind them, in the bank building, and had become alarmed. Little did they know that a battle was being waged in the corner building with only five surrounded Soviet scouts and that somehow these Russians had come from the Germans' own rear.

The infantry were hurrying along the street and straight across the courtyard to the corner building, guided by the sounds of the firing. Globa and Chkheidze were running toward the building along with the soldiers. They reached the bank. Germans were hustling around it, firing their submachine guns at the windows of the upper floors. Vasiliy Globa brought his submachine gun up and fired a burst. Aleksey Chkheidze, pulling a grenade from the pocket of his pea jacket, ran first to the entrance. At the threshold of the carved oak doors, torn from their hinges and splintered by bullets, were the remnants of the cabinets and tables that barricaded the entrance from within. In the spacious vestibule, lying behind the railings of the stairways, were several Germans furiously firing their submachine guns upward. Taking cover behind the doorpost, Chkheidze threw in a grenade. Globa, who had caught up with Chkheidze, threw his grenade in at the same time. Two explosions rang out. Remnants of the stair balusters flew about in the black smoke. Several bursts of submachine gun fire were directed into the still hanging smoke. And the two sailors, along with the infantry, burst into the vestibule.

"Where are our men!" Chkheidze asked Globa in alarm, running up the stairs. Who of their five comrades remained alive?

Up above, around the corner of the stairway, on the fourth floor landing, a grenade exploded, covering the shouts and shots coming from that quarter. Debris flew past Globa and Chkheidze with some force. A dead German fell at the feet of the sailors as they ran upward, his helmet bouncing off the steps as it rolled downward.

Globa and Chkheidze ran to the fourth floor landing.

"Zhora!" they shouted in joy, as they spotted the tall figure of Veretenik in the doorway leading into the corridor. His leather jacket was tattered; his hair, tangled and plastered with dust, fell from his uncovered head onto his forehead; his face looked black, as if covered with soot.

"You've arrived!" Veretenik shouted.

"Where are the others?" Chkheidze asked him.

In place of a response, Veretenik motioned with his hand, pointing upward on the stairs. Everything changed in the bank building from the moment when, after the explosions of the two sailors' grenades, Globa, Chkheidze, and the infantry ran into the vestibule. The attacking Germans now became the defenders. Those of them who had moments before been pressing the five sailors from below had been destroyed by the grenades and sub-machine gun bursts. Those who had remained uninjured had fled. Those Germans who had earlier made their way into the upper floors by the fire escape were now cut off from below.

Going around the infantrymen running up the stairs, Veretenik, Globa, and Chkheidze hurried to the aid of their comrades. Encouraged by the rapidly arriving help, the other four scouts threw themselves with double effort at the enemy who moments ago had been so persistent but now was slinking away.

Now no longer defending but pursuing, Kalganov forgot about the pain of his wounded arm and ran along the steep iron steps that led to the highest landing in the attic and fired a fanning burst into the semidarkness. Not a shot was fired in response. The iron roof above Kalganov's head rattled with the muffled sounds of men running across it.

"There you are!" Arming his last grenade, he hurried toward the dimly lit opening at the end of the attic, which was a half-opened door. Pushing on the door with his hand, Kalganov looked out at the sloping roof with its fresh covering of snow. Several Germans were running at full speed toward its edge, above which protruded the round handrail of the fire escape, leaving the dark spots of tracks behind them in the snow. Summoning all his strength, Kalganov threw his grenade right behind them and, recoiling from pain in his agitated wound, started back down the steps into the darkness of the attic. Past him, toward the exit onto the roof, burst Veretenik, his submachine gun at the ready, and behind him yet another sailor. Kalganov looked around in the semidarkness of the attic: Globa and Chkheidze! Did this mean that they had brought help?

Not ten minutes had passed from the moment that Globa and Chkheidze had burst into the bank with the infantry. During this time the outcome of the battle had been decided. Not a single

German remained in the building—only their bodies piled up in the vestibule, on the stairway, in the corridors, in the attic, and on the roof. Kalganov had the scouts quickly collect the documents and medals from the dead. He took four iron crosses and several identification booklets. The senior lieutenant opened one of them. It was not an ordinary soldier's identification booklet, but that of an SS soldier, with a portrait of Hitler on the inside cover. This was the enemy they had been engaging!

Now they could not waste a moment. The enemy, alarmed that an entire Russian unit had broken through into his forward edge, had opened heavy fire on the bank building with machine guns and submachine guns. Running Germans were seen through the windows of adjoining buildings, in the courtyards, on the other side of the fences. With each second, there were more of them. The captain who commanded the infantry company said to Kalganov:

"They are cutting us off. We must withdraw before it is too late. You who are wounded should withdraw first."

The infantry and sailors abandoned the building, covering each other with fire. The enemy, who had brought in fresh forces, had begun to move in from several directions.

Comrades helped their wounded to walk. Chkheidze supported Nikulin, and Globa assisted Maksimenko, who had lost a lot of blood. Veretenik carried Malakhov. During the entire course of the battle, but especially after Malakhov had been wounded, Veretenik tried to remain close to him and give him encouragement.

It was not easy for one man to carry Malakhov, and Veretenik tired. The enemy was firing not only at the bank building but also at the street intersection near it, trying to cut this sole path of retreat. They had to cross an open area that was under fire as rapidly as possible.

"Drop me!" Malakhov said to Veretenik, "or we'll both go down. Leave me here, then pull me out later."

But how could he leave his friend under fire?

It is not known what fate would have befallen these two inseparable friends if assistance had not arrived—a female medic and two Hungarians, residents of a nearby building, who voluntarily came out to help her. They placed Malakhov on a stretcher and the four of them, with Veretenik's help, carried their patient from the intersection under fire on the run. Fortunately, no one was hit.

Several minutes later, Malakhov and everyone who had carried him were safe.

Thus, on 17 January 1945, concluded the patrol that had lasted for three days. Leaving the hospital, Kalganov turned over to headquarters both maps, paid for with his blood and the blood of the sailors who had accompanied him. These were the navigational chart of the Danube and the marked map of enemy positions in the area of Erzhebetheid bridge.

CHAPTER FIFTEEN

BUDAPEST UNDERGROUND

Kalganov buried his chin in the dry, biting snow. Bullets whistled over his head with a nasty, ripping sound. A German machine-gun hammered somewhere up ahead, quite near. It seemed that it would not stop its tiresome, dangerous firing.

The snow driven into his patchy beard made his chin cold. But he had to lie immobile: the machine-gun continued to fire. "What's he going to do, fire the whole belt?" Kalganov was annoyed. "My beard will freeze to the ground while he finishes." Carefully rotating his head, he looked to the flanks. Sailors Globa and Chkheidze also lay spreadeagled several paces from him in the snow, which at night appeared blue-gray. Up ahead a hundred paces were the blackened skeletons of a totally burned-out two-story building and a half-destroyed stone fence. The machine gun was pounding from somewhere in these ruins.

"We have to pull back! As soon as this firing stops."

The machine gun's hammering abruptly ceased.

"Pull back one at a time!" Kalganov shouted in half voice.

Pushing himself from the snow-covered ground with both hands, tall Globa quickly jumped up. Crouching over, he rapidly made his way past Kalganov. At that same instant, as if suddenly remembering, the machine gun again hammered from the burned-out building.

Turning his head, an agitated Kalganov followed Globa with his eyes. Would he make it? He did make it. Globa should wait where a German tank, destroyed some time ago, was silhouetted on the edge of the square. The rallying point was behind the tank.

The machine gun was quiet again.

Light on his feet, Aleksey Chkheidze immediately broke for the tank. His modest, adroit, youthful figure in a tightly belted smock rushed toward the hulk like a whirlwind. Machine-gun bullets marked his route. But Kalganov was confident that Aleksey would make it.

"Now it's my turn."

Kalganov managed to make it part way. Because of his height, he perhaps was more noticeable than the others. A machine-gun burst stitched the snow nearby. Kalganov hit the ground, then jumped up again when the machine gun stopped firing. He ran toward the tank hull. Another machine-gun burst. But he had already run behind the tank, when suddenly his foot fell into something and he felt a sharp pain in his knee. He could hear the bullets splattering with a hollow sound on the tank's armor above him. "Let them!" He was already safe behind the tank.

"What did I run into?" Kalganov looked around. "Ah, a man-hole!" He pulled his foot from the crack between a dislodged round manhole cover and the edge of the hole. He crawled toward the sailors who had sought shelter behind the huge black tank, its top sprinkled with snow.

Other machine guns joined the weapon that was still firing at the tank. The enemy was taking this seriously. Now, a white, rapidly spreading radiance flickered beyond the tank—the Germans had fired an illumination rocket.

The flare went out, and the machine guns ceased firing. The enemy was calming down. The scouts looked at their comman-der in anticipation. But he said nothing. He ran his fingers across his frozen beard, combing the snow out of it. The senior lieutenant had still not decided whether to repeat the attempt somewhere else. How much ground they had covered over the past four nights here, in the southern part of Budapest, in Budafok, trying to penetrate through the enemy's forward edge! It was now more difficult to do this than at any previous time. The encircled Germans, pressed in from all directions, driven from almost all sections of the city, were still holding on to the right bank, in Buda. Their positions extended along the steep Fortress Hill, bounded by a high stone wall. Behind this wall was the enormous Royal Palace and many other old buildings, constructed long ago.

All the enemy forces that remained in Budapest were drawn toward Fortress Hill, where Colonel General Wildenbruch, the commander of the surrounded enemy grouping, had his headquarters. The circle of his defenses had been reduced, but this enabled it to be more dense. Each meter of space in front of the forward edge was inspected by a host of enemy eyes both day and night and subject to observed fires.

In addition, our command, to finish off the enemy's Budapest forces more quickly, had to know where and how the artillery batteries were disposed in Buda and what forces the Germans had in various sectors of the defense. The Soviet command also had to find out the enemy's plan. Did he intend to break out toward his own forces who were attempting to relieve him?[1] To answer these questions, knowledgeable "tongues" had to be captured. The scouts of our units operating in Budapest had already attempted to reach Fortress Hill through enemy positions many times. But the enemy's defensive ring was too dense.

All attempts were unsuccessful. And, therefore, because other scouts had failed, the mission was assigned to Senior Lieutenant Kalganov's Danube scouts, about whose successful patrols even the *front* commander was well aware.

Kalganov's scouts had now attempted to carry out this difficult task several times. They tried to make it to Fortress Hill through the German forward edge by vacant lots and courtyards or to go through attics and basements—all to no avail. The enemy, sensing his end was near, had become vigilant as never before.

It was quiet. Only isolated rifle shots rang out infrequently somewhere, or a muffled short burst of automatic weapons fire was loosed.

Should they try again? Kalganov looked into his scouts' faces, glowing whitish in the semidarkness under their black naval pile caps. If he gave the order, they would follow him under enemy fire again. But did he have the right to risk their lives in vain? People would die, and the mission would remain unaccomplished. They had to try again, but not this night. Now the alerted Germans would remain on their guard until morning.

"We are going back!" Kalganov said unhappily.

Thirty minutes later, they arrived at their apartment, situated deep in the courtyard of a building on the outskirts of Buda. Here the scouts rested, discussed their actions on patrols, listened to political information briefings provided from time to time by Gura, Maksimenko, or their commander, and prepared for new missions.

When Kalganov, Globa, and Chkheidze came in, a fire was burning brightly in the stove and a large teapot snorted away happily. Those who had remained behind at the "base" were awaiting their return. They did not question the arriving scouts as to the success of their effort. Their appearance spoke clearly— they were empty-handed again.

Kalganov refused tea and food and a hot cup to warm himself. He hung his submachine gun by its sling on the bedpost and collapsed on the cot in his quilted jacket. One of the scouts caringly spread a cloak over their commander.

Disappointment and anger gnawed at him and kept sleep away. Moreover, his knee, twisted on the edge of the manhole, hurt, and still more his right arm—the bullet wound he had received three weeks earlier in Pest, during the engagement in the bank building, had not healed. Kalganov had been forced to go to the hospital with a gunshot wound near his elbow. The bone was injured. They put a cast on his arm and told him it would take some time to heal. But when he learned from his visiting scouts that the command had given the scout detachment the mission to penetrate to Fortress Hill, he firmly resolved to participate in the patrol. The doctors protested. They wanted to evacuate him to the rear and not return him to duty. But Kalganov was firm. They removed the cast and placed a bandage on his arm. He returned to his sailors with his arm in a sling and the same day reported to the command: "I am ready to accomplish the mission."

Now, he lay covered from the neck down, disappointed and angry, having lost any hope of sleep. Feeling the dull pain in his wounded arm, he agonizingly thought about how to capture a "tongue." Day after day, crawling under fire along and across no-man's land, they had been unable to penetrate to Fortress Hill. Then he had stumbled into the manhole and banged up his leg. He stretched out his arm to rub his twisted knee and froze, captured by a thought that came to him suddenly. "What if?"

Unbelievable! Could it work? What if they got to Fortress Hill not through the German forward edge, but under it? They could climb down into a manhole and walk through the sewer pipes. He recalled how, when they were still fighting in Pest, several times they had to look into the manholes along the roads. Fairly large pipes ran between the manholes—large enough for a man to move through. Perhaps it was the same here in Buda?

"We'll try it!" Kalganov grew excited. "But we have to find out how to get there. The underground sewer system is certainly an entire network. If we proceed without a plan, we might end up somewhere where we don't want to go, or nowhere at all. We want to come out in the area of the Royal Palace, where Wildenbruch's headquarters is most likely to be. Only there can we capture the most valuable 'tongues.' If only we could find someone who knows the layout of the underground sewer system! Who knows how much time it would take us to reconnoiter the system on our own!"

Now Kalganov was wide awake. The thought that perhaps they could get to Fortress Hill under the ground would not leave him.

In the morning, having given the concept much consideration during the night, Kalganov shared his idea with his comrades. Everyone liked it. But how would they find a reliable route underground? They pondered together over this for a long time. Finally, the commander said:

"We have to go around to all the cellars where people are hiding. Ask for a specialist on the sewer system, but don't say why a specialist is needed. There may be some enemy hiding among the population."

The remainder of the night and all of the following day, the scouts went around to basement after basement. It was unbearable to the population to be huddled together in shelters for now the third month, starving and awaiting death by aircraft bomb or artillery shell. The uninvited "defenders"—the Germans—had long ago grown tired of the people, who were waiting impatiently for the end of the Germans dug into Fortress Hill and for peace to come to the city. The residents of Budapest were glad to give the Russians all the help they could.

Around evening, the sailors finally brought in two men to the senior lieutenant. Kalganov questioned them with the assistance of Lyubisha Zhorzhevich. One turned out to be a sheet metal repairman. But it became clear that he knew absolutely nothing about the layout of the sewer system in Buda, and he was dismissed immediately. The other, already somewhat senile, explained that he was a pensioner and had worked many years in the Budapest municipal department as an engineer responsible for the sewer system. He expressed willingness to help the Russians. When asked whether he knew the layout of the sewer pipes and manholes that led to Fortress Hill, he gave an affirmative response. "What is the diameter of the pipe?" Kalganov asked. The old man replied, "It varies. In some areas, one can move at a crouch." Kalganov put paper and pencil on the table in front of the old man and asked him to draw a precise sketch of Buda's sewer system and mark on it the pipe diameter and the manhole locations. The old engineer, stretching his memory, worked several hours on the sketch. Although he did not know why the Russians wanted this information, he surmised it was needed for some military purpose, and he feared making a mistake. They did not rush him. Let him recall everything exactly.

The sketch was finally ready. Kalganov thanked the old engineer and dismissed him. The scouts generously provided the old man with bread and canned meat from their ration packets.

The scouts' commander sat over the sketch for a long time, cross-checking it with his map. If the sketch was accurate, they could move through the sewer system, hunched over to be sure. If the pipes were not full of sewage, they could make it to the manholes located close to the Royal Palace. They could hope that the passageways, which lay sufficiently deep in the ground, were intact and not caved in as a result of bomb or artillery shell detonations.

Kalganov put together a plan that envisioned emerging from a manhole somewhere near the palace, capturing a "tongue," and returning with the "tongue" by the same route. For this mission he had to take several of his toughest and cleverest scouts. Kalganov informed the command of his plan, and they approved it.

Before they could begin such a risky patrol, the men had to be prepared and to conduct preliminary reconnaissance. Kalganov had thoroughly studied the sketch drawn by the old pensioner. When it got dark, so as not to alert the enemy, Kalganov led his group toward the destroyed tank—the same spot where their last effort to make it to Fortress Hill had ended unsuccessfully.

The enemy could not see the scouts behind the tank. According to the sketch, they could begin their route at the same manhole where Kalganov had twisted his knee. They moved the heavy manhole cover aside, and the commander, turning on his flashlight, climbed down into the deep chamber on iron rungs affixed to the stone sidewall. At the bottom of the chamber was knee-deep, stinking slush. Apparently, during the fighting the sewer system had been damaged somewhere, and in some places the sewage had stopped flowing out of it. Kalganov shone the light on the wall. As indicated on the sketch, a one-meter-diameter pipe went through the chamber toward the German side. Crouching, Kalganov resolutely crawled into this pipe.

Time and time again bumping his head on the slimy ceiling of the pipe, Kalganov walked forward, moving his boots through the motionless, foul-smelling slush. With each step the stench became more unbearable. It became increasingly difficult to breathe. There was almost no good air in the pipe.

But Kalganov continued to move straight ahead. He did not keep his flashlight on but only infrequently shone it for a second or two to light up the path in front of him. He was worried about the sudden appearance of another chamber in front of them.

Occasionally he turned around and listened—were the rest moving? They were coming! But with each step he became more convinced that there was no point in going on. He took a breath and almost passed out. Finally, he stopped and turned around.

"We are going back!"

With difficulty, the scouts turned around and went back to the chamber. Some were barely breathing and had to be dragged out. Having climbed back up to the destroyed tank, they all lay exhausted in the snow, greedily gulping the fresh, frosty air.

It was clear to Kalganov that not everyone he had brought along this time would have the strength to make the difficult journey, even if they wore gas masks. Would a gas mask even help them? He had to select the toughest of the tough, the strongest of the strong. This time they had moved not more than two hundred meters, and many of the men were almost completely exhausted. The route to the Royal Palace would be many times longer, and, perhaps, the farther they moved, the more unbearable would be the condition of the pipes.

The mission was set to depart the following night, the night of 7 February [1945]. They had to hurry. The day of the final assault on the last German positions in Budapest was approaching.

Kalganov devoted an entire day to preparation. Of those who had gone into the sewer with him, after the "test" he selected the strongest: Andreev, Gura, Kotsar, Globa, Chkheidze, Nikulin, and Malakhov. Of course, Lyubisha Zhorzhevich was included in the group. Lyubisha was clever and strong. Before the war, he had been a boxing champion in Belgrade. If they were to capture a prisoner and tie him up, Lyubisha would be a good man to have along. In addition, Lyubisha knew both German and Hungarian and would be irreplaceable in the event they had to monitor German conversation or interrogate a prisoner on site.

Kalganov divided the scouts into two groups and placed one under the command of Andreev. He commanded the second group himself. Several men from the naval infantry brigade were also included in the group, along with the scouts. Both groups were to commence movement together and, upon reaching a juncture in the sewer system, separate so that each came to the surface at a different point near the Royal Palace.

The manhole through which Andreev's group was to surface was, according to the sketch, behind Magdalene Church, near Capistrano Square, not far from the palace's internal gates. Kalganov's group was to reach the manhole located near the King Mat'yash Well, not far from the internal gates of the castle. Kalganov selected these two as the most suitable of all the exits to the surface.

The scouts set out on this unusual patrol at nine o'clock in the evening of 6 February, when the darkness of the winter night lay securely over the city, broken infrequently by tracer shells and rounds. They carried gas masks and a supply of ammunition and grenades. Just before their departure, as they always did, they conducted a short, all of five minutes, party-Komsomol meeting. "Remember," the commander said, "we are setting out on a mission like no other that we have ever done. The most important thing is to preserve our composure. Everyone keep your wits about you. If one person loses self-control, it will prevent everyone else from moving. There is no place to turn around in the pipe. Maintain your courage!" "We will be strong!" was the sailors' response. But they understood that it would be difficult.

The scouts moved to the destroyed tank that stood in no-man's land undetected by the enemy. Several sailors accompanied them, and Kalganov ordered them to take up positions around the tank and guard the manhole until the scouts returned. This precaution was necessary because the enemy was nearby.

Kalganov climbed down into the chamber first. He turned on his flashlight and, crouching down, began crawling through the pipe. Behind him proceeded the remaining men. Last came a communications specialist with a telephone set and wire reel on his back. The wire came off the reel and fell into the slush on the bottom of the pipe, then stretched back toward the manhole. From the manhole, the wire went from no-man's land toward our front line and beyond to the command post of the general officer who commanded the units preparing to attack Fortress Hill. The general, whom Kalganov had briefed before departure, said that he would wait next to the telephone. It was recommended that the initial report concerning the results of the reconnaissance be transmitted by telephone directly to the general. Upon completion of the mission, if it was possible, they should leave observers near the Royal Palace who would continue to report anything worthwhile by land line.

The scouts moved slowly along the pipe. They went past the spot they had reached the last time. An unexplored route lay ahead. Kalganov used his light with great care, turning it on only for a second or two and lighting the area not directly in front of him but to the side, on the wall of the pipe covered with globs of slime.

He warned his subordinates that no one except him was to use a light. They proceeded, observing the utmost quiet. Only the slush splashing under their feet and heavy breathing through their masks could be heard.

They had to move crouched over the entire time, except when they went on all fours, involuntarily plunging their hands into the cold, sticky goo to support themselves on the bottom of the pipe. The stench penetrated through their gas masks. Now and again, it was unbearable, and their hands went up to their masks to tear them off.

Their energy was being expended quickly. Kalganov decided to call a short break. Removing the sweat-streaked rubber mask from his mouth, he passed the word along the file:

"How is it in the rear—is everyone keeping up? Does the telephone work?"

"Everyone is moving!" he heard in response. "But the telephone doesn't work."

The telephone operator reported that he was unable to communicate with the command post because there was a leakage of current, perhaps because of a break in the insulation somewhere in the wire.

"The insulation can't bear up under these conditions, but we can!" Kalganov thought to himself.

They would move on without communications. The telephone operator went back; he had become superfluous. After a short rest, the group moved ahead. Everyone was tired. It was not easy to move constantly bent over in the terrifying closeness and stench. And they needed to conserve their strength. By Kalganov's calculations, based on the sketch, they had to move underground in these conditions for several kilometers and the same distance on the return trip. And they needed some energy to operate above ground. Perhaps they would have to fight to capture a "tongue" or break away from pursuit.

Kalganov provided for additional short breaks to conserve energy. During these moments of rest, the commander did head counts to ensure that no one had fallen behind or lost consciousness because of the foul air. They had now been moving more than two hours. Everyone was holding up.

By his reckoning, they had long ago passed under the enemy's defensive line and were probably already in the rear of his forward positions. Several times they listened as the ground shook over their heads, followed by a deep rumble. This should be shells fired by our artillery deep into the enemy rear.

They passed through several chambers that joined the pipe with a manhole to the street surface. Approaches to these chambers were made especially carefully. Passing through one of these chambers, they heard the snow alongside the manhole cover crunch under heavy footfalls. They heard the muffled sounds of voices several times through the walls. Perhaps in these places the pipes passed close to underground bunkers in which the surrounded Germans were huddling together.

After three hours of movement, they reached the juncture in the pipe where the group was to divide. Before this, they had come upon other branches and intersections of the underground pipes.

Under the light of his flashlight, Kalganov had compared these with the sketch he had received from the old engineer before crossing them so as not to veer off track.

They stopped for a moment. Shining his flashlight on the sketch, the commander confirmed that he was not mistaken. In a whisper, he ordered:

"Andreev—to the left!"

The order was quietly passed along the file. Kalganov moved into the pipe that went off to the right, with the scouts of his group behind him.

According to the sketch, just a short distance remained from the branch to the manhole where they were supposed to surface. The sewage standing in the bottom of the pipe now did not reach their knees—this section of the sewer system was apparently situated higher than the previous sections. It would have been easier if the journey up to this point had not already worn the scouts down. The gas masks did not protect them from the stench, and they began to feel lightheaded. The men forced themselves to move forward only by the force of their will. Their backs and legs hurt, and they desperately wanted to stand erect. But there was no place to stand up—their shoulders were hard up against the round stone arch.

But here Kalganov took several more steps and impatiently straightened up to his full height. The pipe had ended and he was standing in a chamber. The stagnant air of the manhole chamber seemed fresh and clean to him after the suffocating atmosphere of the pipe. It was pitch dark all around and above him. Kalganov turned on his flashlight and shone it around. The blackened circular brick walls that had been laid long ago were crumbling in some places. Right-angled iron rungs driven into the masonry led upward to a tightly closed manhole cover. There were not many rungs—some had long ago fallen out of the water-soaked bricks. The yellowish light reflected off the sewage. Kalganov extinguished the flashlight and looked at his illuminated watch face. It was two o'clock. They had been moving through the sewer system for approximately four hours.

The remaining scouts crawled from the pipe into the chamber. It was difficult for everyone to fit in the chamber; they stood pressed tightly against each other.

It was quiet as before. They all remembered the order they had received about silence. The enemy could be directly overhead.

Lyubisha Zhorzhevich attempted to climb the iron rungs, but could not—too many rungs were missing.

"Stand on our shoulders!" Kalganov said to him.

The scouts stood next to the wall, pressed even more closely together. Lyubisha scrambled up on their shoulders and reached up to the manhole cover. He pressed his ear against it and listened for some time. He heard no sounds from the ground level except occasional small arms firing from somewhere at the forward area. Apparently there were no enemy near the manhole cover. Zhorzhevich, bracing his arm against the top rung, pushed up on the manhole cover with the other arm. It did not budge. He pushed again. The manhole cover was firmly in place. Perhaps something was holding it down?

Pushing with his shoulder on the manhole cover with all his might, Lyubisha tried to dislodge it. The cover held on as though it had been welded in place. Exhausted, Lyubisha jumped down from his comrades' shoulders. Another scout climbed up to the manhole cover in his place. He pushed for some time but could not move it.

Kalganov impatiently glanced at his watch. They had been working on the manhole cover for almost half an hour! How much longer would it take? Would they have to return empty-handed and would this entire difficult journey have been made in vain?

"We'll have to knock it out!" Kalganov decided. Under their feet, several bricks that had popped out of the chamber facing lay in the mud at the bottom of the chamber facing. They gave one of these to Zhorzhevich, who had once again climbed up on his comrades' shoulders. Zhorzhevich began carefully, so as not to make any loud noise, to beat on the bottom edge of the manhole cover with the brick.

The muffled, somewhat ringing blows of the brick on the iron struck alarm in the hearts of everyone. Would the enemy up above hear these blows? Perhaps, attracted by the suspicious noises, the Germans were already standing at the manhole cover, holding their weapons at the ready.

There was a sharp, scraping noise overhead. A gust of fresh, frosty air blew in. They had finally succeeded in dislodging the frozen manhole cover.

Lyubisha levered the crumbled brick into the gap formed by the edge of the manhole and its cover. Widening this gap, he carefully moved the manhole cover aside. Those standing in the darkness below could not see what Zhorzhevich was doing, but they listened as he crawled outside. Making an effort not to drop the manhole cover loudly, he again moved it back in place.

It was deathly silent. The scouts waited. Zhorzhevich should be looking around to determine if the remaining scouts could come to the surface. Agonizing minutes passed. The scouts listened in silence. There was not a sound on the surface.

What was happening with Lyubisha? Had the enemy taken him? Five minutes passed, then ten. There was a light tap on the iron lid overhead. Then another and another. As agreed upon, this was the three knocks on the manhole cover by Zhorzhevich. This meant they could come out.

The manhole cover scraped as it was moved aside. The dull gray circle of the aperture appeared. Rain clouds covered the night sky. Into the opening, into the faces of the scouts, fell large, ragged clumps of wet show—it was falling everywhere. The silhouette of a head in a pile cap showed on the dark gray background of the sky at the edge of the manhole. It was Zhorzhevich. He whispered loudly:

"Come out."

Malakhov and one of the naval infantrymen climbed on their comrades' shoulders toward the manhole opening and crawled through it. They closed the manhole cover behind them so that an open manhole would not attract the attention of any Germans who might pass by. Kalganov and Nikulin remained in the chamber below, as a reserve. The senior lieutenant had correctly decided that small groups of two or three men could operate more successfully on the surface.

Lyubisha and the two with him, after closing the hatch, quickly ran behind a low parapet that bordered a small square. The dark mass of the palace, covered by a thin layer of untouched snow, rose up dimly in the overcast winter night beyond the parapet. "I've looked around," whispered Lyubisha. "There are no Germans in the immediate area. We have to search them out."

On the opposite side of the small square from where the scouts were positioned were the dark contours of closely standing multistory buildings. On that side, explained Lyubisha, he had heard someone's footfalls. It appeared that the path from the palace toward the front line crossed this very place. And in general, here in their own rear, around their headquarters, the Germans had to think they could move about freely. If only the hour were a bit later. But a headquarters hardly sleeps at night, especially now, when the Germans were being compressed in an encirclement; they should not be sleeping.

The scouts quickly ran across the square toward the buildings. They crowded under the arch of the nearest gate, the iron-latticed doors of which stood half open. They crept up and listened.

They had to wait for some time. Snow continued to fall in large, congealed lumps. Their clothing that had become thoroughly wet during their journey was quickly turning white, and severe cold was taking hold of their feet in their wet boots, swollen from sewer water. The scouts were frozen. Their bodies quietly shivered in the effort to get warm.

Then they heard steps at the far end of the pavement. Several people were coming toward them. The steps approached quickly. The scouts readied themselves. Now the walkers were at the gate.

Lyubisha, his back pressed to the wall, extended his arm back in warning and touched the arm of Malakhov, who was standing behind him. This meant "get ready!"

A group of German soldiers walked past the gate. Their figures, in baggy capes with high-peaked caps worn low, appeared fleetingly one behind the other on the other side of the whimsically decorated gate. Was this the changing of the guard? Reinforcements to the front line? There were too many of them to attempt a capture. And there was no point in taking a "tongue" from among simple soldiers. An officer was required, and not an ordinary officer, but a staff officer, one who would be well-informed.

Agonizing minutes of anticipation passed. Then Lyubisha turned around and nodded his head at the scouts standing behind him. Two quarreling voices could be heard from the same direction the Germans had come a short while ago. They were arguing in Hungarian. Lyubisha understood immediately: Salashisty! It would not have been difficult to handle these two, even though they were drunk. But was it worth it to take any of them? The Germans would hardly trust these stooges with serious military information.

The Salashisty passed near the gate. From their arguing, Lyubisha caught that they were returning to the front line and for some reason were very unhappy with each other.

The Salashisty disappeared, and their drunken voices grew quiet.

The minutes again dragged on in anticipation.

Finally, new footfalls were heard approaching the gates. One man was walking alone, quietly, unhurriedly. He came even with the gates. Hiding in their shadows, Lyubisha looked him over. A *furazhka* with a high crown, a broad cloak. An officer!

Lyubisha waited. The walker passed the gates. Lyubisha slipped out of the gate behind him and with a calculated movement struck the German on the back of the head with the butt of his submachine gun. Malakhov threw himself at the German at the same time and, grabbing him, fell on the pavement. The German's *furazhka* flew from his head. Stunned, he did not utter a sound. They dragged the "tongue" to the gates, gathered up his *furazhka* so as not to leave any signs, put it back on the officer's head, firmly pushed a gag into his mouth, and tied his hands behind his back. He still had not come to. Lyubisha was worried: had he struck him too hard? No, he was breathing.

Taking advantage of the fact that there was no one else on the square, they quickly dragged the prisoner over to the manhole. No one noticed the scouts in those seconds when they were running across the square. They dropped their prize on the ground alongside the manhole and gave the agreed signal to those waiting below—three taps with a buttstock on the manhole cover.

"Take our catch!"

They lowered the "tongue" into the chamber and climbed down behind him themselves. They again moved the manhole cover back into place.

His head lowered lifelessly, the German sat in the muck, which was just below a man's knees on the bottom of the chamber. He would have fallen had scouts not been standing tightly all around him.

"Bring him around!" ordered Kalganov. They began to rub the prisoner's ears. Finally, he shook his head and mumbled something.

"He's coming to!" those around him exclaimed happily. Kalganov turned on his flashlight. In its light they could see the German's wildly blinking eyes. He was grinding his teeth and jerking, and an expression of terror appeared on his face. A moment ago he had been walking along the street. All around it was quiet and calm, and suddenly he was sitting in muck, his clothes were soiled, he was icy cold, and some people with black faces and black clothing were standing around him in a tight circle.

Everything that the German now was seeing must have seemed to him like an underworld into which he had suddenly fallen. Perhaps he believed that he had not gone to hell but into captivity, after Lyubisha explained this to him in German. The officer tried to stand up but fell helplessly back into the muck. His legs would not hold him.

They searched the prisoner. Kalganov inspected his documents in the light of the flashlight. He was First Lieutenant Reinrohr. On Kalganov's instruction, they removed the crumpled, slobbered-on gag from his mouth. Through Lyubisha, Kalganov began to question the lieutenant. He immediately informed them that he was an officer from the operations section of Wildenbruch's staff. Kalganov was happy. This was a very valuable "tongue," the kind they needed.

If only the telephone communications worked! They could have interrogated him and reported directly to the general by land line. They still did not know what might happen on the return trip. Would they be able to drag their "tongue" back, and would they make it back themselves?

Andreev's group was operating at the same time. After beating their frozen, snow-covered manhole cover off with some difficulty, they looked around. Through the slowly falling snow, in the night darkness they saw that they were at the end of a narrow lane, alongside a small church with a half-destroyed bell tower. This was the Magdalene Church, their designated objective. The church stood on the corner of a lane and a square, whitened by the falling snow. On the opposite side of the square they could make out a three-story building with columns and alongside it a monument. On the left, at the edge of the square, stood several large cannons in firing positions. The scouts counted: eight 150mm guns—two batteries. Two tracked prime movers were parked nearby. German soldiers were bustling around them, unloading crates of ammunition. Not far from the guns, in front of the three-story building, stood a tank with an antiaircraft machine gun in the turret. The scouts' attentive eyes caught everything. On one of the streets that came into the square they spotted seven six-barreled mortars.[2] A bit farther along this same street they could see elevated upward the long barrels of three 200mm cannons, prepared for firing. It was clear that a large quantity of enemy artillery was concentrated here. The Germans, pressed into a circle on Fortress Hill, already had insufficient space for minimal dispersion of their artillery.

What the scouts had already seen was valuable information for the command. They did not need a "tongue."

Carefully slipping out of the manhole, Andreev, Globa, and Chkheidze replaced the cover with the help of those who remained below. Skirting around the church and staying in the buildings' shadows, they moved by the perimeter of the square on the opposite side of the cannons. Then they turned around the corner. Earlier, they had noted that Germans appeared on this street infrequently. The scouts hid in the shadows by the corner watching for an officer.

After a fairly long wait, they spotted a person coming out of a multistory building that stood not far away. They looked closely—it was a soldier. But this German could hardly have been in the building alone. Would anyone else come out? The scouts moved closer to the entrance along the wall.

Their supposition proved correct. At brief intervals, individuals and pairs left and entered the building. But as far as they could determine in the darkness, these were common soldiers, perhaps runners or communications personnel. Or were they simply dropping in on a cold night to warm up? Perhaps there was a headquarters in this building?

Finally, two men came out of the building's door and, quietly conversing, headed toward the square. They passed close to the scouts. One was of medium height, fat, in a black leather coat and uniform peaked hat. The other was tall, heavyset, in a long cape and officer's *furazhka*.

In an instant, two shadows separated from the wall and slipped in behind the walkers. An instant later, another shadow appeared in front of them. They operated in the normal fashion for capturing a "tongue."

Chkheidze, who along with Globa had run up behind them, gave the tall one a short but powerful blow on the head with his buttstock. He fell but not all the way to the ground, staying on his knees. They had not managed to grab his arms before he managed to strike Aleksey Chkheidze with his fist in the chest, directly on the solar plexus, with all his might. For an instant, Chkheidze almost lost consciousness from the pain. But overcoming this, he threw himself on the tall one, trying to help Globa subdue him. The enemy was strong, agile, and clever. He resisted violently, striking out with his fists and attempting to cry out.

Globa pressed his broad palm against his mouth. But the German twisted away. Fearing that he would raise the alarm with a shout, Globa struck him with a knife. The German collapsed in a heap.

At the same time, Andreev firmly held the fat one. Globa and Chkheidze arrived to assist Andreev. They tied the prisoner up and shoved a gag in his mouth.

In several minutes, the scouts were already back at the manhole with their prizes. Their comrades awaited them.

The fat one in the leather coat, finding himself in the chamber, twisted his head in bewilderment and fright, mumbled, but offered no particular resistance. They had dragged the German in the coat to the manhole and dropped him through—they could not leave the body on the street to alert the enemy and enable him to raise the alarm and begin pursuit. Andreev removed the dead man's documents from his pockets to hand over to their commander.

The mission had been accomplished. Now it was time to return.

Thirty minutes after Andreev, Chkheidze, and Globa climbed into the manhole with their prize, both groups of scouts linked up at the juncture of the pipe to return to base together. Andreev gave Kalganov both Germans' documents. The fat one in the leather coat turned out to be Major Shtrunk from the headquarters of the 239th Storm Artillery Brigade. The dead German whose corpse lay covered with muck at the bottom of the sewer was a Sergeant Weis from the SS Motorized Division Feldernhalle.

They ordered the captured Germans into the pipe. The fat major had difficulty crouching over and, groaning, submissively crawled into it, splashing in the muck with his corpulent body. The first lieutenant was stubborn at first. But they nudged him with a buttstock, and he complied.

The return journey through the pipe was even more difficult. They became totally exhausted in the suffocating atmosphere and cold muck, which had soaked their clothing, and from moving in a hunched-over position for almost the entire night. Kalganov had to permit breaks more often now than on the journey toward Fortress Hill. They sat with total indifference, submerged up to their waists in the stinking slush and, resting their backs on the curved walls of the pipe, took short rests. When the break was over, some were able to get up only with the help of their stronger comrades.

Along the way, first one and then another broke down, stumbled, and fell. But they got up again and went on.

At the very beginning of the journey, the captured major began to gasp for breath—there was no spare mask for him. Chkheidze, moving at the rear, took off his mask and gave it to the major. This valuable "tongue" must be delivered alive at all costs. But Chkheidze himself quickly began to gasp for air. Then Globa gave him his gas mask. Thus, using one gas mask for two men by turns, they moved forward with their prisoner. The second prisoner also was unable to move without a gas mask. Lyubisha Zhorzhevich gave him his.

It was five o'clock in the morning when the scouts finally returned to the manhole near the burned-out tank. Their comrades waiting for them on the surface helped them climb out. The scouts could barely stand up, and not everyone had the strength to climb up by himself. Some of the scouts lost consciousness as soon as they hit the fresh air. All of their outer garments were worn through on the back from rubbing against the stone arches of the sewer system.

But they pulled the prisoners out of the chamber first. The scouts were more concerned for the prisoners' lives and health than for their own.

They led the captured "tongues" to the command post of the general, who had anticipated the scouts' return all night. The major and the first lieutenant had still not regained their senses. When someone offered the major a cigarette "to raise his spirits," his hands were so shaky that he could not hold it. Coming around somewhat, the major declared, "I'll tell you everything. But first let me wash and change clothes." The first lieutenant, making the same request, could not stop expressing surprise: "Did I really come out of that hell alive? No, that was worse than hell. It is probably cleaner in hell."

At the limits of their endurance, dirty, their clothing tattered, the scouts returned to their apartment. Their comrades were anxiously awaiting their arrival. Water was boiling in tubs on a fired-up stove. Two large bottles of eau de cologne, obtained from a pharmacy supply house, stood ready. All the clothing that had become thoroughly saturated with stinking sewage was immediately discarded. Vigorous bathing commenced.

At the same time, interrogation of the two "tongues" brought back by the scouts was proceeding at headquarters. The major and the first lieutenant pointed out on a map where and how artillery was displaced and the locations of command posts and shelters on Fortress Hill. They helped pinpoint the front-line trace, recounted what kind of forces the German command had available in Budapest, and told what they knew of the plan for breaking out of the encirclement.

When the day of the decisive assault on Fortress Hill—the last German stronghold in encircled Budapest—arrived, the Soviet guns struck squarely on those targets on Fortress Hill that the sailor scouts had themselves noted and those pointed out by the "tongues" they had captured.

By this time, Kalganov was once again in the hospital. His wounded arm, which had become infected after crawling through the pipes, required treatment. In addition, he had received yet another wound. In the very last days of the battle for Budapest, an enemy bomb fragment struck him in the leg.

The scouts visited their commander in the hospital every day. On 13 February, the day the enemy in Budapest was finally defeated, several of Kalganov's sailors visited him. They carried a large, wrapped container into his room and ceremoniously positioned it alongside their commander's bed.

"What is this?" The senior lieutenant did not understand at first.

"It's from us!" he heard in reply.

"Booty?" The perplexed Kalganov stroked his beard and arched his eyebrows. In the detachment, the pursuit of trophies [booty or confiscated property] was strictly prohibited. During the entire period, there had not been a single "booty dealer" among the sailors, and suddenly—this! They had dragged in some kind of booty, for him.

"Who dared do this?" Kalganov questioned sternly.

"As a sign of respect."

"A sign of respect? What is it?"

"A bed from the Royal Palace! From [Admiral] Horthy's apartment! Don't you, our commander, deserve to lie in a good feather bed? Weren't we the first of our forces to reach the palace?"

This sentiment came so much from the heart that Kalganov began to laugh.

"All right, show it to me."

The sailors adroitly unwrapped the container. Indeed, it contained a luxurious feather bed, pillows, linens, and pillow cases with intricately embroidered monograms and crowns on them. Though there had not been a king in Hungary for some years, it was still considered a monarchy, and all the appropriate paraphernalia had been preserved in the Budapest palaces.

"Well, why are you bringing me such excesses?" Kalganov disdainfully looked at the royal sleeping accessories. "I have hospital issue."

The sailors forced the issue.

"What hospital issue? Your mattress is pitiful! You can lie on that with a wounded leg?"

In the end, Kalganov had to agree, and they bedded him down in all the royal accessories, after disinfecting them at his request.

The sailors departed, satisfied.

Indeed, he was very comfortable lying in the royal feather mattress and luxurious pillows. But the next day, Kalganov demanded that they give him the standard hospital mattress and pillows. The countless visitors had tired him. Having heard that "the Beard," the commander of the scouts, lay on a royal bed, many had come by to look in on him since the fighting in Budapest had ended.

Kalganov had to recuperate longer than he had planned. Spring came. Our offensive moved forward everywhere, pushing the enemy toward his last positions. Kalganov still had to remain in his hospital bed. No, he had not thought that the reconnaissance in the pipe would be his last. But the scouts had gone ahead without their commander.

CHAPTER SIXTEEN

HUNGARIAN COMRADES

The final days of existence of the encircled German forces in Budapest were passing. Compressed from all sides into a small area of Buda around Fortress Hill, the Germans had not yet lost hope for relief. The worse their situation became, the more savagely they launched attacks to discover weak areas in the encircling forces.

On 11 February, two days before the final defeat of the enemy in Budapest, Chkheidze, Globa, and Nikulin, appointed senior, were sent out on reconnaissance into Buda with the mission to capture a "tongue." The command needed to know where the enemy was preparing his next attacks.

At about 2200, the three scouts arrived at the front line to select the spot where it would be best to make their way over to the enemy side in the darkness of the winter night.

The forward edge passed along one of the blocks of the northern part of Buda, where it adjoined the city's oldest quarter, Obuda. Ancient buildings of heavy construction stood close together, with buildings of newer construction squeezed in here and there. There were narrow streets and small squares.

Here our forward positions were close to the enemy positions. In many places, only a courtyard or narrow lane separated them. At the spot where our scouts decided to cross the forward edge, our forces occupied positions in a large, multistory building. Behind the building, at an intersection, stood two of our howitzers in firing positions.

It did not present any particular difficulty to these experienced scouts to work their way toward enemy positions, the more so because the winter night was dark and there were no fires coming from the German side.

Approximately an hour after the scouts had moved beyond the forward edge, the infantry occupying defensive positions at the building's windows heard hurried steps. The soldiers recognized the figures running toward the building as the sailors who had only a short time ago gone in the other direction.

"Stand clear, infantry! The Germans are launching their attack!" the sailors shouted, running into the building. The soldiers had barely managed to get ready when the dark, crouching figures of Germans were intermittently spotted in the courtyard adjoining the building.

Submachine guns chattered from the building's windows, interspersed with rifle fire.

Nikulin wanted to tell Globa and Chkheidze: "Let's go back to the detachment. This isn't our fight any longer." But the Germans were attacking so violently that the scouts had to take up arms. It was too late to leave.

The scouts had detected these Germans—there were many— alongside the adjacent building already prepared to begin their attack. Therefore, Nikulin gave the command to withdraw slowly to warn the infantry.

The situation grew more complicated with each second. The Germans rushed the building in a frenzy. Their losses did not slow them down. Shots were already ringing out on the upper floors, and muffled grenade explosions were heard. The enemy had penetrated through one of the platoons into the building. Shaggy crimson flames flickered from the window of a lower floor, driving the night darkness away. The Germans had tossed several Molotov cocktails into the building.

Using his large numerical superiority, the enemy drove the infantry from the building. Nikulin, Globa, and Chkheidze, still firing, were among the last to abandon the building.

When the three scouts ran out of the building, they saw that the enemy had already broken through their rear, toward the intersection where the two howitzers were parked. In the light of the flames that were licking out of the windows of the building the soldiers had just abandoned, they could see that many artillerymen had already been killed. Those who were still alive were taking shelter behind their guns and firing back.

No, there was no way the scouts could avoid the fight. They could not abandon their army comrades, who had always been ready to help them.

Nikulin ran toward the intersection first and, angling toward the corner of a building, threw a grenade at the Germans who were running toward the guns firing their submachine guns.

The explosion, flashing in the night darkness, dispersed the enemy. Two more grenades—Globa's and Chkheidze's—exploded right behind Nikulin's. The scouts dashed through the smoke of the detonations toward the artillerymen. Taking cover with them from enemy bullets behind the large gun assemblies, they opened fire with their submachine guns on the Germans who were once again surging toward the intersection. The Germans were forced back.

There was a lull in the fighting, but it could end at any moment. It was already after midnight. Tracer streams marked the black sky in all directions. Dull reddish reflections from the fires that had been started in the abandoned building ran along the snow-covered pavement, along the shields and barrels of the two howitzers, behind which were hiding three scouts and several artillerymen.

The scouts probably could have left during this lull. No one required them to remain and continue the fight. But their soldierly honor required them to remain. Taking advantage of the break, they looked around. Having noted that a barricade made of bricks cordoned off one of the narrow streets leading away from the intersection, some seven meters wide, Nikulin pointed it out to his comrades.

"Let's go there. It will provide better cover than these guns."

The breather did not last long, perhaps three or four minutes. The silhouettes of German soldiers slinking in the shadows of walls appeared in front of the barricade in the darkness at the far end of the street. They were the source of the ominous glow of tracer bullets.

A new attack began. Bullets made staccato slaps on the brick barricade. Sharp fragments of broken brick struck their faces and arms. Enemy soldiers ran down the narrow street, taking cover behind building entrances. Burst after burst was fired at the scouts. But there were only three men behind the barricade. And near the artillery pieces were only three or four artillerymen and two or three infantrymen who had joined them from the building, which was now in enemy hands.

Fire from the barricade prevented the Germans from exposing themselves. But they ran from building to building along the street, and in the black casements of the windows the muzzle flashes came closer and more frequently.

From behind them ran up a soldier with a trophy light machine gun. He laid down next to the scouts and exclaimed in surprise: "Sailors? Where from?"

He thrust the bipod of the machine gun between the bricks, readied the weapon, and fired a long burst.

The scouts were glad. Help had arrived!

But their joy was short-lived. The crimson flash of a German grenade extinguished it. The machine gunner rolled over, pulling his machine gun down after him. At that moment, cries in a foreign language were heard behind them. The scouts looked around: soldiers in yellow Magyar capes were running across the intersection with submachine guns and rifles at port arms.

Salashisty? They have come around to our rear!

No, these were not Salashisty. The men in Hungarian uniforms were firing on the run in the same direction as the scouts. When these men reached the barricade and lay down behind it, the scouts could see that each of them had a broad red armband on his sleeve. One of the Magyars pulled the morbidly stiff finger of the dead soldier from the light machine gun and began to set it up again on the barricade.

"Where are you from?" Globa asked him.

The Magyar, judging by everything, did not know the Russian language, but he understood Globa's question.

"Budapest!" He pointed at himself, and asked Globa, "Moscow?"

"Moscow!" Globa replied, though he was born in the Ukraine. But Moscow, both for him and, apparently, for this Magyar, meant more than simply a city. The Magyar fired sparingly in short bursts, skillfully moving the barrel from target to target. It was apparent that he had been a soldier.

Before this day, the scouts were accustomed to seeing people dressed in Hungarian uniforms as enemies. And now here, it turned out, they had found allies among them.

About a company of Hungarian soldiers came rushing forward to the aid of the intersection's defenders in a timely manner. A captain thirty-five years of age commanded them, a regular offi-cer as best could be determined. All of his soldiers appeared to be experienced fighters. The scouts later learned that these soldiers, and a majority of the residents of Budapest and the surrounding area, had gone over to our side along with their commanders and were already fighting against the Germans.

The fire of the light machine gun, directed by the experienced hand of the Magyar soldier, the fire of his comrades and several of the artillerymen, and of the three scouts, stopped the enemy. Not one German showed himself in the dark street in front of the barricade.

Nikulin looked at the illuminated dial of his watch. Three o'clock. Not yet close to dawn. Perhaps the enemy would calm down and not come at them again. "Can we return to the detach-ment? But, should we leave the Magyars here alone?" Nikulin looked at his comrades. Clinging to his submachine gun, Globa looked out from under his tilted pile cap over the barricade.

Chkheidze, having removed the drum from his submachine gun, was busily recharging it with cartridges. They accepted it as a given that they would defend this intersection and the two guns here. Almost no one remained of the artillerymen, and the infantry were defending other positions. No, they could not leave yet.

"Do you hear it?" Nikulin touched Globa's arm.

In front of them, from somewhere in the gloom at the far end of the street, came a muffled rumbling and clanking, like a large beast crawling in the night, quietly, but growling evilly, grinding its teeth.

"Tank!" whispered Globa to Nikulin.

The now aroused Chkheidze hurriedly reloaded his drum and put it back in his submachine gun.

The clanking sounds of track and the snarling of an engine grew louder. The men who were hunkered down behind the barricade froze.

"Can our gunners fire at it?" Globa looked with hope over to where the two howitzers were sitting.

"Who is left to man the guns? Our gunners have been killed," Nikulin replied, and asked: "Do you have an antitank grenade?"

"Yes!" Globa unfastened a weighty antitank grenade from his belt and readied the fuse.

"And you, Aleksey?" Nikulin asked.

"I'm ready." Chkheidze showed his.

The motor growled louder.

The outline of an angular, low silhouette appeared from around the corner in the night darkness at the opposite end of the street. The silhouette enlarged rapidly, moving along the narrow street. Now, even in the night darkness, it was clear that this was not a tank but an armored half-track.

The scouts waited, ready to throw their grenades. But the armored transporter did not approach to within grenade range. It stopped about forty meters in front of the barricade. At that same instant, several explosions occurred on the barricade, and bricks and fragments flew in all directions. The half-track had opened fire with an automatic cannon. The scouts and Hungarian soldiers were now pressed to the bricks, shielding their heads and weapons.

Several more cannon bursts and the barricade would be destroyed by shells, none of its defenders remaining alive. Perhaps, even before that, taking advantage of the fact that no one could fire from behind the barricade, the Germans would rush it.

An explosion above, almost on top of Globa's head, showered him with several bricks. But he quickly recovered, opened his eyes, and exchanged glances with the Hungarian lying next to him, the same one with whom Globa had been conversing not long ago and who was now skillfully firing his light machine gun. In the soldier's open eyes, in his thin face, his cheeks covered with many days of black stubble, Globa read the same emotions the Magyar could see in his glance at that moment—fear and resolve. Fear that they would perish and still not delay the enemy, and resolve not to wait for death to come but to do everything to divert it from themselves and their comrades.

The soldier made a sign with his hand somewhere off to the left, and, in response, Globa pointed to the same place. They understood each other. They knew that in these decisive moments they were fighting in one formation, and they shared the same fate.

The Hungarian soldier handed the light machine gun to one of his comrades and, taking that man's submachine gun, ran along the barricade. Globa followed behind him, holding an anti-tank grenade in his hand.

They ran over to the wall of the building and, pulling themselves through a burned-out windowsill, jumped inside. Globa and the Hungarian soldier rushed through the rooms of the half-destroyed building, across fallen beams and collapsed ceilings along the wall adjoining the narrow street. They listened to the frequent barking bursts of cannon fire from the armored transport and feared that the barricade and everyone defending it would be destroyed while they were trying to get to an attack position.

They reached the last room. A courtyard was visible through a broken window in the night semidarkness. In the middle of it sat the shell of a car with open doors and bulging fenders, black against the white snow. Near the opposite side of the courtyard, behind a stone barrier with many holes, the frequent close shots of the half-track resonantly pounded.

As a precaution, Globa fired a short but widely dispersed burst along the black windows of the building on the other side of the courtyard. It seemed to him that someone had moved in one of them.

Globa was not wrong. In reply, they had fleeting glimpses of intermittent muzzle flashes in the dark openings. Bullets struck the wall with a dry staccato from outside the building, not far from the window behind which Globa and the Magyar were concealed.

It was clear. Germans were preparing to attack with the support of the half-track and assembling in the building on the other side of the courtyard.

What could they do? Go back? No!

"Cover me!" Globa shouted to the Magyar, pointing to his submachine gun. The soldier understood. He took a position near the remnants of the window frame. Holding tightly to his submachine gun and grenade, Globa rolled out into the courtyard through the adjacent window and fell in the loose shallow snow. Not hesitating a second, he ran across the courtyard. It seemed that they were firing at him—up ahead, low to the ground, was a yellowish line of tracers, particularly bright at this night hour. Globa dodged and ran to the wreckage of the automobile, then fell behind it.

A submachine gun chattered behind him. It was the Magyar firing, attracting the Germans' attention to himself. Globa leaped up and in several paces covered the distance to a stone fence that separated the courtyard from the street. He huddled down in a gap and sprawled in the snow in the deep shadow of the fence.

Now several meters separated him from the half-track. Globa crawled toward it, trying to remain in the shadow of the fence. Ephemeral reddish reflections passed in front of his face along the snow, which appeared gray—the reflections of the half-track's cannon's muzzle flashes.

"Can I throw it yet?" Globa raised his head and took stock. The half-track was ten to fifteen paces away in the middle of the street. "I can reach it!" Resting the palm of his left hand on the snow that had just fallen, Globa pulled out the cloth loop of the safety with his teeth, and, turning over, hurled the grenade to the front portion of the vehicle. Angry, dull flames danced along the thin barrel of the automatic cannon that hung over the edge of the vehicle's side. The grenade was still in the air, and Globa, grabbing his head with his hands, pressed his face into the snow, protecting it from the explosion.

The snow shook under him; the concussion struck his ears sharply. Globa looked up and saw nothing in front of him except black smoke. It seemed to him that someone was shouting amid the smoke where the half-track stood.

"Are you alive? I'd like to give you another grenade!"

But Globa did not have a second grenade. He pulled his last grenade, a fragmentation grenade, out of the pocket of his pea jacket and, after arming it, threw it almost by guess into the heart of the smoke. A flash and a loud explosion followed.

Black smoke—thick, tightly swirling, covered both the half-track and the entire street in front of it. Yellowish purple flame showed through the smoke periodically, throwing weak reflections on the snow.

Picking up his submachine gun, Globa, crouching, ran back. He jumped into the hole in the stone wall and tried to gauge how quickly he could run to the automobile hulk and then from it to the half-destroyed building in which his Magyar comrade was waiting. What about the Germans in the building deep in the courtyard? He looked at the dark square windows. There was no one there. Perhaps the Germans, seeing their half-track burning, had withdrawn? If only!

Jumping up, Globa ran toward the car with all his might. Hardly had he reached it and thrown himself into the snow behind it when they peppered the ruined body with bullets, like a handful of rocks. "The Germans have not fled! They won't let me get away."

But a familiar submachine gun chattered again from the half-ruined building, from where Globa's new comrade was waiting for him. The submachine gun fired a long, continuous burst. It was firing, most certainly, at the windows where the Germans were. Not hesitating for a moment, Globa pushed himself off the soft snow and scurried toward the place from which the Hungarian soldier's submachine gun was firing, as if beckoning him.

Jumping through the window, Globa ran several more steps. Behind him, the submachine gun fired two or three more seconds and then fell silent. Globa stopped and turned around. The Magyar was coming toward him, catching up. He raced toward Globa and, shouting something enthusiastically, grabbed him in an embrace.

From everything that the Magyar shouted, Globa understood only a single word, which he repeated especially frequently: "*Keshenem!*"—thank you. He squeezed the soldier in his powerful arms.

"Thank you, friend! Thank you for opening fire!"

They returned to the intersection. The firing in the vicinity had grown quiet. It was getting light. Behind the almost destroyed barricade sat Nikulin and Chkheidze, two artillerymen—the last of them—nearby, and three Magyars, holding their weapons at the ready. The remaining Hungarian soldiers had taken up positions in the corner buildings that abutted the barricade. Their captain, with the white face of one who has lost a lot of blood, sat with his back up against the gun carriage of a howitzer, holding his right arm out in front of him. It appeared strangely short. Blood was dripping through the thick layer of bandage. One of the Hungarian soldiers, holding the captain's arm, was applying a fresh bandage to it. It turned out that a fragment from a shell fired by the half-track had torn off his hand. But after being bandaged, he had continued to command his soldiers.

The three scouts remained at the intersection with the artillerymen and the Hungarian soldiers until six o'clock in the morning, when our infantry arrived. Now their consciences allowed the scouts to depart. They were sure that with the arrival of the infantry, the enemy not only would not capture the intersection and two howitzers but also would be driven from those positions he had managed to capture at night.

The three sailors said good-bye to those with whom they had stood shoulder to shoulder in the long and difficult night fight. The two unwounded artillerymen pressed their hands and thanked them:

"Thank you for helping us to defend our guns!"

Globa and the Magyar soldier parted friends. The two of them had gone together to blow up the half-track. They slapped each other on the back and hugged. They only regretted that they could not understand each other's language. But Globa, who had learned some Hungarian words during the time of fighting in Budapest, understood that this soldier wished the same for him as he did—to remain unwounded until victory. Just a short time ago, they had been enemies and, perhaps, had shot at each other.

Gesticulating profusely, Globa's new friend tried to explain something to him, pointing in the direction of one of the streets coming into the intersection. At first, Globa could not understand what the Hungarian wanted to tell him. But he finally guessed: he was inviting Globa to his house. Like many soldiers of his company, he was a Budapest resident. Globa answered with a smile.

"Thank you, friend! As soon as we beat the Germans."

CHAPTER SEVENTEEN

SIX LIGHTS

The last ice was floating down the Danube. The snow had already melted off the Hungarian fields. Forces of the Third Ukrainian *Front,* who had just fought off an enemy onslaught between Lakes Balaton and Velentsa, intended to break out toward the Danube, were moving westward along the drying roads west of Budapest, toward the Austrian border and Vienna. Sensing that the end was near, the enemy was putting up a fierce defense. He was still holding on in the Hungarian city of Esztergom on the right [south] bank of the Danube thirty-five kilometers northwest of Budapest. But Soviet forces had destroyed the enemy defense south of Esztergom. Going around the city to the west, near the Hungarian town of Tata, they were pressing from three sides toward the Danube against a grouping of German divisions. They needed to attack these divisions from a fourth side, from the Danube. Then the enemy, caught in a "sack," would face inevitable defeat.

To inflict such a blow, an amphibious assault had to be landed on the right bank, west of Esztergom, near Tata. This mission was assigned to the Danube Flotilla.[1] It would not be easy to accomplish. The enemy was occupying both banks of the Danube several kilometers east of Esztergom, holding the entire channel under his artillery sights. And the main reason it would be difficult was

because, as they had done on the Danube on more than one previous occasion, the Germans had created an obstacle for our vessels at Esztergom by blowing up a railroad bridge. The massive
girders dropped into the water formed, as it were, an iron fence.
We had to find a gap in this fence of just five to six meters width
and a depth of not less than one meter, through which armored
cutters could pass.

A gap had been sought in the Esztergom bridge for some time.
The flotilla's scouts closely inspected each span of the bridge in a
battery commander's stereoscopic telescope from the heights along
the river at our forward edge. By the position of its half-submerged
girders and the frothy waves of the rapid Danube water, the
observers attempted to determine where the girders lay and if an
armored cutter could pass over the top of or between them.

But observation alone could not provide adequately precise
data. Nor was aerial photography, which our pilots attempted several times, sufficiently clear. It was necessary to deceive enemy
monitoring, go to the bridge, inspect it, and take measurements.
Who better to do this than the sailors of the reconnaissance
detachment? They were experienced in such matters.

There was little time. An end had to be put to the German
grouping west of Esztergom, near Tata. A formation of vessels commanded by Hero of the Soviet Union Captain Second Rank Pavel
Ivanovich Derzhavin received an order: at night on 20 March, they
were to pass through the Esztergom bridge into the enemy's rear,
toward Tata, and land an amphibious assault. The detachment's
scouts received the mission from the staff: before the armored cutters with the amphibious force commenced movement, find a passage through the destroyed bridge. Upon approach of the armored
cutters, mark the route to the bridge and passage land with signal
lights. Maintain the lights until all armored cutters have passed
through the lane.

On the night before the night of the intended execution of the
amphibious landing, a rubber boat departed from a dock located in
the rear of our front-line units in the Hungarian town of Sob, on the

Czech border on the left [north] bank of the Danube. Turning, it went upstream toward Esztergom. Three scouts were aboard the boat: Lyubisha Zhorzhevich, Vasiliy Globa, and Aleksey Chkheidze.

Holding to the middle of the river, the rubber boat rushed along toward the bridge. The dark night and great speed were its only defenses. If the enemy who was monitoring the river from the shores had heard the sound of its motor, he hardly could have taken the rapidly moving boat under fire.

They passed unnoticed through the enemy's forward positions on the banks. It was dark all around. But at any moment illumination rockets could be fired from either bank. Up ahead, extending along the river, the low black strip of an island could be seen. The bridge was a bit farther upstream. They noted sparse, black vegetation in the darkness on the barely whitish sandy strip. The rubber boat moved along, holding close to the left shore of the island. They passed the island. Up ahead, dimly outlined against the background of the night sky, the obscure features of high bridge piers loomed like towers. The girders dropped from them were sticking out of the water.

Reducing speed, they approached. With the motor at idle, they could hear the sound of the rapidly flowing water as it raced between the steel beams of the submerged girders and surged up against the stone pilings. The noise of the water across the destroyed bridge was so loud that the enemy on the shores certainly could not have heard the quiet puttering of the rubber boat's motor as it carefully moved from pier to pier. The three scouts were seeking a reliable passage lane for the armored cutters.

They found a lane between the third and fourth piers, counting from the right bank. But they had to establish for certain if there were any steel beams under the surface that might tear into the bottom of an armored cutter. They not only had to measure with rods but also go into the water themselves, holding onto the side of the boat, and feel with their feet what was down below. They had done this some time ago at Prakhovo. The water was still winter-cold. After only several seconds, their legs began to go numb. Climbing back on board, the scouts warmed up with gulps of booty rum from a flask and again went down into the freezing cold water. In the end, they confirmed that the passage was completely safe and returned to their base at full speed.

On the following night, which was just as dark, an armored cutter departed from the dock at Sob. Two small launches were tied up to its left side. They were intended for Kotsar and Malakhov, who were on the same cutter. At first, the leader did not want to take Malakhov along. The leg wound he had received in Budapest had still not healed. But nonetheless, he persisted and was now back with his comrades.

Veretenik, Gura, and Zhorzhevich went on the same armored cutter with Kotsar and Malakhov. The armored cutter was to land them en route to the island, and Kotsar and Malakhov in their launches were to remain alongside the passage discovered by the scouts between the piers of the destroyed bridge on the previous night.

Still earlier, a rubber boat had departed with a small launch in tow. Aleksey Chkheidze sat next to the helmsman, and in front was Globa.

Each one, except Chkheidze, was to occupy a designated post and, as soon as the ships approached, turn on a signal light. After everyone else had assumed their positions, Chkheidze was to return alone in the rubber boat to the formation commander and report readiness. Going aboard the lead cutter, he was to guide the column to and through the passage.

When Globa had anchored his launch below the island and all the scouts were in their designated places, Chkheidze guided the rubber boat downstream to the base at full speed. Quiet reigned over the river as before. The enemy still apparently suspected nothing.

The six scouts were prepared to perform their duty. Each had a powerful light, which until it was time, of course, no one turned on. All were armed with submachine guns and grenades, in the event there was a confrontation with the enemy. Kotsar was to mark one side of the passage next to a girder protruding from the water. Malakhov was positioned at the opposite side of the passage in the other launch, along the bridge pier. Zhorzhevich took a position at the end of the island oriented toward the bridge. Veretenik and Globa were farther downstream on the island, at the edge of the shore, some distance from each other. Globa was waiting in a launch below the island, the first scout on the armored cutters' route.

When the sound of the motors of the expected vessels was heard, six signal lights would be turned on in the darkness over the river. They would form an extended chain along the channel. The armored cutters would move from one marking light to the other toward the bridge.

Holding their still dark lights in readiness, they scouts waited, each at his post, shivering from the river chill. They were intently listening to the night silence. Could they make out the familiar rumble of motors? They pressed their fingers on the button, ready to turn on their lights. But only when the boats were close. Not a minute earlier, so that the enemy could not fire at the moving ships.

The quiet embraced the river, which was cloaked in the black cover of night, over the hidden danger that was invisible in the darkness on the banks, over the destroyed bridge, alongside which the Danube water churned and burbled, lapping at its piers and making its way through the steel superstructure of the spans. Only somewhere far, far away, upstream, could the muffled rumble of a cannonade barely be heard. It was in the Tata area, to which our armored cutters were moving to assist our army units who were pressing the enemy toward the Danube. The battle did not ebb for a minute through the night hours.

When Aleksey Chkheidze arrived at the base in his rubber boat, he saw that the assault troops were loaded on the ships, and the ships were ready to depart. The commander of the formation was waiting anxiously for a report from the scouts. As soon as Chkheidze reported that the path to the passage lane was marked, they sent him to the cutter commanded by Hero of the Soviet Union Captain-Lieutenant Konstantin Ivanovich Vorob'ev. This cutter was to lead.

It was three o'clock in the morning when the lead vessel approached the bridge, the remaining cutters following in a trail formation.

The enemy concealed on both banks was silent. The darkness hid the small vessels moving in the middle of the river. The muffled sounds of their motors probably did not reach the shore. The enemy could hardly consider that the Soviet sailors would risk moving through the destroyed bridge, the iron barrier of which extended in the water across the Danube, on this impenetrable dark night. At the same time, all the Germans' attention was drawn to the forward edge. They had every reason to fear that our units in the positions in front of Esztergom could go over to the offensive at any moment.

Aleksey Chkheidze stood in the commander's wheelhouse next to the helmsman, giving him directions. Nothing was visible up ahead in the narrow opening of the vision slit. Only one who had traveled here before could have found the necessary route. Chkheidze, like his comrades in reconnaissance, could see more in this pitch darkness than those who were moving through here the first time.

The contours of the destroyed bridge were still totally indistinguishable up ahead on the background of the night sky and the dark banks. The island that lay on the route to the bridge also remained unseen. But Chkheidze had already surmised that it was close. Somewhere nearby, concealed in the darkness, Globa, Zhorzhevich, Kotsar, and Malakhov were waiting at their posts. Peering into the night, they were listening for the sound of the motors. And when they heard it, each scout would turn on his signal light. A constellation of six lights would be shining in the middle of the black river, indicating the route to the vessels. Of course, these lights would be seen not only on the ships but by the enemy on the banks. They would spot them, wonder why they were lit, and then begin to fire at them to put them out. Aleksey Chkheidze felt more and more concern for his comrades waiting up ahead. Turning on their lights, they would unavoidably draw enemy fire on themselves.

Up ahead, slightly to the left of the ship's course, a tiny white flash gleamed in the night darkness. "Globa's flashlight!" Chkheidze announced.

There, where the light burned, a little bit above it, straight reddish lines of fire instantly showed and then quickly died. "They are firing tracers!" Aleksey's heart skipped a beat. His comrade was under fire!

Beyond Globa's light, slightly upstream—on the island now—three more lights flashed one after the other, forming a widely spaced file chain stretched along the vessels' path. Three lights were from Veretenik, Gura, and Zhorzhevich. There were two more lights at the far end of the chain, close to each other—Kotsar and Malakhov. Six lights pointed out the route.

Purplish and white lines, continuously cutting through the darkness from the left and right, came together, intersecting, as if someone wanted to cross out the six immobile lights flickering up ahead.

Closer, closer, the first light—Globa's flashlight—was dead ahead. The flickering light could be seen on the black water. The lead armored cutter turned a bit to the right—Globa's light was now along the left side. They could hear the evil whistle of a passing shell and low-flying bullets hitting the water.

Chkheidze peered out of the wheelhouse to the left, toward the reflections of Globa's light, twisting like gold snakes on the dark water churned up by explosions. Chkheidze saw Globa. He was sitting in his launch, bobbing up and down in the wake of the larger vessel, with one hand holding onto the side of his boat and the other holding his signal light up high. The cutter passed close to the launch, six or seven meters. Globa seemed to be shouting. But the rumble of the vessel's motors and the scream of shells and bullets made it impossible to hear. "Has Globa been wounded?" Chkheidze was concerned. He wanted to call out to his comrade. But the yellowish reflections of Globa's flashlight dancing on the water were already behind them. Neither the reflections, the light, nor his boat were visible.

Choosing the path, the lead cutter hurried toward the bridge. Three lights were shining from the left, on the dim outline of the island strip. The cutter hurried past them, holding a course between the lights that marked the edges of the passage lane.

Pointing out to the helmsman how he should steer the vessel, Chkheidze simultaneously followed his comrades' lights. The fire of enemy machine guns and guns was now being directed at them from both shores. Zhorzhevich's light fell and went out. No, it did not go out, it was raised up again. Malakhov's light went out! It flickered again. It went out again! Had Arkadiy been wounded? Killed? Kotsar's light could not be seen. What had happened to him? The island slid past.

The bridge!

The armored cutter moved precisely through the middle of the passage. The tower of a pier flashed by, coming up out of the water high into the starless sky. The angled contours of half-sunken girders were visible for a moment. The cutter passed through. The noise of the water surging between the steel beams and slapping against the rocks grew quieter.

Gunfire and explosions rang out behind them. Our artillery, positioned in front of Esztergom, opened fire on the enemy batteries. The Katyusha rockets, fired by the artillery support vessels, cutters moving behind the assault force, passed overhead with a roar.

The lead armored cutter had already sailed upstream far beyond the bridge. The next vessel moved behind it, almost in its wake. The enemy, caught unawares, was hardly able to inflict any losses on the ships that passed through the bridge. But what happened to the six daredevils who so bravely stood watch under enemy fire? Their lights were excellent beacons for German artillerymen and machine gunners. Concern for his comrades pulled at Chkheidze's heart. He looked around. Were his friends all right? Were their lights still burning?

Lights were still burning, but not all of them. They were shining under machine-gun fire, under shell and mortar bomb detonations launched from the shore. They burned until all the armored cutters had passed through the passage reconnoitered in the bridge. The courage of those who had held the lights, surprise, and the precise actions of those aboard the vessels determined the success of the operation.

The sailors had accomplished their assigned mission. The amphibious assault, supported by the fire of shipboard guns, was landed at the designated site and hour, in complete accordance with the plan developed by the flotilla staff. This determined the outcome of the battle. Pressed toward the Danube, the enemy grouping was liquidated.

Before dawn, one of the armored cutters returning downstream went to the island and recovered the scouts. They took them aboard like heroes, led them into the warm crew quarters, and fed them. Zhorzhevich had a fresh, bleeding wound in his shoulder, which was bandaged. They laid Globa, who had received a serious contusion and a wound in his hip, down.

The mission had been carried out; the ship took the scouts back to base. But they were not happy. Arkadiy Malakhov was missing. They found his pile cap, submachine gun, and grenades in the launch he had signaled from, which was full of holes from shell fragments. There was no doubt that Malakhov had been seriously wounded or killed by a close explosion, then thrown into the water along with his light. Of course, he could not swim in that condition. Even had he been thrown into the Danube alive, he would have been in no condition to survive long in the icy water. And there was no one to help him.

The loss of a comrade dampened the happiness of their success. Everyone in the detachment loved this resourceful and sharp-thinking young man from Leningrad. Arkashka the artist, they called him, because he loved to draw in his free time, in quiet moments. He always had a notebook in the pocket of his sailor pants, in which he already had collected many sketches: portraits of his comrades, Danube scenery, and the streets of Hungarian cities. Arkadiy Malakhov was one of those who made up the fighting core of the detachment. Like many of his comrades, he had seen the front and had begun to fight earlier than his draft cohort. Still as a schoolboy, in the summer of 1941, he had captured an enemy agent who was signaling enemy bombers with a flare. At the age of seventeen, he had already become a soldier in a security battalion, then constructed defensive lines around Leningrad. Evacuated from the besieged city, he quickly became a naval infantryman and took part in the landings at Kerch and across the Dniester estuary.

Veretenik in particular grieved for Malakhov. They were the closest of friends from the moment they had first met in the fall of 1944 on the Danube, on the captured enemy monitor to which they were both assigned. Veretenik and Malakhov were transferred together from the monitor to Kalganov's detachment. They had gone out on patrol together in Budapest and on more than one occasion had helped each other. The last time was the memorable engagement in the bank building. Veretenik had carried Malakhov, wounded in the leg, out from under fire.

The scouts reported to Kalganov, still recuperating in a hospital in Budapest, that Malakhov was no longer with them. The commander was very sad. Malakhov was a faithful comrade, reliable in battle, one of the cleverest scouts, who frequently made his own ingenious contributions during the accomplishment of the assigned mission. The commander accepted his suggestions on more than one occasion.

Kalganov wrote to Malakhov's mother in Leningrad with an aching heart. "Accept my sorrowful sympathy on the brave death of your son. I knew him as an exceptionally simple, courageous, and quick-witted soldier-scout. I went with him on combat missions many times, and was always surprised by his happy demeanor. His positive attitude encouraged the soldiers in battles, and this was sometimes at the most difficult moments. Our memory of Arkadiy and his combat deeds will be with us to eternity. For his brave deeds, he has been recommended for a decoration. Eternal glory to him."

An official notification of the death of her son was also sent from the headquarters.

Malakhov's comrades took an oath to avenge his death. And they kept their promise in new battles, when the flotilla's vessels again proceeded upstream along the Danube, leaving Esztergom far behind.

On one of the days of this offensive, the flotilla commander, Rear Admiral Georgiy Nikitich Kholostyakov,[2] was handing out awards in front of a formation of sailors to those who had distinguished themselves in battle. The awardees were summoned forward out of the formation one after the other, and the admiral pinned an order or medal on each of their chests.

Here is how it went:

"Seaman Malakhov!"

"He died a hero's death!" the formation responded in unison.

The flotilla commander, frowning, looked at the brand new Order of the Patriotic War, Second Degree, which he was already holding in his hand. Then he laid it off to the side, and instructed:

"Send it as a memento to his family!"

Then a letter suddenly arrived from Malakhov, with a return address of a nearby unfamiliar unit.

"Arkashka has been raised from the dead!" the sailors rejoiced, and, of course, Zhora Veretenik most of all.

What had happened to Arkadiy Malakhov?

The water raised by a nearby explosion poured into the boat. It knocked Malakhov's pile cap off and threw him overboard, along with the light that he had tied to his gear with a cord. When he surfaced, he could no longer see the boat. A bridge pier loomed darkly nearby. Several powerful arm strokes and Arkadiy grabbed on to the slippery, cold stones. The current was trying to tear him away from the rock wall and carry him into the black expanse of the river. His fingers rubbed raw and bleeding, Malakhov crawled with difficulty onto a small ledge, in the form of a narrow cornice under the water's surface around the circumference of the pier. Pressed up against the cold stones, he felt for his light. It was still in one piece. He had to continue performing his duty. Explosions were going off in the water around him. Something whistled above his head and snapped dryly on the stones—bullets or fragments? "The cutters are coming," Malakhov thought. "I can already hear them. They're coming! I have to give my signal. I have to turn on my light."

Moving hand over hand along the stone wall, pressed to it so as not to be pulled into the water, Malakhov moved along the ledge to the other side of the pier, which was the boundary of the passage lane prepared for the armored cutters. Through the noises of nearby explosions and the crash of the water displaced by them, through the whine of shell fragments and bullets, through the boiling Danube water swirling around the bridge pier, he thought he could hear the familiar, growing ever louder, rumble of cutter motors. Straining his vision, he could already see increasingly clearly in the darkness the silhouette of the lead cutter approaching the bridge. Malakhov turned on his light and raised it up.

The lead cutter was already close. It was important that it enter the passage lane precisely, not deviating a single meter. Error would be disastrous. Malakhov waved the flashlight back and forth several times to his right—this was the agreed-upon signal. Now the vessel would not err.

He came to in the water without his light, which he had just been holding. Silence struck him; all around was total silence. He could see only the fleeting, flying color of tracer bullets, carrying low over the water. He understood that the firing had not stopped, but it had stunned him so that he heard nothing. Did this mean that he had been thrown into the water by an explosion a second time and survived? He was lucky! He pulled off his water-soaked pea jacket.

The current was carrying Malakhov downstream. He did not fight against it: he would not overcome the Danube.

Armored cutters were coming toward him, hurrying toward the bridge. The vessels were passing close to Malakhov. At times, the current carried him so close to some of them that just a bit closer and he could have reached out and caught someone's arm if the bow wave from the fast-moving vessel had not washed him aside or submerged him altogether. Something struck him in the hip. A shell fragment or a bullet? Malakhov thrust his hand into the water and touched his hip. It hurt. Perhaps it was bleeding.

Surfacing, he saw the hulls of armored cutters passing close by, at times illuminated by dull flashes of tracer shells and bullets. He saw the assault troops lying on the decks, saw the signalers standing on their mounts behind the wheelhouses.

He shouted: "Throw me a rope!"

But no one on the ships could see or hear him.

It would have been difficult to see him in the dark night water. Sounds were already coming back a little—the confusion, it seems, was not so strong, and now he could hear firing and the rumble of the motors of the last of the vessels proceeding past him fading in the distance.

The water, which had brought him back to consciousness so quickly, now was numbing his body with cold. His swollen boots became like cast iron and pulled him down like weights. He managed to pull them off with difficulty. Struggling with the numbness that was slowly but inexorably taking over his body, Malakhov vigorously moved his arms and legs. But his strength faded with each minute. The confusion was taking its toll, along with the wound he had just received. Malakhov could feel his blood draining into the Danube's cold waters. It was becoming more difficult for him to swim.

He held toward the left bank but decided not to swim to it because he didn't know if the current would carry him there and if our forces or the enemy's were on that bank.

Malakhov was exhausted, and he lapsed into unconsciousness. Later, as he recalled, he felt his shoulder hit something solid. The current had dragged him up onto the sand. "The shore!" flashed through his clouded brain. "But whose?"

When Malakhov regained consciousness and opened his eyes, he saw above him a dimly illuminated gray concrete ceiling. He heard a conversation in an unintelligible language. "Have I fallen into the hands of the Germans?" He struggled to get up. A blow struck his head, after which he fell into a semiconscious state, barely seeing or hearing what was happening to him. It was already day. His hands were tied behind his back, and he was being dragged across a field, past rows of barbed wire. He was pulled into a building, next to which cars were standing and Germans were crowded around. He was shoved into a room.

Malakhov looked at all of this like a terrible nightmare. He had fallen captive to the Germans! He ground his teeth in anger and disappointment. He did not want to live. If he had known that this would happen, then that night, there on the river, he would not have tried to survive in the water. It would have been better to drown than to fall into the hands of the Germans! Sailors do not surrender! Never before had one of the flotilla detachment's sailors been captured. But he, Arkadiy Malakhov, was now a prisoner.

They pushed him into a room where an officer with a cape thrown over his shoulders sat behind a table with two field telephones.

"Sailor?" the officer asked in Russian, pointing at Malakhov's uniform.

"Sailor!" Malakhov replied with a challenge. He had nothing to lose. He had no hope that the Germans would keep him alive.

"What were you doing in the Danube?"

"Swimming!" Malakhov answered with a smile.

The officer put several more questions to him, and Malakhov replied with the same taunts to each of them.

The officer finally lost his patience. He shouted something to the guards standing outside the door. They struck Malakhov in the back with their rifle butts and dragged him away. They tied him up, then pushed him into the sidecar of a motorcycle, face down. A German sat on top of him, and the motorcycle sped away. Again some kind of headquarters. More unsuccessful interrogations and insults. A cubicle without a window. Again interrogations and again taunts. Malakhov did not understand why they were interrogating him so persistently. Perhaps it was because he was the only sailor that had fallen into the Germans' hands. Perhaps they were guessing that he was not a common sailor but a scout? Or they hoped that through him they might learn something about the flotilla's activity?

During countless interrogations, they beat him in the stomach and knocked out his teeth. He was spitting up blood. Malakhov told the enemy nothing and gave up no military secrets. Barefooted, with his hands tied, he was finally pushed into a column of prisoners whom the Germans, retreating, were driving out of camps deeper into their own rear.

Malakhov's sailor *tel'nyashka* attracted special attention from the military police guarding the column. First, they tried to displace all their anger for having to retreat on the sailor. They put Malakhov in the first row of the column and struck at him more often than the others. With glee, they stomped on his bare feet with their boots.

They drove the prisoners westward, through Czech towns and villages. The local inhabitants peered out at them with sympathy from behind fences. They attempted to throw the prisoners crusts of bread or parcels with food without being seen. But the guards would not allow it.

Malakhov did not think he would last long. He was receiving too much attention from the military police in comparison to the other prisoners. But just the same, he held on until the day when they reached the prisoner-of-war camp. They drove Malakhov and hundreds of other prisoners into a large warehouse building that did not have a single window. The other men advised Malakhov: "It would be better if we hid you!" They put him in a far corner and threw the hay that was scattered around on the floor on top of him. They placed several wounded prisoners on the hay so that Malakhov would not be seen if one of the guards came in. A doctor from among the prisoners of war bandaged their wounds, using paper. There were no actual bandages. One time a day— when they fed the prisoners—his comrades slipped a mess tin with a thick broth to Malakhov under the hay.

Days passed. The prisoners listened with hope for the rumble of battle, to hear their forces advancing toward them.

On one of these nights of worried anticipation, the warehouse doors burst open. The light of a flashlight passed across the prisoners' faces. A frightened and angry voice shouted:

"Russians, get up! All of you! Quickly!"

They decided to hide Malakhov and several other wounded who could not walk. The Germans would rush the column and shoot those who lagged behind. They hid the wounded in the hay, of which there was an abundance. It was not only thrown all over the floor; bales of hay filled entire stables. The wounded hid behind them.

The Germans were in a hurry. They did not even take time to count the prisoners. When the warehouse was empty, one of the guards looked around and then shouted something. No one responded. Just to be sure, the guard fired a submachine gun burst around the interior of the warehouse. But the hay bales protected those hiding behind them from the bullets.

Waiting until the voices and commotion of the departing column had died down, Malakhov, who could barely walk, and one other wounded prisoner made their way outside. It was already light. There were no Germans. A small village was close by. Having made their way through backyards to a poor-looking hut, Malakhov and his comrade cautiously knocked at the door. A woman opened the door and was frightened when she saw what was in front of her. But she immediately took them in. The woman was speaking Czech, Malakhov and his comrade Russian. But they understood one another, for the two languages were similar. The woman fed the starving men and told them that the German rear service troops who were in the village had already left. But their units retreating from forward positions were still passing through the village heading west.

Malakhov feared for his comrades who remained behind in the warehouse building. What if the retreating Germans should spot them and finish them off? He shared his fears with the woman. She ran to her neighbors. Soon all the wounded—thirty men— were safely hidden by the residents of this Czech village.

But Malakhov and his new friend did not remain there. They decided to walk as far as they could toward their own forces. They moved all day, through patches of woods, remaining concealed and constantly on the lookout. At night they walked along a road, ready at a moment's notice to hide in the roadside bushes or in the ditch. They saw Germans, hurriedly retreating from the forward area, walking and driving toward them.

On the morning of the next day, Malakhov and his partner encountered Soviet forces. Ten days had passed since that memorable Esztergom night. So few, but so many.

Malakhov was quickly assigned to reconnaissance in one of our army units. From there, he wrote to his old comrades. Arkashka the artist was once again moving westward. But how sorry he was that he was unable to rejoin his own detachment before the end of the war!

CHAPTER EIGHTEEN

TO THE LAST BORDER

A pril. The high springtime sun burned brightly in the clear sky, and, beneath it, the flowing Danube waters sparkled and glistened in a silvery spray. The hills along the banks were already touched in green. Farther upstream, they became steeper and more crowded in on both sides of the river. The Alps, where the Danube began its journey in Switzerland and southern Germany, were getting closer.

Esztergom, Tata, the Hungarian city of Komarom, and its Czechoslovakian sister city on the opposite bank, Komarno, were left far behind. The bridge between them had been saved by the scouts' bravery. Veretenik had raced onto it first under a rain of bullets and pulled an already lit fuse out of demolitions prepared by enemy sappers.

The bows of Danube Flotilla vessels had crossed Hungary's western border some time ago, leaving Bratislava [Czechoslovakia] behind. The sailors, who had walked along their last Czechoslovakian shore, had done their part for the liberation of this city. Now Austria was on both banks of the river. Vienna was just up ahead. With each day, the forces of the Second and First Ukrainian *Fronts,* advancing along the Danube, moved closer to the Austrian capital. With each day, the flotilla's vessels, staying on line with the ground forces, also drew closer.

As always, the scouts of Kalganov's detachment were always in front. But, like before, they were not all together. Some continued to reconnoiter the route for the ships. Others were conducting reconnaissance for the *BOS*—the shore escort detachment [*beregovoy otryad soprovozhdeniye*], which was proceeding along the right [south] bank.

It was 7 April. No matter how hard the enemy tried, he could not hold the ground in front of Vienna. Soviet forces, having broken through all the enemy's defensive lines, had come around into the Austrian capital from the northwest. Infantry and tanks had broken into the city from several directions.

Danube scouts were among those who entered Vienna first. Globa, Gura, and others were reconnoitering for the ground escort detachment, whose self-propelled guns were moving to Vienna along a highway that followed the river. The scouts were to give the self-propelled guns early warning of what threatened them along their route and find targets for their fire.

Proceeding carefully along the route, hiding in villages and patches of woods, the scouts reached the first buildings on the eastern outskirts of Vienna. The self-propelled guns were moving a short distance behind the scouts.

It appeared that there was no one up ahead on the road or in the buildings along the side. But the scouts knew what it would cost to expose the self-propelled guns. Germans lying in wait could fire at them a with a *panzerfaust* [man-portable antitank rocket] from any window or from a well-concealed antitank gun.

The scouts moved forward, inspecting every building, every window grating, and every window. Up ahead, on the right side of the road, was a white, two-story building. The glassless windows looked like dark squares. What was inside the rooms?

Globa, taking cover behind a small stone bridge across a ditch, fired a burst into the windows just to be sure. A machine gun barked out a long burst in response. It was firing from the attic window. Could there be a *faustnik* [*panzerfaust* gunner] there also?

Pulling a flare pistol out of the top of his boot, carried for the purpose of designating targets for the self-propelled guns, Globa fired a flare into the window. Smoke soon came out of the window. Apparently, the flare had struck some flammable substance. Heartened by this stroke of luck, Globa reloaded the flare pistol and fired another round through the window. At the same time, his comrades opened fire with their submachine guns.

After firing several flares through the windows, Globa saw that he had not wasted them. The building was on fire. All firing from it had ceased. The path was clear for the self-propelled guns.

Kalganov's scouts continued to advance from building to building, from street to street, clearing the path for the *BOS*'s self-propelled guns. They were among the first to reach Vienna's Northern [railroad] station, inciting panic among the Germans who had crowded into it. The self-propelled guns, destroying by direct fire enemy firing points along the path cleared by the scouts, followed in their tracks.

Globa and his friends raced to lead the self-propelled guns to Imperial Bridge—the only one of five Vienna bridges the enemy had not blown up. The German command was saving it for a connection with their rear and in the event they had to withdraw from Vienna. It was obvious that, after withdrawing, the Germans would attempt to blow this last bridge behind themselves to delay our advance. The scouts were rushing to lead the self-propelled guns to Imperial Bridge because at that time their comrades— sailors and soldiers who had landed from armored cutters the evening before and boldly broken through the front line to the bridge and captured it—were holding it.

Everyone who had landed knew that they still had to repel an enemy onslaught aimed at recapturing the bridge. They knew that the ships had departed and were not coming back, that help was not coming on the river. The enemy had cut the channel again with fire and would not allow them to cross through a second time. But they had hopes that their comrades advancing through the city's streets would break through to relieve them. They were coming. But when?

The assault force at the bridge withstood five attacks during the day. Fewer and fewer of them remained capable of fighting. Toward evening, there was a lull—the enemy broke off his attacks.

The night passed in nervous anticipation. The assault force listened with hope to the rumble of battle in the city. Were their comrades far away? Would they break through soon?

Morning came, the morning of 12 April. It began with a new enemy attack. They fended off continuous attacks. Almost completely out of ammunition, less than half of the assault force remained.

Night came—the second night. It did not bring a respite. The enemy continued his attacks. He launched a particularly fierce attack in the early morning.

The night dragged into day; fewer and fewer men capable of holding a weapon remained to defend the bridge. It had now become clear that if the enemy attacked and fired with the same effort, the force could hardly hold on to the end of the day. But this thought did not weaken their hands. On the contrary. It forced them to grasp their weapons more firmly and to expend each remaining bullet more carefully.

The enemy began his attack after noon, the strongest and most violent of all his attacks over several days. It was clear that the German command had decided to capture the bridge again, to capture it at any price.

Even the seriously wounded returned to their positions to beat off this attack. Everyone knew that there was nowhere to retreat to, and help had not yet arrived.

It was already clear that this time they would not be able to hurl the enemy back; too little strength remained to do so. Many of the assault force had already put aside their last bullet for themselves.

And suddenly the attacking Germans fled. A booming cannon shot was fired, then another. It was a self-propelled gun, firing at the fleeing enemy. This was the first of the *BOS*'s self-propelled guns that the sailor scouts Globa and Gura had led through the Viennese streets.

It was a joyful meeting on the square next to the bridge of those who were holding it and those who had arrived to relieve them.

Vienna was now behind them. A short distance remained to the German border, the last border on the route of the advancing forces. It was already known that the Allied American and British forces were moving toward them. The enemy was withdrawing, but was still fighting, clinging to his last defensive lines.

The vessels and the ground escort detachment, cooperating with the advancing forces, were moving beyond Vienna. And, as always, the scouts—the eyes and ears of the flotilla—were moving ahead of them.

The town of Tuln, an important road junction west of Vienna on the Danube, had been taken. The armored cutters were already approaching Lintz, some fifty kilometers from the Austrian-German border.

The scouts had been inseparable on the entire stretch of the fight up the Danube, all the way from the Black Sea. But in the end, the fortunes of war had separated them. Some, like Kalganov, Kotsar, and Nikulin, ended up in hospitals. Malakhov served in another troop unit after his flight from captivity. The remainder continued to perform reconnaissance duties, some in the ground escort detachment, others in ship units. But wherever they were, not one of the scouts forgot about his comrades in the detachment—not about those who continued to go forward or about those who were forced to languish in a hospital bed. Of course, the scouts did not forget about their commander. Kalganov, who was still continuing his recovery in a combat hospital, was now in Czechoslovakia and often received updates from his scouts. He was sorry that he could not be with them to the end, to greet the now approaching victory day with his men. He greedily questioned every newly arriving patient at the hospital to learn what he could about his friends. He listened closely to the latest news reports, trying to guess what battles the sailors of his detachment were participating in now.

One predawn hour, firing awoke Kalganov. Cannons and machine guns were firing, there were submachine gun bursts, rifle shots rang out, and a shower of flares burst in the sky. "The enemy? An air assault?" Kalganov grabbed his crutches and thrust his hand under the mattress, where he had a pistol hidden.

The door to his room opened, and someone shouted: "The war is over!"

The wounded who were able jumped from their beds and hugged each other. Kalganov slid off the bed to the floor and, leaning on his crutches, went over to the window, opened it, and emptied an entire magazine into the whitening sky in joyful excitement. This was his victory salute.

Music floated in over the hospital walls. Kalganov hurried out into the street with the other patients. A crowd of Czechs—residents of the town where the hospital was located—was gathering around the entrance. Many of them were carrying national three-colored flags. They waved their flags in greeting when the wounded showed up at the hospital doors.

A crowd assembled later that morning in Kalganov's room. A grand ceremony took place. Kalganov sat on a chair in the middle of the room, his casted leg stretched out in front of him. The hospital barber was fussing over him. Pieces of his famous beard, which Kalganov had grown and saved for four years, were dropping from his face onto the floor. Now, finally, had come the day that he had awaited so long, the day on which he could shave it off.

EPILOGUE

Those who had gone to war as young people were already in their thirties. The babies that had been born after the last shots were fired were already young people. Fifteen years had passed. Life had scattered these comrades in arms—the Danube scouts, who at one time had shared a wartime fate—to the far ends of the country. Each of their lives was now unfolding.

But no one's life had taken such a hard turn as that of Aleksey Chkheidze. Unscathed through the war, after the war's end he was injured by an accidental explosion. He lost his sight, hearing, and both hands. He was treated in hospitals and clinics for more than a year. The doctors made every effort to partially restore him to health. They removed several bomb splinters from him, but not all of them. They were able to restore some hearing in one ear. But the doctors were unable to return his vision to him.

In the summer of 1946, Aleksey—at that time he was nineteen years old—returned to Tbilisi to his parents. The first day, as soon as his return became known, his girlfriend from his school years came to visit him. He had waited the entire war for this meeting with the girl who had answered his front-line letters, full of love. "Despite what has happened, we will still be together," she said. "No!" he replied, gathering up all his courage. "You should not suffer your whole life because of me." She disagreed with him, but he stood his ground.

A wounding of the spirit was added to the young sailor's broken body. But he courageously endured this also.

His torn-up body required continued treatment. There was still some hope that the doctors could restore some sight in one eye. Chkheidze went back to a hospital room.

In a Moscow clinic ward, he made friends with a neighbor in the next bed, a Spaniard, Carlos Asin, who had become an invalid in childhood. A fragment from a German bomb had maimed his right hand. Carlos had been evacuated to the Soviet Union along with other Spanish children. He had found his second home in our country. This Spaniard and the Georgian were united not only by similar fates but also because they had one homeland and the same enemy.

When both were released from the clinic, Aleksey began to spend his entire days and be himself again in Carlos's family. The two friends had one hand between them.

What could be more difficult than to live without sight and without hands? But Aleksey Chkheidze, a man of great will and vitality, did not give in to despair or depression. He had found many friends, who did not leave him by himself. Valentina Nikolaevna Guseva became his faithful helper in life. Carlos, his wife, Maria Danilovna, and their son Serezha read books and newspapers to Aleksey and wrote letters for him. Carlos became a constant companion and guide.

All the years after the war, Chkheidze dreamed of finding his friends from the detachment. Recalling who was from where, he sent out inquiries. Many of them turned up nothing. Not everyone had returned to his home of record, and many had changed their address more than once. But the search continued.

Vasiliy Globa was found first. It turned out that he was working in Dnepropetrovsk at an electric locomotive assembly plant, in the casting shop, leading a team of foundrymen who had achieved the rank of Collective of Communist Labor. Chkheidze found Grigoriy Kotsar, who after the war had become an attendant in a station at one of the Krivy Rog mines. He heard from Aleksey Gura—a party worker in Berdyansk. The address of Nikolay Maksimenko, also a party worker, in Nikolaev oblast, was also discovered. Georgiy Veretenik, who worked as a driver in Kherson, wrote a letter. Vasily Nikulin, a union worker on the railroad, was found in Moscow. Sonya Dubova turned up at a military base not far from Moscow. After the war, Sonya finished a military institute, served in the fleet for a long time, and had recently retired at the rank of captain. It had been more difficult, of course, to find her than some of the others. He had looked for her as Dubova, and it turned out that she had been Osetrova for some time and had two sons. Valya Morozova was found. She had safely recovered from the serious wounds she had received on the road to Sevastopol. Her husband was easily recognized as that lieutenant to whom she had said good-bye over the open hatch of an aircraft on that night forever memorable to both of them. Now they had two large sons. They heard from Captain Aleksandr Morozov from the Caspian Flotilla in Baku. Captain-Lieutenant Vladimir Kalinichenko called from the Northern Fleet.

The detachment commander was also found—in Leningrad. Viktor Andreevich Kalganov was still on active duty in the Soviet navy at the rank of engineer-captain second rank. After the war, he graduated from a higher naval academy, received an engineer specialty, and was conducting research work. Several important improvements were credited to his name. He had achieved success not only in the sciences. He was an outstanding skier and scuba diver, and if that was not enough, he had successfully entered the amateur art field.

Arkadiy Malakhov, Arkashka the artist, also turned up in Leningrad. He had become a professional artist, although after the war he had completed not an art school but a law school. Malakhov specialized in the layout of books.

And, finally, after long searches, Chkheidze managed to find Venedikt Andreev in the Siberian city of Kurgan, where Andreev was the director of the House of Culture.

Thus the detachment was "assembled" once again.

Only Lyubisha Zhorzhevich could not be tracked down. After the war, he returned to his homeland, to Yugoslavia. He corresponded with Kalganov at first but later dropped out of sight.

In the winter of 1959, the first time after fifteen years apart, the scouts gathered in Moscow. Kalganov, Sonya, Chkheidze, and Nikulin came from Leningrad to meet their former flotilla commander, Vice-Admiral Kholostyakov, and the former flotilla chief of staff, Captain First Rank Sverdlov. Morozov arrived from Baku to see his wartime friends. Veretenik drove in from Kherson in his truck, completing a scheduled intercity trip. Andreev and Malakhov arrived later.

A feeling of comradeship, a feeling of old, unfaded through the years, naval friendship, a friendship tempered by many experiences united them all. In the most direct sense, they had passed arm in arm through the fire, water, and the pipe—the fire of combat engagements, the rapid water of the Danube, and the underground pipe of Budapest. And though more than a few years had passed, in many villages and cities along the Danube, whether it be in Romania, Bulgaria, Yugoslavia, Hungary, Czechoslovakia, or Austria, the people remember these brave Soviet sailors who, led by a young bearded commander, were the very first messengers of freedom on cutters more than once marked by bullets and shell fragments.

NOTES

Translator's Introduction

1. The best history of this detachment is F. F. Volonchuk's *Po tylam vraga* [In the enemy's rear area] (Moscow: Voyenizdat, 1961).

2. Strekhnin is the author of several works of Soviet military history: *Cherez shest' granits* [Across six borders] (Moscow: Voyenizdat, 1955); with F. Suryadov, *Bronekatera v boyakh za Stalingrad* [Armored cutters in battles for Stalingrad] (Moscow: Voyenizdat, 1947); *Korabli idut v Berlin* [Ships sail to Berlin] (Moscow: DOSAAF, 1977); and *Yest' zhenshchiny v russkikh seleniyakh* [There are women in Russian villages] (Moscow: Sovietskaya Rossiya, 1970).

3. The first memoir to be published on the Baltic Fleet scout detachment was *Surovyye tropy: zapiski razvedchika* [Difficult paths: Notes of a scout] (Moscow: Voyenizdat, 1961), by Hero of the Soviet Union V. D. Fedorov. Fedorov later authored a second work on his wartime experiences, *Devyat'sot dney razvedchika* [Nine hundred days of a scout] (Moscow: Voyenizdat, 1967). This appearance of three memoirs and Strekhnin's secondary account in just five years suggests a concerted effort by the Soviet military establishment to publicize the combat actions of these elite forces.

4. The most detailed World War II history of this flotilla is I. I. Loktionov's *Dunayskaya flotiliya v velikoy otechestvennoy voyne (1941–1945gg.)* [The Danube Flotilla in the Great Patriotic War (1941–1945)] (Moscow: Voyenizdat, 1962).

Foreword

1. The Great Patriotic War is the conflict between the Soviet Union and Germany that began with the German invasion of the USSR

257

on 22 June 1941 and ended with Germany's surrender on 9 May 1945. World War II began with Germany's invasion of Poland in September 1939 and ended with Japan's surrender in September 1945. This translation observes this distinction.

2. The Order of the Red Banner dates from 1 August 1924 and was awarded to persons and units for a variety of accomplishments related to courageous performance in combat.

3. The Order of Nakhimov dates from 3 March 1944 and was awarded to naval officers and units for outstanding successes in the development, conduct, and support of naval operations that resulted in the defeat of an enemy offensive, the support of active fleet operations, or the inflicting of significant losses on the enemy while preserving one's own force.

   The Order of Kutuzov dates from 29 July 1942 and was awarded to military commanders and units for excellence in planning and conducting an operation that resulted in significant enemy losses while preserving one's own force. This award was intended for army units but was awarded to the Danube Flotilla because of its participation in ground operations with Red Army forces attacking along the axis of the Danube River.

4. Komsomol is short for *Kommunisticheskiy soyuz molodezhi* (young communist league), the organization that prepared young people for subsqent Communist Party membership. *Komsomolets* is a male Komsomol member, *Komsomolka* is a female Komsomol member.

5. A *front* was roughly equivalent to an American or British army group. *Front* commanders responded to orders issued by Stavka of the Supreme High Command in Moscow, either directly or promulgated through a Stavka representative who personally traveled from Moscow to the *front* command post.

Preface

1. *Cherez shest' granits: Ocherki o boyakh dunayskoy flotilii v 1944–1945 godakh* [Across six borders: Outline of battles of the Danube Flotilla in 1944–1945] (Moscow: Voyenizdat, 1955), by Yu. Strekhnin.

2. The Russian here is *yazyk,* and it means literally "tongue," like the tongue in a person's mouth. This term was used in both the Red Army and navy to refer to a live prisoner, one who could speak, as opposed to a dead prisoner, who could not.

3. The *tel'nyashka* is the striped T-shirt that all naval infantrymen and sailors wear. This clothing item was added to the uniform of Soviet airborne troops in the 1970s, apparently at the insistence of the late Army General V. F. Margelov, himself a naval infantryman from the

early days of World War II. The two T-shirts are easily distinguishible by their colors: the naval version has dark blue stripes and the airborne version a lighter shade of blue.

Chapter 1. To the Aid Station

1. The standard issue submachine gun at this time was the *PPSh-41* (*pistolet-pulemyot Shpagina*—submachine gun of the Shpagin design), a 7.62mm weapon with a 71-round drum (disk) magazine. Other standard small arms included the 7.62mm Tokarev semiautomatic rifle; the 7.62mm 1891/30 Mosin bolt-action rifle; and the sniper version of this same rifle.
2. After the Germans captured Sevastopol on 3 July 1942, the remaining forces of the Black Sea Fleet were deployed to ports on the east coast of the Black Sea. On 28 July 1942, Stavka combined the ground forces of Southern and North Caucasus *Fronts* into a single North Caucasus *Front* and operationally subordinated the Black Sea Fleet to this *front*. Thus the fleet's naval infantry units were operating ashore, often in support of Red Army units.
3. This "Islamic Legion" cannot be readily identified. These men could have been conscripts from German-occupied Soviet territory (many Tatars lived in Crimea) or Red Army prisoners of war who had become *hilfwilliger* (voluntary laborers). Only in February 1943 did Heinrich Himmler authorize the recruitment of large numbers of Moslems from the population of Bosnia. They were formed into the 13th *Waffen Gebirgs Division der SS* and employed primarily for antipartisan duties in Yugoslavia. See Gordon Williamson, *The SS: Hitler's Instrument of Terror* (Osceola, Wisc.: Motorbooks International), pp. 122–23.

Chapter 2. Iron Souvenir

1. The sniper version of the 1891/30 Mosin Nagan bolt-action rifle fired the 7.62 x 54mm rimmed cartridge and differed from the standard-issue rifle in having a more carefully bored barrel, a turned-down bolt handle (to clear the scope), and an optical sight.
2. There is a clear reference in Soviet sources to a detachment of sailors, based on Kronshtadt Island near Leningrad, who attacked Finnish rear areas on skis during the Soviet-Finnish War of 1939–40. See *Pobeda* [Victory] (Moscow: DOSAAF, 1975), p. 18. It cannot be ascertained if Yusupov belonged to this unit.
3. An abatis is an obstacle created on a forest road or trail by piling or stacking trees across the trail, normally used to block vehicle movement.
4. This officer, who joined the Red Army in 1921, died on 21 February

1944 in a Moscow hospital as a result of wounds received in battle. He was posthumously awarded Hero of the Soviet Union on 13 May 1971. See *Sovetskaya voyennaya entsiklopediya* [Soviet military encyclopedia] (Moscow: Voyenizdat, 1977), 4:623–24. During this period, his 18th Army occupied the left (coastal) flank of the North Caucasus *Front*, to which the Black Sea Fleet was also subordinated. This senior army commander's personal interest in the scouts and Kalganov suggests that Kalganov's mission was in support of 18th Army headquarters.

5. The Order of Aleksandr Nevskiy dates from 29 July 1942 and was awarded to commanders from division down to platoon level for demonstrating personal courage and bravery and skillful command that ensured their unit's success.

Chapter 3. Watch over the Sea

1. Strekhnin does not provide the name of this lieutenant, but S. Slavich identifies one Aleksandr Tarutin as the parachute instructor for another group of scouts who jumped into Crimea during this same period. He was a master of sport in parachuting. See *Posesloviye k podvigu* [Postcript to a feat] (Simferopol': Izdatel'stvo "Tavriya"), pp. 248–49.

2. The mission to which Strekhnin specifically refers in this passage is discussed by Slavich in *Posesloviye k podvigu*, pp. 248–72. This jump occurred on 11–12 June 1943.

3. This could well have been F. F. Volonchuk's group, which also was inserted into the Black Mountain area of Crimea in June 1943. See *V tylu vraga* [In the enemy's rear] (Moscow: Voyenizdat, 1961), p. 134.

4. The Black Sea Fleet intelligence chief was Colonel D. B. Namgaladze. This reference, along with Kalganov's participation in this covert operation, is the first hard evidence that he was by this time a member of the Black Sea Fleet reconnaissance detachment.

5. Kalganov's group clearly linked up with Volonchuk's group of twelve scouts that were inserted in June 1943, along with the initial group of four that were inserted on 11–12 June 1943.

6. A great number of Spanish nationals fought on the Soviet side in this war, including a group that was inserted into Crimea from Adler airfield on 4 March 1943 to engage in partisan operations. See Serna Roke, *Ispantsy v Velikoy Otechestvennoy Voyne* [Spaniards in the Great Patriotic War] (Moscow: Progress, 1986), pp. 232–42.

7. Veretenik's early war experiences are described in detail in Slavich, *Posesloviye k podvigu*, pp. 205–43.

8. This is the same Aleksandr Morozov who appears in several places in Volonchuk's *V tylu vraga*, a memoir account of the Black Sea Fleet reconnaissance detachment from July 1941 to January 1944.
9. Named for its designer, V. M. Petlyakov, the *Pe-2* was a twin-engined dive-bomber, armed with three 12.7mm and two 7.62mm machine guns, that could carry 1,200 pounds of bombs. It had a top speed of 340 miles per hour at 16,000 feet.
10. In all historical texts, Soviet authors label irregular forces operating in the countryside as "partisans" and irregular forces operating in urban environments as "the underground." Partisans were usually constituted as units or detachments, with a military or paramilitary chain of command, and lived clandestinely in swamps and forests. Members of the underground lived a bifurcated life, performing clandestine acts only when called upon by their leadership. Partisan detachments were frequently commanded by NKVD officers inserted into the German rear to perform this duty. Underground groups were frequently commanded by local Communist Party leaders who remained behind or were inserted into the German rear to perform this duty.
11. This incident has all the ingredients of a communist morality play: member violates socialist legality and is caught, confesses to the collective in a public forum, and is "forgiven" contingent on subsequent appropriate behavior.

Chapter 4. Trust

1. This is the same Revyakin, also known as Sasha Orlovskiy, with whom other members of the Black Sea Fleet reconnaissance detachment made contact in December 1943. See Volonchuk, *V tylu vraga*, p. 138.
2. This and other euphemisms are used throughout this translation to indicate that the German combatants or other prisoners were shot. In the case of German combatants, neither the laws of war nor the Hague Conventions were recognized by the warring sides on the eastern front. In the case of Soviet citizens who were suspected of collaborating, it was official Soviet government policy summarily to execute these "enemies of the people."
3. *Osobyy otdel* [special departments] were formed by the NKVD in all Soviet army and navy units. Their function was to seek out and apprehend traitors and enemy agents.
4. Another source indicates that Anastasia Pavlovna Lopochuk shared the same apartment with Revyakin. See Volonchuk, *V tylu vraga*, p. 139.

Chapter 5. Nord

1. The Border Troops of the KGB had a long history of using of dogs for border patrols.

Chapter 6. Greetings, Sailors!

1. This is the black, peakless cap with ribbon tails worn by all Soviet sailors. Their fleet or flotilla of assignment is stenciled in gold letters on the ribbon that is the band of the cap.
2. The Danube Flotilla had been reestablished on 13 April 1944 on the base of the Azov Flotilla. Its commander at this time was Rear Admiral S. G. Gorshkov. For a concise history of this flotilla, see Strekhnin, *Cherez shest' granits*, and Loktionov, *Dunayskaya flotiliya* .
3. The cutter had formerly belonged to the German SS liaison officer to the Romanian Danube Flotilla, under the name *Nochtung*. See M. N. Kudrya, *Chernomortsy na dunaye* [Black Sea sailors on the Danube] (Odessa: "Mayak," 1990), p. 97.
4. The flotilla was subordinated to this *front*, which at this time was commanded by Marshal F. I. Tolbukhin.

Chapter 7. A Second Line

1. A general description of the seizure of Raduyevats and Prakhovo by ground and riverine forces can be found in Loktionov, *Dunayskaya flotiliya*, pp. 131–37, with a map on page 133. This account includes a paragraph on page 136 describing the role of Kalganov's scouts.
2. This is the disabled veteran whom Strekhnin introduced in his Author's Foreword. Chkheidze's own memoir was published under two titles: *Zapiski razvedchika* [Notes of a scout] (Moscow: Voyenizdat, 1981), and *Zapiski dunayskogo razvedchika* [Notes of a Danube scout] (Moscow: "Molodaya Gvardiya," 1982). His writing largely parallels Strekhnin's account through to the end of the war.
3. A typical armored cutter in 1944 was armed with two 76mm or 100mm guns and two 12.7mm machine guns, all in turrets or behind armored shields. This vessel was designed specifically for fire support of ground forces and ship-to-ship engagements with small vessels in rivers or coastal waters.
4. I had the opportunity to meet Derzhavin in Odessa in October 1990. He recalled Kalganov with great fondness and respect.

Chapter 8. Reinforcements Have Arrived

1. According to the map in Loktionov, *Dunayskaya Flotiliya*, p. 133, Mikhaylovats was in the sector of the 299th Rifle Division, 75th Rifle Corps.

2. The *katyusha* was a multiple rocket launcher, normally mounted on the back of a Studebaker truck. The flotilla also had several armored cutters so equipped. The standard launcher had eight rails and could "ripple" launch (in seven to ten seconds) sixteen 132mm rockets, each with a warhead weighing 5 kilograms to a range of 8.5 kilometers.

Chapter 10. *Ghosts of the Danube*

1. This army was named after its principal leader, the former Red Army general A. A. Vlasov. A talented commander and one of the heroes of the Battle of Moscow in December 1941, Vlasov was captured by the Germans in June 1942 while trying to break out of an encirclement with remnants of his 2d Shock Army. The Germans exploited Vlasov's disillusionment with his former masters and assisted him in organizing the Russian Liberation Army. Vlasov was captured by the Allies at the end of the war and repatriated to the Soviets, who executed him after a trial.
2. When applied to the "traitor" standing before them, the Soviet sailors used this respectful form of address in total derision.
3. There is no indication as to why they believed this prisoner to be a Jew. It does seem to reflect the anti-Semitism that was widespread in Soviet society.
4. This is another example of the execution of prisoners, in this case former Soviet citizens who now were considered traitors.

Chapter 11. *A Bridge near Belgrade*

1. According to Loktionov, *Dunayskaya flotiliya*, p. 148, this mission occurred on 17 October 1944.

Chapter 12. *Operation "Flour"*

1. It is unclear here why Strekhnin labeled Veretenik a "rookie." He had been with the detachment for approximately a year, having participated in the parachute insertion into Crimea for the coast-watching mission in the hills above Yalta.
2. The Salashisty were a Hungarian irregular force that supported the Germans.
3. This scene is strongly reminiscent of a similar incident that occurred in the Northern Fleet in November 1945, in which the scouts of the Northern Fleet reconnaissance detachment opened a warehouse containing food and turned the contents over to the Norwegian population of a small village on the Varanger Peninsula. See Viktor Leonov, *Blood on the Shores: Soviet Naval Commandos in World War II* (Annapolis: Naval Institute Press, 1993), p. 122.

Chapter 14. Two Maps

1. According to Slavich's account of this battle in the bank, in *Poslesloviya k podvigu*, p. 285, it was at about this point that Veretenik burst into a room on this floor where a Vlasovets was concealed. In his fear at coming face to face with a Soviet sailor, the Vlasovets quickly retreated to a broken window and jumped to his death from the fourth floor.

Chapter 15. Budapest Underground

1. German forces were at this time conducting a major counteroffensive west and south of Budapest, in an effort to reach the Danube River and relieve encircled Budapest.
2. This was the German Nebelwerfer, a 150mm multiple rocket launcher mounted on a two-wheeled trailer.

Chapter 17. Six Lights

1. This operation is described in detail in Loktionov, *Dunayskaya flotiliya*, pp. 225–44.
2. Admiral Kholostyakov had assumed command of the flotilla from Admiral Gorshkov in December 1944.

ABOUT THE TRANSLATOR

James F. Gebhardt enlisted in the U.S. Army infantry in 1966 and served for three years, including one year in South Vietnam. He was commissioned in the armor branch in 1974, and commanded a tank company in Germany in 1982–83. From 1983 until his retirement in 1992, he served in Soviet Foreign Area Officer positions: that is, as a research fellow and instructor at the Command and General Staff College; a military analyst at the Soviet Army Studies Office; and an escort officer for the On-Site Inspection Agency. Gebhardt earned a BA degree in political science from the University of Idaho in 1974 and an MA degree in history from the University of Washington in 1976. He is now employed by a defense contractor at Fort Leavenworth, Kansas. His previous publications include several articles on Soviet tactical art and special operations and *Soviet Breakthrough and Pursuit in the Arctic, October 1944* (U.S. Army Command and General Staff College, 1990). Gebhardt also translated *Blood on the Shores* by Viktor Leonov, which was published by the Naval Institute Press in 1993.

Translator's note: Early in the summer of 1996, Yuriy Strekhnin passed away in Moscow.

The **Naval Institute Press** is the book-publishing arm of the U.S. Naval Institute, a private, nonprofit, membership society for sea service professionals and others who share an interest in naval and maritime affairs. Established in 1873 at the U.S. Naval Academy in Annapolis, Maryland, where its offices remain today, the Naval Institute has members worldwide.

Members of the Naval Institute support the education programs of the society and receive the influential monthly magazine *Proceedings* and discounts on fine nautical prints and on ship and aircraft photos. They also have access to the transcripts of the Institute's Oral History Program and get discounted admission to any of the Institute-sponsored seminars offered around the country.

The Naval Institute also publishes *Naval History* magazine. This colorful bimonthly is filled with entertaining and thought-provoking articles, first-person reminiscences, and dramatic art and photography. Members receive a discount on *Naval History* subscriptions.

The Naval Institute's book-publishing program, begun in 1898 with basic guides to naval practices, has broadened its scope in recent years to include books of more general interest. Now the Naval Institute Press publishes about 100 titles each year, ranging from how-to books on boating and navigation to battle histories, biographies, ship and aircraft guides, and novels. Institute members receive discounts of 20 to 50 percent on the Press's nearly 600 books in print.

Full-time students are eligible for special half-price membership rates. Life memberships are also available.

For a free catalog describing Naval Institute Press books currently available, and for further information about subscribing to *Naval History* magazine or about joining the U.S. Naval Institute, please write to:

Membership Department
U.S. Naval Institute
118 Maryland Avenue
Annapolis, MD 21402-5035
Telephone: (800) 233-8764
Fax: (410) 269-7940
Web address: www.usni.org